POPULIST
NATIONALISM

Recent Titles in
Contributions to the Study of World History

POPULIST NATIONALISM

Republican Insurgency and American Foreign Policy Making, 1918–1925

Karen A. J. Miller

Contributions to the Study of World History, Number 69

GREENWOOD PRESS
Westport, Connecticut • London

Library of Congress Cataloging-in-Publication Data

Miller, Karen A. J., 1953–
    Populist nationalism : Republican insurgency and American foreign policy making, 1918–1925 / Karen A.J. Miller.
        p.   cm.—(Contributions to the study of world history ,
0885–9159 ; no. 69)
    Includes bibliographical references and index.
    ISBN 0–313–30776–8 (alk. paper)
    1. United States—Politics and government—1913–1921.   2. United States—Politics and government—1921–1923.   3. United States—Politics and government—1923–1929.   4. Borah, William Edgar, 1865–1940.   5. Johnson, Hiram, 1866–1945.   6. Progressivism (United States politics)—History—20th century.   7. Republican Party (U.S. : 1854–   )—History—20th century.   I. Title.   II. Series.
E784 .M55   1999
320.973′09042—dc21   98–41419

British Library Cataloguing in Publication Data is available.

Library of Congress Catalog Card Number: 98–41419
ISBN: 0–313–30776–8
ISSN: 0885–9159

First published in 1999

Greenwood Press, 88 Post Road West, Westport, CT 06881
An imprint of Greenwood Publishing Group, Inc.
www.greenwood.com

Printed in the United States of America

The paper used in this book complies with the Permanent Paper Standard issued by the National Information Standards Organization (Z39.48–1984).

10 9 8 7 6 5 4 3 2 1

Copyright Acknowledgments

The author and publisher gratefully acknowledge permission to use the following material:

Excerpts from the Hiram Johnson Papers (BANC MSS C-B 581), The Bancroft Library, University of California, Berkeley. Reprinted by permission.

Excerpts from the Henry Cabot Lodge Papers, Massachusetts Historical Society, Boston, Massachusetts. Reprinted by permission.

to my parents

Contents

Preface

The Republican party's foreign policy program at the end of World War I was marked by a paradox. Most Republican politicians favored U.S. entry into the League of Nations, albeit an entrance limited by moderate reservations. These supporters of the international organization included the luminaries of the party. Those who had participated in the prewar construction of a Republican foreign policy, such as William Howard Taft, Elihu Root, and Henry Cabot Lodge, built a partnership with the postwar architects of Republican foreign policy, Charles Evans Hughes and Herbert Hoover. These policy makers understood that U.S. membership in the League would enhance the nation's influence in international relations and strengthen the popular appeal of the Republican party. Entry into the League of Nations was endorsed by Will Hays, the chairman of the Republican National Committee, as well as the members of the platform committees for both the 1920 and 1924 conventions. Yet, the United States did not join the League of Nations. How was it that despite the overwhelming support of the leadership of the party, the Republicans failed to secure full American participation in the League?

The question of United States membership in the League of Nations was introduced in the hostile environment of a divided government. Partisan conflict poisoned relations between the Democratic White House and the Republican Senate, rendering ratification of the Versailles Treaty impossible. However, partisan hostility does not provide a complete explanation for the absence of American participation in the League of Nations. After the election of 1920, the Republican Senate majority leader, Henry Cabot Lodge, and the Republican secretary of state, Charles Evans Hughes, supported entry into the League under the guidelines of Republican reservationism.

These two men molded an activist foreign policy marked by cooperation with international organizations. The U.S. government cooperated in the postwar occupation of Germany, maintained observer status in most League agencies, and consulted with the Reparations Commission to stabilize the European economy. Furthermore, it was responsible for multinational agreements that promoted American power in international politics. The most significant of these occurred when the United States initiated a reconfiguration of balance of power in Asia through the Washington Conference. Despite this record of international activity, and in violation of their own best intentions, Hughes and Lodge failed to preside over a Republican-sponsored entry into the League of Nations.

The leadership of the Republican party—that loose configuration of floor leaders in Congress, members of the executive cabinet after 1921, and party strategists in the National Committee—could not construct a Republican-sponsored entrance into the League of Nations. They failed because of their fear of intraparty conflict. Between 1909 and 1912 the party was ravaged by factional strife as progressives and conservatives vied for control. This internal turmoil led to the Democratic election victories of the 1910s. The vivid memories of the Taft insurgency and the subsequent rise of Woodrow Wilson forced them to place the interests of party solidarity over any policy objective.

The memory of the Taft insurgency held a powerful influence over the Republican party leadership after World War I. When it first came into being in 1909, it possessed a clear political agenda that had its ideological roots in the populist movement. However, in the eyes of Republican party leaders, the insurgency had taken on wider dimensions. It was no longer defined by its political agenda, but by its style of obdurate confrontation. Its influence had spread beyond a particular party faction and had become an awesome force that had driven the party to self-destruction. The insurgency inspired the worst elements of the political man, promoting disunity and eliciting acrimony. All had fallen victim to the force, emboldening even the genteel Elihu Root to respond to the president of the Senate, "If the presiding officer means I am to keep quiet, I yield to his superior authority; if he means I am to listen to that damn bore, he can go to hell." Insurgency had devastated the Republican party by the end of the Taft administration. The resumption of Republican power only could be achieved with the sublimation of insurgency.

Those Republican politicians who watched power slip through their fingers in the 1912 election committed themselves to party reconciliation. Their primary political objective was to end the threat of division engendered by insurgent political rhetoric. The ideology of insurgent politicians might be distasteful, but in and of itself, it was not a problem. The problem lay in the insurgency's rhetorical appeal to confrontation and obstructionism. To effectively deal with this threat, the Republican leadership chose to embrace the full spectrum of opinion within the party and placate those who were disaffected. The resulting reconciliation within the Republican party had important repercussions for the insurgency as a political movement.

The Taft insurgency had been founded in a set of political ideals. Members of the movement sought to democratize Congress by limiting the power of the Speaker of the House and restructuring the committee system. They hoped to curtail the power of the wealthy by changing tariff law and creating an income tax. Most of the members of the insurgency came to Congress by virtue of the support of rural constituencies. They represented western states where populism had been an important political force a generation earlier and where antipathy toward eastern business interests still existed. At its inception the Taft insurgency was a small rural movement that called for federal protection of the common man. By the end of the congressional elections of 1910, it had taken on far larger proportions in the eyes of party leaders. As the insurgency's image overshadowed its political reality, the leadership came to fear that most members of the party would be swept into the tumult of the insurgency. No ideological or geographical litmus test determined membership. Politicians became insurgents when they challenged the authority of party leadership or condemned party consensus.

Under this definition, the power of the insurgency took on a vague and menacing form between 1913 and 1924. The insurgency had no defined membership. It never became a caucus or a bloc or a party. Although all Republicans from western states who had progressive leanings were studied for signs of insurgency, such urban Republicans as Fiorello LaGuardia could be considered part of the movement. This lack of a litmus test for membership was the greatest strength of the insurgency. In the postwar period, the Republican leadership reflexively assumed the movement was potentially large and dangerous. As a result, the party's leaders were cautious not to promote policies that might provoke an insurgent outcry.

The party leadership's reluctance to trigger an insurgent protest provided an important weapon to Republican politicians who opposed League membership for the United States. Republican opponents of the League discovered they could use the specter of party disharmony to their political advantage. William Borah proved to be particularly adept in forcing concessions from both the Senate's floor leadership and the Republican administrations.

Borah recognized that the party leadership's commitment to harmony had particular consequences in foreign policy making. One of the strongest advocates of reconciliation was Henry Cabot Lodge, who served as both Senate majority leader and as chairman of the Senate Foreign Relations Committee. Borah quickly learned that he could use the threat of insurgency to force concessions from Lodge. This had profound implications during the Versailles Treaty debates, when Henry Cabot Lodge's role in the Senate made him the architect of the Republican foreign policy position. Borah's threats continued to have influence after the election of 1920. Lodge's susceptibility to the specter of insurgency led him to advocate foreign policy changes only when the danger of party division had been stifled. This caution discouraged Secretary of State Charles Evans Hughes from engaging in confrontations over U.S. entry into the League of Nations. Rather, Lodge and Hughes advocated internationalist policies that circumvented the League issue. They only risked a confrontation with Borah when they believed he could not provoke an insurgent response.

The resulting Republican foreign policy was molded by the ebb and flow of domestic politics. When issues such as campaign finance reform, aid to farmers, or political corruption preoccupied voters, the threat of insurgency over U.S. entry into the League of Nations held its greatest force. As national elections approached, the Republican leadership deferred the initiation of stronger ties to the League. Republican proponents of the League of Nations found the opportunities for promoting U.S. entry limited.

The formulation of Republican foreign policy was a shared responsibility. Those who had the greatest institutional authority, Henry Cabot Lodge and Charles Evans Hughes, often ceded control to William Borah. The ability to initiate policy shifted from one Republican to another, leading to an ambiguous commitment to the League of Nations and an irresolute foreign policy.

This analysis falls within a recent body of literature dedicated to understanding dissenting voices in the policy-making process of the 1920s. Charismatic politicians of the populist left have come under increased scholarly examination in the last decade. Richard Lower's *A Bloc of One*, Robert Johnson's *The Peace Progressives and American Foreign Relations*, and David Horowitz's *Beyond Left and Right* provide sophisticated analyses of this undercurrent in 1920s politics. These recent historical studies demonstrate that their subjects cannot be dismissed as "isolationists." Rather, these dissenters had articulate, complex world visions that could accommodate neither Wilsonian internationalism nor the Republican Ascendancy's corporate hegemony. They sought to create their own new world order as a remedy to the foreign policy being proposed by the executive branch.

The particular contribution of these recent works is the demonstration that men like Hiram Johnson, William Borah, and Robert LaFollette were driven by ideas. As such, these works constitute a history of political ideology. I do not dispute that these men were driven by a vision of a new world order. My argument rests on that assumption. However, the political influence of these dissenters did not rest solely on their ideology.

The insurgency did not exist as a conventional political movement. Its membership was uncertain, ebbing and flowing from one crisis to the next. With no clear criteria for membership, the insurgency's self-proclaimed leadership often found it difficult to translate ideals into policy. Robert Johnson suggested that these "peace progressives" were influential because they functioned as "a well-organized congressional bloc." He proved that his subjects did behave consistently; each of their actions in proposing legislation, engaging in debates, and voting demonstrated a regularity born out of ideological commitment. However, they also had difficulty delegating legislative responsibilities, engaging in the construction of compromise, and deferring to authority. In many respects, they behaved less like a congressional bloc and more like a herd of like-minded cats.

The key to understanding the influence of the insurgents lies in an examination of the political ideology of the Republican party's leadership. Above any policy concern, the leadership of the Republican party between 1918 and 1924 sought political victory. They wanted to wrest control of the White House and Capitol Hill from the Democratic party and relegate the Democrats to a permanent minority status. As long as the party leaders used elections as the primary means of measuring political success, insurgents had the potential to construct foreign policy. Astute politicians like Hiram Johnson and William Borah could use the fears of party leaders to transform their political ideals into national policy.

This is essentially a case study. It examines the failure of the United States to join the League of Nations as a consequence of ideology. William Borah and Hiram Johnson presided over a collection of American senators who believed that the greatness of the United States rested not on its economic power, but on its historic commitment to individual liberty. These men feared that U.S. entry into the League would drag the nation into the power politics of imperialism. More importantly, it looks at the political tactics that enabled this small group to effectively thwart the will of three presidents. Not only were these men of complex ideas; they were remarkably skillful practitioners of institutional politics.

Acknowledgments

I would like to take this opportunity to thank those who have helped me with this project. I have been through various stages of frustration, anxiety, and despair. I have finished only because of the support others have given me.

My research was facilitated by a host of librarians. The staffs for the manuscript collections at the National Archives, the Library of Congress, the Massachusetts Historical Society, and the Bancroft Library at the University of California at Berkeley provided invaluable support.

My colleagues at Montgomery College and Oakland University gave me unflagging encouragement. They offered me sound advice and helped me when it seemed my administrative and teaching duties would inundate my research. I consider myself very lucky to have worked with two such collegial groups of scholars.

I also benefited from participation in two seminars sponsored by the National Endowment for the Humanities—one led by Charles Neu concerning the organizational dimensions of foreign policy, and the other led by Thomas Kessner concerning modernization in early twentieth-century American culture. The occasion to spend two summers devoted to the intense discussion of historical problems gave me priceless training.

Several historians read the manuscript and identified problems in the construction of my argument. I would like to thank Charles Neu, Walter Metzger, John Cooper, Thomas Kessner, Donald Ritchie, Alan Brinkley, James Shenton, and Richard Pious. All of these academicians have raised questions that triggered important revisions to the text. The resulting book is far better than anything I could have produced without their help. This assistance in content was augmented by Laura Miller, who provided extensive support by editing the rhetorical style of the manuscript.

I have also received important moral support from a number of people. John Cooper, Charles Neu, Thomas Kessner, and Linda Hall have all given me encouragement. They have listened to me, chided me, saluted me. In short, they would not permit me to quit. Their confidence in my ability was resolute, and I owe them all a great debt of gratitude.

I would also like to take this opportunity to thank the members of my family for their support. My parents, husband, and daughter suffered all my frustrations, anxieties, and despair. I know that they will enjoy the publication of this book as much as I will.

1

The Insurgency and Republican Politics

Has the Senator ever heard of the adage that "he laughs best who laughs last"?

—Nelson Aldrich

During the 1920s the Republican party was the majority party. It consistently controlled the White House and both houses of Congress. As a consequence, the Republican party determined U.S. foreign policy in the aftermath of the First World War.

Despite the predominance of a single party during this period, U.S. foreign policy often was confusing. Goals were often unclear and continually subject to change. The lack of coherence in policy grew out of the basic lack of coherence in the Republican party. A superficial examination would indicate that the party was invincible; it won presidential elections with extraordinary margins of victory while maintaining solid majorities in Congress. However, this power at the polls did not easily translate into public policy. No one politician led the party; rather, it was characterized by strong factions that fought for dominance. This factionalism was rooted in the battles over progressive reform. The Republican party of the 1920s was still trying to solve the problem of prewar insurgency. This characteristic was nowhere more apparent than in the Senate.

The Republican party regained control of the Senate in the election of 1918. Although the party had been steadily rebuilding ever since the Taft-Roosevelt split had permitted the election of Woodrow Wilson in 1912, no tangible shift of power occurred until the sixth year of the Wilson administration. This new Republican majority in the upper house of the Sixty-sixth Congress contained a large number of freshmen, but none of the newcomers could be described as a neophyte. They had all participated in the tumultuous politics of progressive reform under the earlier Republican presidents. When they cast their votes, their decisions were informed by the politics of insurgency.

THE FORMATION OF THE TAFT INSURGENCY

The first decade of the twentieth century marked a consolidation of power by the Republican party. Not only did the party maintain a constant supremacy over the Democrats, but power was focused in the hands of a few senior members of Congress. The rules of both houses gave the floor leadership enormous power. By 1908, Speaker of the House Joe Cannon (R, Illinois) and Senate Majority Leader Nelson Aldrich (R, Rhode Island) controlled committee appointments, the interpretation of rules, and the flow of legislation from committee to floor. These men could mold legislation passing through Congress, and because of their power, even Theodore Roosevelt deferred to their will.[1]

Cannon and Aldrich were the undisputed leaders of the Old Guard, that wing of the Republican party that served as the last bastion of nineteenth-century Republican conservatism. They believed government existed to protect property rights, and argued that the increasing scale of business activity constituted no threat to the American public. Unlike their predecessors of the previous century, Cannon and Aldrich presided over substantial Republican majorities in their respective chambers. While the Republican Speakers and majority leaders before them had had to maintain constant dialogue with all members of the party in Congress, these floor leaders of the early Progressive Era felt they could exclude some members of their own party from policy councils without risking encroachment by the Democratic members of Congress.[2] Cannon and Aldrich resisted progressive initiatives to regulate railroad freight rates, increase prosecutions by the Department of Justice's Anti-Trust Division, and conserve natural resources on federal land. They effectively used their positions to defend the power of the conservative Old Guard and to stifle progressive legislation.

This consolidation of conservative power against reform engendered frustration. The rise of a reform-minded element in Congress was not a political anomaly, but rather a reflection of growing public concern. The American people were becoming aware of the dangers of monopoly, and new Republican congressmen were frequently elected on platforms advocating federal control over commerce and reductions in the tariff rates. These issues, first raised during the Populist Era

---

[1] Randall Ripley, *Majority Party Leadership in Congress* (Boston: Little, Brown & Company, 1969), 24–25. See also H. W. Brands, *TR: The Last Romantic* (New York: Basic Books, 1997), 424. Roosevelt fully accepted this relationship and often defended the prerogatives of Cannon and Aldrich. When David Graham Phillips published his indictment of Aldrich's behavior in the Senate, *The Treason of the Senate*, Roosevelt condemned him as "the man with the muck-rake."

[2] The office of majority leader was not created until the Progressive Era. However, the role of majority leader did exist in the late nineteenth century. The earlier party structure in the Senate called for a chairman of the Republican Caucus who functioned as a majority leader. For a thorough explanation of party structure in the Senate in the late nineteenth century, see David Rothman, *Politics and Power: The United States Senate, 1869–1901* (Cambridge: Harvard University Press, 1966).

of the late nineteenth-century, had their greatest following in the agricultural areas of the Mississippi Valley and Far West. A form of agrarian progressivism emerged in these states. Borrowing from populist rhetoric, this new generation of reformers sought to protect the American farmer from monopoly power in manufacturing, transportation, and banking. They shared the populist ideal of an American political supremacy born out of the economic independence of the privately owned family farm. Their belief in the unique character of the American political economy engendered a strong sense of nationalism. These agrarian progressives joined with progressive politicians from urban constituencies to advocate strong federal regulation of the railroad system, more rigorous enforcement of antitrust laws, and lowering the tariff on manufactured goods.

As Cannon and Aldrich were solidifying their control over legislative institutions, they were facing a growing faction of reformers in their own party who were dedicated to the end of conservative government. These two political forces were ideologically incompatible, and both were dedicated to the control of policy making within the Republican party in Congress.

In 1908 the tensions between these two wings of the Republican party erupted into an open attempt to curtail the power of the Speaker of the House, Joe Cannon. Western representatives were confounded by Cannon's use of the rules of the House to prevent floor discussion of their proposed reform programs. Frustrated by the obstructionism of Cannon, these progressive Republicans declared themselves to be in a state of insurgency. They planned to rebel against the Speaker and make government more responsive to popular will. In an effort to open the legislative process, the insurgents proposed rule changes that would eliminate the Speaker's ability to appoint members to standing committees and create a new Rules Committee. This first effort failed in February 1909 when Republican conservatives substituted a weak compromise. The House insurgents recognized their tactical mistakes and began to organize themselves for a second attempt.[3]

The House insurgents recognized that any assault against the power of the floor leader would have to be well coordinated. On the most widely supported issues, the insurgents comprised approximately 20 percent of the Republican membership in the House; as a group they could not control the party, but they could alter party policy.[4] Their power could only be derived through an alliance—or the threat of an

---

[3] James Holt, *Congressional Insurgents and the Party System, 1909–1916* (Cambridge: Harvard University Press, 1967), 17. See also Kenneth W. Hechler, *Insurgency: Personalities and Politics of the Taft Era* (New York: Russell & Russell, 1940), 44–48.

[4] Before 1911 the insurgency existed as an informal group, not a formal bloc or caucus. This first formal meeting of an insurgent Republican caucus included forty-one representatives and ten senators. The members of this caucus who had prior congressional experience had participated in insurgent attacks on the Republican party leadership in the first half of the Taft administration. See Holt, *Congressional Insurgents*, 46.

alliance—with House Democrats. George Norris (R, Nebraska) emerged as the leader of the insurgents in the House. His plan was to concentrate on procedural rules, not policy objectives. It was assumed that if the legislative process became more deliberative, if debate were encouraged, then progressive reform measures would result automatically. The first success came in 1909 with the institution of "Calendar Wednesday," a day on which any member could move legislation from committee to the floor. This broke Cannon's total control of the House calendar. A more significant victory came in 1910, when Norris proposed a major restructuring of the Rules Committee. Under this reform, that committee would become a large bipartisan group free from the Speaker's domination. The Speaker would be specifically denied membership. More important, he would no longer appoint members of the Rules Committee; rather, committee members would be elected according to geographic considerations. Faced with a combined attack by insurgents and Democrats, the Old Guard was not able to block the Norris proposal.

Although the insurgents in the House were in a state of revolt against the authority of Joe Cannon, most of them did not contemplate a total break with the Republican party. In response to the changes to the Rules Committee structure, Cannon stepped down and declared the Speaker's chair vacant. Faced with the prospect of a Democrat leading the chamber, all but nine of the insurgents quickly declared their support of Cannon as the head of their party. Assuaged by promises of intraparty cooperation, members of the insurgency were willing to accept the leadership of the Old Guard as long as that leadership was not despotic.[5]

An insurgent movement similar to that in the House formed in the Senate during the Taft presidency.[6] Like their counterparts in the lower chamber, the Senate insurgents sought ultimately to change the relationship between the federal government and business. Monopolies would lose their protective tariffs and wealth would be taxed. As a result, the average citizen would be saved from the avarice of Wall Street. The more deliberative nature of the Senate—a result of unlimited debate, longer terms, and a separation between the roles of presiding officer and floor leader—channeled insurgency in the upper chamber to debates over legislation, not institutional procedure.

During the campaign of 1908, the Republican party had committed itself to a

---

[5] Hechler, *Insurgency*, 27–82. See also Holt, *Congressional Insurgents,* 16–27. The leader of the anti-Cannon movement, George Norris, would not break party ranks to vote for a Democratic Speaker.

[6] The senators who were considered the core of the insurgency included Albert Beveridge (R, Indiana), *William Borah* (R, Idaho), Jonathan Bourne (R, Oregon), Joseph Bristow (R, Kansas), Norris Brown (R, Nebraska), Elmer Burkett (R, Nebraska), Moses Clapp (R, Minnesota), Coe Crawford (R, South Dakota), *Albert Cummins* (R, Iowa), Joseph Dixon (R, Montana), Jonathan Dolliver (R, Iowa), *Asle Gronna* (R, North Dakota), *William Kenyon* (R, Iowa), *Miles Poindexter* (R, Washington), and *John Works* (R, California). Two leading figures in the House insurgency—*George Norris* (R, Nebraska) and *Irvine Lenroot* (R, Wisconsin)—were elected to the Senate during the Wilson administration. Those italicized were still in the Senate in 1918.

revision of the protectionist Dingley Tariff. Progressive Republicans continued to advocate protectionism for infant industries and for natural resources, but argued that protective tariffs for established industrial sectors defied sound economic logic. High tariffs on items such as textiles and paint assured unduly high consumer prices and guaranteed excessive profits to industry.   The new tariff would reestablish true equilibrium between consumer and manufacturer.

However, it was not a progressive who defined the Senate's position on tariff reform. Nelson Aldrich was the Republican senator responsible for the text of the new tariff. As chairman of the Finance Committee, he controlled the drafting process; as Senate majority leader, he dominated floor debate. Aldrich did not share the progressives' vision of encouraging competition by lowering tariffs.   He recognized that protection of the economy was unbalanced, with manufacturers holding an unreasonable advantage. Aldrich's reform, however, was not to lower the protection for manufacturing industries, but to balance these rates with protection for mining and agriculture.[7] In an effort to assure that his philosophy would dominate tariff debate, Aldrich prevented the assignment of progressives to the Finance Committee.   Jonathan Dolliver (R, Iowa), a progressive with substantial seniority, sought to become a force for reform in the committee, but he was denied a seat.

The text that the Finance Committee submitted to the Senate was nothing more than a restructuring of the established tariff schedules. Although the tariff rates for a few items were lowered, most either went unchanged or were raised slightly. Furthermore, classifications of products were changed and these reclassifications almost always provided greater protection for American manufacturers.   The Aldrich version of the tariff was a reassertion of the principles of the Dingley Tariff, with no provisions for removing the competitive edge provided by the tariff to established industry.

Progressive Republicans, viewing the tariff draft as a presumptuous use of the leader's power, felt that Aldrich had misused his control over the Finance Committee to thwart the declared goals of the party, and that he was attempting to use his position as majority leader to silence the objections of the progressives. Determined that Aldrich would not go unchallenged, progressive Republicans organized an open rebellion against the leader's tariff. These insurgents in the Senate became well coordinated during the tariff battle. Under the leadership of Robert LaFollette (R, Wisconsin) and Albert Beveridge (R, Indiana), the Senate insurgents became a systematic political force. They met regularly, divided tasks, and maintained discipline.[8] They would attempt to use this organizational base in subsequent party disputes.

Despite the efforts of progressive reformers, the Payne-Aldrich Tariff became

---

[7] Nathaniel W. Stephenson, *Nelson Aldrich, a Leader in American Politics* (New York: Charles S. Scribner's Sons, 1930), 358–360 and fn. p. 478.

[8] Hechler, *Insurgency*, 99–145, and George E. Mowry, *Theodore Roosevelt and the Progressive Movement* (Madison: University of Wisconsin Press, 1947), 46–65.

law.   It marked the triumph of the conservatives over progressive reform. However, this defeat did not break the insurgents, but instead induced them to expand their efforts. As the insurgents were losing ground on the tariff issue, William Borah (R, Idaho) and Albert Cummins (R, Iowa) proposed the creation of a progressive federal income tax. This tax—an effort to reduce individual wealth and redistribute income—was anathema to the arch-conservative Aldrich. The Old Guard quickly searched for an alternative revenue scheme and settled on a corporation tax. Once again, the conservative Republican leadership prevailed, leaving the insurgents with the feeling that they had been stifled.[9]

In both the tariff and income tax cases, Senate insurgents showed no inclination to desert their party, just the leadership of Nelson Aldrich. The Democrats could be used as leverage against the Old Guard, but the Democratic party was not perceived as a safe haven for disaffected Republicans. The insurgents continued to strive for a reformed Republican party that would generate policy in a rational fashion, not through the manipulations of senior members of the party.

Between the conservative Old Guard and the insurgency lay the amorphous center of the Republican party. Approximately half of the members of the party were caught between these two factions. These Republicans were likely to be conservative, but their conservatism was different from that of the Old Guard. They believed in classical economics, and feared the class warfare of socialists and single-taxers.   They had faith in the ability of American business to bring well-being to the entire population and believed that the government's duty lay in the protection of free enterprise. While they did not seek the same substantive political changes the insurgency envisioned, they did question the dictatorial power of the floor leadership. The main body of the Republican party in Congress believed in rational competition. Just as they suspected that monopolies tended to undermine legitimate business competition and genuine growth, they doubted that the power of Cannon and Aldrich was conducive to rational government. These men in the middle were not a cohesive group united by a single ideology. Their actions in the two years between 1909 and 1911 can be characterized by grudging support for the insurgency's attack on procedural rules, but a reluctance to support the substantive changes to tariff law and regulatory legislation proposed by these reformers.

The products of the insurgency's attacks were satisfactory to no one. The power of the floor leadership was weakened; the membership of committees reflected the political and geographical balance of the entire chamber; legislation could move more easily from committee to the floor. However, the legislation passed during this period of turmoil was still fundamentally conservative. The Old Guard retained considerable control over the substance of legislation, a situation symbolized by the passage of the protective Payne-Aldrich Tariff.

The conflict that had begun on Capitol Hill became a nationwide dispute by

---

[9] Hechler, *Insurgency*, 146–153.

1910. The Old Guard dedicated itself to eliminating the insurgency in Congress. As part of this effort party conservatives solicited the aid of the White House. President William Howard Taft had not been a supporter of the legislative agenda of the western progressives. However, it was the insurgents' unwillingness to adhere to party direction that cemented Taft's decision to support Cannon and Aldrich. He was willing to tolerate debate, but not to the detriment of party rule. Using its influence over the Republican National Committee, the Old Guard supported conservative Republican candidates who were willing to challenge the reelection of insurgent Republicans. Although a few insurgents lost their seats in Congress, the Old Guard's effort was a failure. Not only did the insurgency continue to exist, but its opposition to the party leadership intensified.[10]

THE INSURGENCY AND THE ELECTION OF 1912

Debates over the control of the legislative process and the role of the federal government exploded in 1912. Intense conflict over progressive reform had been building at the state and local levels. In California, Iowa, and Pennsylvania accusations of despotism and corruption were hurled at conservative Republicans who defended property interests. Progressive politicians at all levels began to see a systemic problem within the Republican party. The revolt had expanded in scope and was no longer simply targeted against Cannon and Aldrich; President William Howard Taft was branded as the ultimate reactionary.

The Republican nominating convention of 1912 would become one of the most bitter in the party's history.[11] Taft's incumbency did not lead to automatic nomination. Progressive Republicans searched for their own candidate to unseat Taft. The former president, Theodore Roosevelt, became a key figure in this search.

Theodore Roosevelt had been absent at the outset of the insurgent revolt. While the insurgents organized against the power of Joseph Cannon, Roosevelt hunted game in Africa. During his return trip, he was intercepted in Europe by Gifford Pinchot. Purged from the Department of Interior for his attacks on more conservative superiors, Pinchot had strong opinions regarding the insurgency. He provided Roosevelt with a complete, if not unbiased, account of the general turmoil

---

[10] Lewis L. Gould, *Reform and Regulation: American Politics from Roosevelt to Wilson*, 2d ed. (New York: Alfred Knopf, 1986), 140–143. See also Paolo E. Coletta, *The Presidency of William Howard Taft* (Lawrence: The University Press of Kansas, 1973), 113–120.

[11] For detailed accounts, see Brands, *TR*, 707–719; Gould, *Reform and Regulation*, 148–160; John M. Cooper, *The Warrior and the Priest: Woodrow Wilson and Theodore Roosevelt* (Cambridge: Harvard University Press, 1983), 156–163; Francis L. Broderick, *Progressivism at Risk: Electing a President in 1912* (Westport, Conn.: Greenwood Press, 1989), 37–56; and Amos Pinchot, *History of the Progressive Party, 1912–1916* (New York: New York University Press, 1958), 158–163.

in the party. Roosevelt was concerned by Pinchot's report and returned to the United States ready to chide President Taft.

Proximity to the crisis in Washington merely reinforced Roosevelt's concern. His criticism of Taft intensified, and he found that he could not support the president's renomination. As a former president, he was the most senior of all the opponents of Taft and the Old Guard. His charisma was overwhelming.

During the Payne-Aldrich Tariff debates insurgents had begun to consider a challenge to Taft's renomination. The figurehead of the Senate opposition, Robert LaFollette, saw the debates as an opportunity to organize support for a presidential campaign. However, LaFollette's candidacy was immediately eclipsed by Theodore Roosevelt's declaration of candidacy. LaFollette's acerbic personality, combined with a failure to extend his political following beyond Wisconsin, eliminated him as a genuine threat to Taft. As a result, Roosevelt, not a member of Congress, would be the leading challenger at the Republican National Convention.

Although he had extensive support among Republican politicians, Roosevelt lost the nomination to Taft at the National Convention in Chicago. Taft's victory resulted from an institutional quirk in the convention's voting structure, not from widespread support in the party. The size of the state delegations at the convention had been determined by the total state population, not by the number of registered Republican voters. Taft, with his control over federal patronage, had been able to secure the votes of the southern delegates. It was this control over delegations from states where the Republican party was weak that secured the nomination for Taft. In response to Taft's victory, Theodore Roosevelt bolted the convention and formed an independent Progressive party.

The division of the Republican party in 1912 was severe. A significant number of important politicians left the Republican party, but they did not constitute the entire progressive movement. Those who left the party to follow Theodore Roosevelt were likely to hold state, not national, office. Only two members of the Senate—Miles Poindexter (R, Washington) and Joseph Dixon (R, Montana)—left the Republican party to join Theodore Roosevelt's Progressive party.[12] Members of Congress understood the consequences of a bolt. The rank of a congressman was defined by his position within the party. To leave the party meant to abandon seniority; to abandon seniority meant to abjure power. While they might not have campaigned for William Howard Taft, most insurgent Republicans did not break with the party itself.[13] For their reward, they shared in the few perquisites left to

---

[12] Holt, *Congressional Insurgents*, 65. Dixon was not returned to the Senate and Poindexter asked to rejoin the Republican party after the election of 1914.

[13] A few senators, including Norris, Cummins, and Clapp, endorsed Roosevelt, but supported the rest of the Republican ticket. Borah refused to endorse anyone in the presidential race. Works was unusual in that he endorsed Wilson, but supported the rest of the Republican ticket. Holt, *Congressional Insurgents*, 66–70. The Republican/Progressive split had its most dramatic implications for the private life of Nicholas Longworth (R, Ohio),

the Republican party in Congress after Wilson's victory in 1912.

The election of 1912 demonstrated what had been foreshadowed in the debates over the Payne-Aldrich Tariff and the revolt against Joe Cannon. The insurgents opposed, first and foremost, the misuse of power by the party leadership. They found intolerable the manipulation of institutional procedures to thwart the will of the majority. The insurgency was a revolt against the conservative individuals who led the Republican party. Insurgents sought to reform their party, not to abandon or destroy it. They argued that the Republican party was something greater than Aldrich or Cannon or Taft and they resented any Old Guard claims to the contrary. Nonetheless, the division was deep enough. The Taft-Roosevelt split divided the Republican voters, thus permitting the election of the Democratic candidate, Woodrow Wilson.

THE REPUBLICAN PARTY AND THE NEW POLITICS OF CONSENSUS

In 1913 Republicans suddenly found themselves the minority party. Not only had they lost the White House, they lost control of the Senate as well. (The Democrats had taken control of the House of Representatives in the fractious election of 1910.) Nonetheless, the Republicans assumed they would have to endure Democratic control for only a brief period. The divisions at the Chicago convention would be repaired. Errant Progressive bolters would have to be punished, but they would be quickly absorbed back into the party.

The process of reconsolidation was eased by changes in party personnel. In 1911 Nelson Aldrich retired, and Joseph Cannon lost his seat in the election of 1912. With these departures, the insurgency was confronted with a new style of leadership. The regular Republicans began to reconsider the role of the floor leaders and recognized the need for conciliation and compromise within the party. As the insurgency lost its two antagonists, its bellicose nature subsided. The vitriol of the Taft years gave way to protracted negotiation. Only Robert LaFollette refused to give quarter; he alone continued his personal attacks against the conservative leadership of the party and remained the gadfly of Senate politics.

After the election of 1912, Henry Cabot Lodge (R, Massachusetts) took on a role of increasing importance in the Republican leadership. He was one of the principal architects of the plan to rebuild the party, and was largely responsible for securing a role for insurgents. Lodge was in no way an insurgent progressive. He had held a position solidly within the mainstream of the Republican party since the aftermath of the Spanish-American War. He was an early supporter of American commercial expansion into the international market. He advocated an American economic empire based on a strong monetary system, worldwide naval presence, and access to markets throughout colonial areas. Lodge believed the financial and industrial strength of the United States was one of the nation's greatest assets, and

---

who chose to stand with his party and campaign for Taft rather than support his father-in-law, Roosevelt.

constituted no serious threat to the American people. Despite his conservatism, Lodge would seek out opportunities to work with the insurgents for the purpose of party solidarity. Lodge's concept of party structure, not his ideology, made him an important ally of the insurgent wing of the party.

Lodge had witnessed the Republican defeats in both 1892 and 1912. The lesson he had learned in both cases was that the Democrats could only win an election when the Republicans undermined their own party solidarity. Lodge was convinced of the superiority of the Republican party; the conduct of the Democratic party under Woodrow Wilson reaffirmed this notion. Lodge questioned the thrust of Wilson's early domestic program of progressive reform and became vehemently opposed to the president's policy leadership as political attention shifted from domestic to foreign issues. The primary objective of Lodge was to end Democratic control and the only way to achieve that was to unify the party.

The political skill of Henry Cabot Lodge had first been measured on the state level. He had come to office through the maelstrom of Massachusetts politics. Throughout the late nineteenth and early twentieth centuries the Republican party of Massachusetts was badly divided between urban progressives and Old Guard conservatives. To succeed politically, Lodge had to preach compromise in an atmosphere of bitter political antagonisms. The first four times he was sent to the Senate, he was elected not by the Massachusetts electorate, but by the state legislature. This process demanded an acute sensitivity to the rivalries among politicians. This situation did not change until the election of 1916, after the passage of a constitutional amendment providing for the direct election of senators.

Lodge's ability to gain support among Massachusetts politicians was complemented by his ability to maintain support among the general public. He could identify public opinion, and felt free to mold his political image to conform to that opinion. Despite his enthusiasm for liberal British political thought, he routinely pulled the Imperial Lion's tail for the amusement of Irish-American voters. He found it a political advantage to be pilloried by both the Old Guard and the Mugwumps.[14]

It was in the Senate that Lodge's instincts for institutional politics were refined. At the beginning of his career in 1893 he broke the unwritten tradition of the Senate that freshman were to be seen but not heard. His resolution to put an arbitrary end to the debate over the repeal of the Sherman Act (the one providing for bimetalism) was even more dramatic in that it contested the tradition of unlimited debate. The resolution died quietly, but it did serve to pull Lodge out of the shadowy environment of the Senate's freshmen.[15] He had impressed his party's leadership and had become a protégé of the Republican senior members.

Lodge's career was further enhanced by his appointment to the Senate Foreign

---

[14] See John Garraty, *Henry Cabot Lodge: A Biography* (New York: Alfred Knopf, 1968) and William Widenor, *Henry Cabot Lodge and the Search for American Foreign Policy* (Berkeley: University of California Press, 1980).

[15] Garraty, *Henry Cabot Lodge*, 134–136.

Relations Committee. By using the committee as a forum, Lodge had been able to take advantage of his friendship with and intellectual affinity for Theodore Roosevelt. He became a leading proponent of the new style of American commercial internationalism. He helped to lead the drive for a modernized blue water navy, an isthmian canal, and colonial systems that would both open new areas for international trade and uplift non-Western peoples to Anglo-Saxon ideals of democratic government.[16]

Since the Spanish-American War, Henry Cabot Lodge had become a leading figure in determining the direction of American foreign policy. He did not forgo this role after the election of Woodrow Wilson in 1912. Lodge had been one of the leading congressional supporters of Roosevelt's belief that it was America's destiny to lead the world in the twentieth century. He was steadfast in his efforts to promote an active American presence in international affairs. He was particularly aggressive in pushing for American military preparedness and diligent in defending American rights of neutrality. In order to return the Republicans to what he saw as their proper role as the majority party, and to secure the continuation of the Republican foreign policy that he had helped to formulate, Henry Cabot Lodge searched for a reconciliation with the members of the insurgency.

Under the direction of Lodge, conservatives and insurgent Republicans would find their common cause—the defeat of the Democratic party in the 1916 election. To achieve the removal of Wilson, Lodge was willing to make concessions to the insurgency. The movement's members received important committee assignments. William Borah, the insurgent who had generated so much controversy over his advocacy of an income tax, was assigned to the prestigious Senate Foreign Relations Committee in 1913.

The solidification of the Republican party in the Senate was relatively easy; Miles Poindexter was the only senator who identified himself as a member of the Progressive party. Through cooperation with the Democratic party, Poindexter was able to hold onto his committee positions until 1915. In that year he attempted to reenter the Republican party, but was informed by Minority Whip Henry Cabot Lodge that he would pay a price for his disloyalty.[17] Poindexter was stripped of his chairmanship of the Committee on Expenditures in the War Department. He was also denied seats on the Foreign Relations, Judiciary, and Interstate Commerce committees. For one year he served in limbo, denied all assignments he requested. After this brief period of punishment, he was readmitted into the party and placed

---

[16] Lodge's activity as a defender of American maritime interests was not limited to his political activity. His historical writings, such as *Alexander Hamilton*, emphasize the historical importance of international commerce and a strong navy. For an extensive examination of the intellectual roots of Lodge's foreign policy ideas, see Widenor, *Henry Cabot Lodge*.

[17] Normally this task would have gone to the minority leader, Jacob Gallinger (R, New Hampshire); it is unclear why Lodge was given the responsibility, but it is indicative of his importance in the efforts for reorganization.

on the powerful Committee on Committees.[18]

The Republican party courted bolters in an attempt to convince them that a reunified Republican party was a significant improvement over Democratic control of the federal government. Between 1912 and 1916 the Republican party gradually drew the wayward back to the fold. Even Theodore Roosevelt was treated as a prodigal son. Newly elected senators, including former Progressive party leaders like Hiram Johnson (R, California), were welcomed to the ranks of the Republican party in Congress.

The senior members of the Republican party faced significant problems in their drive for reunification. The outline of Woodrow Wilson's reform program included proposals for a downward revision of the tariff, a strengthening of the antitrust laws, and a restructuring of the banking system. This was the nature of reform long advocated by the insurgents of the Republican party. The organization of a cohesive opposition to the substance of Wilson's reform program could prove difficult. As a result, the Republicans chose to focus their reunification efforts not on debates over Wilson's policy, but on Wilson's policy making.

Conservative and insurgent Republicans agreed that policy making under Wilson had placed too much power in the hands of the executive. The election of 1912 not only put a Democrat in the White House, but it radically changed the relationship between the executive and legislative branches. With Democratic majorities of 291 to 127 in the House of Representatives and 51 to 44 in the Senate, Wilson decided that it was safer to work through the structure of his own party than to risk his programs by forming a new progressive coalition.[19]

During the Sixty-third Congress the Democrats came to depend heavily on a binding caucus to ensure solidarity in voting. Wilson had developed a policy of sending entire legislative programs to the Democratic caucus for consideration. Once a final decision was made, all Democrats were bound by the vote of the caucus. Commitment to the caucus decisions was strong. Intraparty differences were resolved long before an issue was discussed in floor debates. As a result, Wilson's authority in the party remained solid and his opponents could be controlled.[20]

Wilson's power was further augmented by the internal structure of the Democratic party in Congress. The party leadership was controlled by progressives with little experience. These progressives were ideologically tied to Woodrow Wilson and had linked their electoral success to his candidacy. John Kern (D, Indiana) was elected Senate majority leader in 1912 with only two years of

[18] Howard W. Allen, *Poindexter of Washington: A Study in Progressive Politics* (Carbondale: Southern Illinois University Press, 1981), 153–171.

[19] Gould, *Reform and Regulation*, 177–178; August Heckscher, *Woodrow Wilson* (New York: Charles Scribner's Sons, 1991), 285–293, 303–321; and Arthur Link, *Wilson: The New Freedom*, vol. 2 (Princeton: Princeton University Press, 1956), 145–175.

[20] Ripley, *Majority Party,* 58–59. See also, Marshall Dimock, "Woodrow Wilson as a Legislative Leader," *Journal of Politics*, 19 (February 1957): 3–19.

experience in the Senate; his Whip, J. Hamilton Lewis (D, Illinois), was a freshman senator.[21]   Although senior members of the party retained control of the committees, they had to share power in the caucus and during floor debate. Most of these senior Democrats were conservatives who were not inclined to agree with progressive reforms. However, Wilson's influence over the caucus and the floor debates was an effective curb on conservative dissent.

This cohesion of party policy around the executive offended those insurgent Republicans who might have been ideological allies of Wilson. To senators like George Norris and William Borah the caucus system smacked of "Aldrichism." The old enemy of despotic control over congressional voting had emerged wearing the Wilsonian mantle.[22] Democrats did not need the insurgency's votes to get legislation through Congress, and made no sustained effort to forge bipartisan progressive legislation. Divisions between the two progressive groups appeared as early as 1913 with the debates over the Underwood Tariff, as insurgent Republicans were frustrated in their attempts to protect agricultural commodities and to increase income tax rates.[23] The separation continued throughout the Wilson presidency.

Wilson was the dominant force in the Democratic caucus and effectively used it to speed legislation past partisan opposition. Republican perceptions of Wilson's control over Democratic members of Congress added a new dimension to their opposition to Wilsonian policies. This opposition originated during the debates over domestic reform legislation, and it intensified as the war in Europe pushed foreign policy questions into the forefront.

THE PRESIDENTIAL ELECTION OF 1916

The efforts to reunify the Republican party were designed to strengthen the Republicans in Congress, but also to replace Woodrow Wilson with a Republican president in 1916. Republicans and Progressives sought to erase the memories of 1912 and reunite the party. This required finding a presidential candidate of

---

[21] Ripley, *Majority Party*, 52–53. See also Link, *Wilson: The New Freedom*, 48.

[22] Holt, *Congressional Insurgents*, 84–85. Albert Cummins denounced Wilson on the floor of the Senate, arguing, "The influence which has been exerted by the President upon members of Congress, an influence so persistent and determined that it became coercive is known to every intelligent citizen of the United States. . . . The President of the United States, assuming to interpret and apply the economic doctrine of his party, has laid the heavy hand of his power upon a branch of the Government that ought to be co-ordinate, but which, in fact has become subordinate. It ought to humiliate us all somewhat when we look around and find that the people generally not only understand the surrender of our rights and privileges but observe it with a certain degree of satisfaction." Lindsay Rogers, "President Wilson's Theory of His Office," *The Forum* 51 (February 1914): 175–176. See also *LaFollette's Weekly* 4 (November 9, 1912).

[23] See Holt, *Congressional Insurgents*, 81–94 and Arthur Link, *Woodrow Wilson and the Progressive Era, 1910–1917* (New York: Harper and Row, 1954), 36–42.

national stature who had been involved in politics during neither the Taft insurgency nor the Roosevelt bolt. The obvious selection was Charles Evans Hughes.[24]

Hughes had impeccable credentials as both a Republican and a progressive reformer. His political career developed in New York State. In 1905 and 1906 he led investigations to determine the role of corruption in the management of public utilities and life insurance companies. The thoroughness of these investigations revealed an extraordinary collusion between wealthy businessmen and Republican politicians. The state leadership of the Republican party realized it could only revive its reputation by making Hughes its candidate for governor in the 1906 election. Hughes won the election and compiled an impressive record as a reform governor. His rising stature within the party led President Taft to nominate him to a vacancy on the Supreme Court in 1910.

Hughes left elective politics just as the Republican party was being torn apart by the disputes between the Old Guard and the insurgency. As a member of the Court, Hughes held himself aloof from partisan politics. He adamantly refused to become involved in the disputes over the tariff, taxation, and party discipline. This detachment was so complete that Hughes refrained from voting in elections for fear that a trip to New York would distract him from the pressing affairs of the Court.[25] He never took a stand against the actions of the Old Guard. Nonetheless, Hughes was able to maintain his credentials as a progressive reformer through his decisions on the Supreme Court. As a justice, he promoted an interpretation of the Constitution that supported increased federal authority in interstate commerce and permitted state protection of workers' interests. In 1916 he was one of the few nationally known Republicans who was respected by progressives and conservatives alike.

Calls for a Hughes candidacy increased in the spring of 1916. Frank Hitchcock, who had been the manager of William Howard Taft's successful presidential campaign in 1908, began to solicit Republican delegates without Hughes's approval.[26] Hughes's viability as a successful candidate was cemented by the climate of reconciliation in the party. Under these circumstances no candidate who had offended another faction could receive a majority of the delegate votes. Furthermore, the National Convention was more impervious to factional manipulation after rules changes in 1913, which weakened the influence of southern delegations. As one prospective member of the Republican National Committee complained during a credentials fight, "Every time we get into a contest

---

[24] For an analysis of the Republican factionalism leading to the formation of a consensus around Hughes, see S. D. Lovell, *The Presidential Election of 1916* (Carbondale: Southern Illinois University Press, 1980), 1–38.

[25] Merlo J. Pusey, *Charles Evans Hughes*, vol. 1 (New York: The Macmillan Company, 1951), 316.

[26] Pusey, *Charles Evans Hughes*, 320.

of this kind we are called upon to do something for harmony's sake."[27]   In a political climate promoting harmony, with no dominant factional leader to contest his nomination, Charles Evans Hughes emerged as the most obvious candidate.

The first ballot at the convention placed Hughes in the lead, with 253 ½ of the necessary 498 delegates for nomination. As the balloting continued, delegates committed to favorite sons shifted to Hughes. In response to the momentum of the convention, John Weeks and Lawrence Sherman withdrew from the race.[28] Recognizing the rising support for the Hughes candidacy, Theodore Roosevelt announced that he would not oppose a Republican ticket headed by the justice and the Progressive party was left to join the fusion or suffer ignominious defeat. This ended any serious threat to the Hughes candidacy from Republican quarters. On June 11 Hughes resigned from the Supreme Court and on June 30 he accepted the Republican nomination with a speech entitled "America First and America Efficient."

The core of Hughes's campaign against the Wilson presidency concerned foreign policy, not domestic reform. During Wilson's first term the Democratic party had lowered the tariff, restructured the banking system, and increased the power of the federal government to prosecute antitrust cases. All of these accomplishments had been sought by progressive Republicans. Although progressive Republicans might be willing to attack the specifics of the Democratic legislation, they would not necessarily ally themselves with more conservative members of the party to propose a Republican alternative. Progressive Republicans were divided in their opposition to Wilsonian reforms, with some charging they went too far, some complaining that they were insufficiently stringent, and some simply regretting their connection to the opposition party. Nevertheless, progressive Republicans agreed that if given the opportunity, the conservatives of their own party would destroy the good that Wilson had accomplished. Domestic reform issues were simply too divisive to form the foundation of the Republican campaign in 1916. However, a broad spectrum of Republicans could achieve a consensus over foreign policy.

Republicans had begun their attacks against Woodrow Wilson's foreign policy from the outset of his administration. Wilson's selection of William Jennings Bryan as secretary of state was met by Republican skepticism. Bryan was inexperienced in diplomacy; his political career had been strictly limited to the domestic sphere. His stature in the party was based on his three failed attempts to be elected president. Bryan could not win the nomination a fourth time in 1912, but had been instrumental in the nomination of Woodrow Wilson. The image of Bryan as secretary of state made it easier for Republicans to attack the substance

---

[27] Minutes of the Republican National Committee, June 10, 1916, p. 58.

[28] The first big shift for Hughes came when the Michigan delegation abandoned Henry Ford, who had won the primary election, and announced support for Hughes. See Lovell, *The Presidential Election of 1916*, 46. For a discussion of the shift of other candidates to Hughes, see Pusey, *Charles Evans Hughes*, 327.

of Wilson's foreign policy. The points of attack concentrated on two main issues. Republicans objected to Wilson's dependency on noncareer diplomats whose commitments were to the defense of the president's political philosophy, not the preservation of established diplomatic relations. In addition, Republicans decried the deficient state of military preparedness and the subsequent inability of the U.S. military to defend American interests abroad.

Wilson had been presented immediately with major revolutions in China and in Mexico. Both were important tests of nonindustrialized nations' attempts to develop modern, democratic governments. In both cases the introduction of republican governments led to a series of civil wars and American lives and property were placed in jeopardy. Wilson was not willing simply to follow the pattern of economic and military intervention that had been established under the Republican administrations; he wanted to create a distinctly different course of action.[29]

Wilson agreed with his Republican predecessors that the United States should defend emerging democracies. He did not share their assumptions of how that defense would be achieved. The Roosevelt and Taft administrations had both encouraged the expansion of American business interests in emerging republics such as China and Mexico, believing that the resulting economic development would provide the foundation for liberal democracy. Republican foreign policy experts were committed to the assumption that democracy functioned best under a rising standard of living and that this required heavy external capital investment.

Wilson questioned this economic qualification for democracy. His experience with recent American politics demonstrated that the presence of corporate influences was more a threat than a support to democratic government. Under Wilson, the Department of State separated itself from American business interests in China and Mexico. Career diplomats, who often had strong ties both to American business and the Republican party, were replaced with political appointees. At worst, these men were political hacks; at best, they were well-intentioned naifs. These new diplomatic representatives were loyal to the president and his democratic ideals, but had limited experience in both information

---

[29] Wilson envisioned a new international order that did not depend on the use of military force or economic coercion. In a general climate of democratic government and healthy economic competition, states would preserve their national honor and self-determination. Conflicts that arose would be resolved through diplomacy and arbitration. Wilson continued to advocate a new international order throughout his presidency, but often resorted to military intervention and economic coercion to attain U.S. foreign policy goals. A substantial body of literature exists on Wilson's foreign policy objectives: see Arthur Link, *Wilson: Revolution, War, and Peace* (Wheeling, Ill.: Harlan Davidson, Inc., 1979); N. Gordon Levin, *Woodrow Wilson and World Politics: America's Response to War and Revolution* (New York: Oxford University Press, 1968); Lloyd Gardner, *Safe for Democracy: The Anglo-American Response to Revolution, 1913–1923* (New York: Oxford University Press, 1987); and Lloyd E. Ambrosius, *Woodrow Wilson and the American Diplomatic Tradition* (Cambridge: Cambridge University Press, 1987).

gathering and negotiation.[30]   Republican politicians were already critical of Wilson's decision not to support American corporate activity in China and Mexico. As a result of his decision to depend on inexperienced diplomats, Wilson lay open to Republican accusations of ineptitude. Republican attacks on Wilsonian foreign policy in China and Mexico would provide much of the foundation for the battle against Wilson's response to the European war.

The assault on Woodrow Wilson's foreign policy was led by the ranking Republican on the Senate Foreign Relations Committee, Henry Cabot Lodge. His efforts were augmented by his old friend, Theodore Roosevelt, who repented his actions of 1912 and hoped to use his charisma to unify the party against Wilson.[31] The Lodge/Roosevelt assault on Wilson's foreign policy was based on the question of preparedness. They believed that the United States had emerged as an international power at the beginning of the twentieth century. This new status carried the obligation to defend American interests with military force when necessary.   It would be inappropriate for the United States to intervene indiscriminately in foreign disputes; intervention risked both human and material resources. However, when the attendant gain outweighed the apparent risk, military intervention could be threatened or used. Lodge and Roosevelt argued that this capacity for intervention required a military force prepared for immediate deployment.

As the presidential campaign unfolded, relations with Mexico deteriorated. In response to Pancho Villa's cross-border assault in the spring of 1916, Wilson sent the Pershing Expedition into Mexico. Deficiencies in training and equipment became apparent and Republicans sharpened their attacks. The inability of the American army to pursue and capture the renegade Pancho Villa, combined with its defeat by the Mexican Constitutionalist army during the incident at Carrizal, did not bode well for any future performance in the European war.

Lodge and Roosevelt found another major point of attack with the question of protection of merchant shipping in the European war zone. German threats to American merchantmen, combined with submarine attacks on Allied merchantmen carrying American passengers, raised questions about Wilson's commitment to defend American lives and property abroad. The *Lusitania* incident provided a

---

[30] See Larry Hill, *Emissaries to a Revolution: Woodrow Wilson's Executive Agents in Mexico* (Baton Rouge: Louisiana State University Press, 1973); Noel Pugasch, *Paul Reinsch: Open Door Diplomat in Action* (Milwood, N.Y.: KTO Press, 1979); and Gardner, *Safe for Democracy.*

[31] The discussions between Lodge and Roosevelt are borne out in their correspondence; see Henry Cabot Lodge and Charles F. Redmond, eds., *Selections from the Correspondence of Theodore Roosevelt and Henry Cabot Lodge*, vol. 2 (New York: Charles Scribner's Sons, 1925), 447–459. John Cooper details Roosevelt's shift in interest away from domestic political concerns to foreign policy beginning in 1914; see Cooper, *The Warrior and the Priest.* H. W. Brands emphasizes Roosevelt's romantic fascination with military valor as the reason for Roosevelt's increasing emphasis on foreign policy after 1915; see Brands, *TR*, 760–775.

focal point for Republican discontent. The death of 128 American citizens triggered a public demand for action. Diplomatic negotiations began between Secretary of State Robert Lansing and German Ambassador Count Johann-Heinrich Bernstorff to end submarine attacks on commercial vessels. The Wilson administration was able to secure a German commitment to end its policy of attack without warning. Despite this success, Republican politicians continued their criticism of Wilson's policy, arguing that it was insufficiently resolute.

As the European war dragged into 1916, most of the Republican members of the Senate came to support Lodge. His pleas for military preparedness appealed to the nationalism of conservative and insurgent Republicans alike. Insurgent politicians assumed the superiority of American democratic institutions, and most accepted as an article of faith that a military defense of American democracy was necessary. A few, like Miles Poindexter, fully supported Lodge's calls for preparedness and a more assertive defense of American neutral rights. William Borah supported a stronger American army, but when faced with the possibility that the United States might enter the European war, he reminded the Senate of the warning of entangling alliances in Washington's Farewell Address. The insurgents were not opposed to armed defense. They believed the United States needed a military force able to defend American lives and property. Their support for a strong military faltered when they realized that only a thin line separated the defense of American lives from the defense of American corporations.

Charles Evans Hughes was able to synthesize a campaign position that accommodated the interests of both conservative and progressive Republicans. The issue of preparedness was key to this synthesis. Virtually all Republicans agreed that the United States needed a substantial military force to defend its national interest. Even those insurgents who were reluctant to send U.S. troops into the European war agreed that the army needed to be large enough to provide a credible deterrent threat. During the campaign Hughes stressed what insurgents considered Wilson's inadequacies in the expansion and professionalization of the United States Army.[32]

Despite this unity over a key foreign policy issue, the Hughes candidacy was weakened by the split between the wings of the Republican party. Although Republicans were committed to the logic of party unification, the acrimony of the Taft insurgency and the Progressive bolt could not be erased completely. The candidate Hughes could not overcome the fundamental mistrust within the party.

This problem of mistrust was most critical in California. The Republican party of that state was split between populist-oriented progressives in the north and conservative business interests in the south. Politics in northern California were dominated by Hiram Johnson, who had been a popular reform governor and ran as Theodore Roosevelt's vice presidential candidate in 1912. He loathed the Old Guard and only supported a fusion of Republicans and Progressives with great

---

[32] Pusey, *Charles Evans Hughes*, vol. 2, 350–359.

misgivings. The situation was further complicated by Johnson's decision to run for a seat in the U.S. Senate in 1916. He originally sought the California Progressive party's endorsement, but after the Chicago convention he decided to cross file as a Republican. In an effort to placate Johnson, the Hughes campaign lobbied California Republicans to accept a fusion endorsement. Dismissing the conciliatory acts of the national Republican leadership, state party leaders, William Crocker and Francis Keesling, fought ardently for the defeat of Johnson.[33] Hughes's campaign in California needed to be conducted with extraordinary tact and sensitivity.

Hughes was not able to negotiate the complexity of party rivalries in California. His campaign tour through the state was swept into the acrimony of the Senate primary race. William Crocker, in his role as Republican National Committeeman, dominated the scheduling of Hughes. As a passionate opponent of Johnson, Crocker sought to deny him the political benefit of appearing in public with Charles Evans Hughes. The tension surrounding the Hughes campaign tour descended to the near farcical during an overnight stay in Long Beach. Those responsible for Hughes's local arrangements chose not to inform the presidential candidate that Governor Johnson was staying in the same hotel. Upon discovering the coincidence, Governor Johnson declined to proffer an invitation, fearing the perfidy of Hughes's conservative escorts. The failure of Hughes to call on Johnson was perceived as a snub. Although Johnson endorsed Hughes and portrayed him as a true progressive, the Progressive voters of California failed to follow Johnson's lead.[34] Hughes lost the state of California in the November election. California's thirteen electoral college votes cost Charles Evans Hughes the presidency.

Wilson's defeat of Hughes in the 1916 election frustrated Republican politicians. They had made tremendous strides in reunifying the Republican party. In many states the old division between conservatives and progressives had been repaired. However, this accomplishment was insufficient. Wilson had won California by a margin of 3,775 votes. The failure of Hughes in that state resulted from the inability of the conservative and progressive factions to work in union.

The Republican party strategy was the correct one. The leadership simply had not accounted for the difficulty of its execution. They understood that the process of reconciliation needed to continue and it would eventually return them to power. Further changes were made in the convention rules of the Republican National Committee. When the Republicans selected a new national chairman after the 1916

---

[33] Crocker was the representative to the Republican National Committee and Keesling was the chairman of the state Republican party; both had strong ties to the conservative business interests of southern California. For a full account of party factionalism in California, see Richard Lower, *A Bloc of One: The Political Career of Hiram Johnson* (Palo Alto: Stanford University Press, 1993). See also Lovell, *The Presidential Election of 1916.*

[34] See Lower, *A Bloc of One*, 65–91 and Mowry, *The California Progressives*, 247–277.

election, the conservative party leadership bowed to the will of important insurgents and chose Will Hays, the candidate proposed by both William Borah and Theodore Roosevelt.[35] Under the direction of Will Hays the party would continue to strive for an end to acrimony and the construction of a new party solidarity. He continued the pattern of reconciliation established four years earlier. Hays affirmed this policy of inclusion to the Republican National Committee by asserting, "There is but one possible rule for a party organization; the rights of the individuals within the party to participate in the management of the party's affairs shall be and remain equally sacred and sacredly equal."[36]

THE REPUBLICAN PARTY AND WORLD WAR I

Shortly after the presidential election, the Republican party faced a reexamination of U.S. foreign policy toward Europe. The international events between 1914 and 1917 forced the insurgents to consider the importance of foreign policy issues, and they found themselves incapable of fully absorbing the bellicose stance of Lodge. The attitudes of insurgent Republicans toward U.S. foreign policy were marked by ambivalence. Preparedness for the defense of the United States might be acceptable to them; the use of a strong army or navy to project American business interests abroad was not. Fearful of being dragged into the defense of a corrupt Europe, insurgents searched for a political direction that protected American national honor.

Members of the insurgency suspected that antidemocratic forces were at work to drag the United States into the European war. The armaments industry was profiting enormously from increased demand; financial institutions were growing more powerful as they negotiated sales to the belligerent nations. Insurgents began to argue that the appropriate response to the carnage in Europe was not American intervention, but diplomatic pressure for an arbitrated settlement. President Wilson's emphasis on arbitration and negotiation with the Germans over neutral shipping rights provided a potential rapprochement. The Republican insurgents found themselves ideologically situated between Lodge and Wilson.

Despite their differences with Lodge, insurgents could not easily reconcile themselves to the full scope of Wilson's foreign policy. They had joined the Republican party in attacking Wilson's policy toward Mexico. They had accused the president of meddling in Mexican domestic problems when he ordered the occupation of Veracruz in 1914. They suggested his vacillating policy toward Pancho Villa had prompted attacks by the Mexican revolutionary. Many criticized

---

[35] Seward W. Livermore, *Woodrow Wilson and the War Congress, 1916–1918* (Seattle: University of Washington Press, 1966), 107–109.

[36] Quoted from Hays' acceptance speech as chairman of the Republican National Committee. Minutes of the Republican National Committee, February 13, 1918, p. 107.

the poor state of preparedness witnessed by the Pershing Expedition. They were dismayed by their belief that Wilson's Anglophilia was tying the United States to British foreign policy. Although many insurgents had supported the president's efforts to arbitrate a settlement in the European war, they became disenchanted with his lack of success, blaming it on his apparent support of Great Britain.

The climax of tension between the insurgents and Wilson came in the spring of 1917 with the debate over the armed merchant ship bill. In response to Germany's decision to resume unrestricted submarine warfare, Wilson proposed the arming of American merchantmen. The mainstream of the Republican party (as well as several of the insurgents, including Borah and Poindexter) approved of the measure as an appropriate defense of American rights. However, a small group of insurgents led by George Norris and Robert LaFollette claimed that the bill would provide a situation even worse than a declaration of war. Under the bill, Wilson would have total control over an undeclared war. Through his power as commander in chief Wilson would determine the scale of combat and its objectives. The opponents of the armed merchantmen bill pointed out that without a declaration of war, Congress would have no role in defining American diplomatic objectives. In an effort to curb Wilson's power and prevent American entry into combat, Norris and LaFollette led a filibuster against the legislation. Wilson was infuriated by the Norris/LaFollette filibuster and condemned its supporters as a "little group of willful men." Although the filibuster did block the passage of the armed merchantmen bill, it did not prevent the eventual arming of merchant ships or U.S. entry into the European war. President Wilson called for a special session of Congress and received a declaration of war against Germany on April 6, 1917. However, the Norris/LaFollette filibuster reaffirmed the image of insurgents as intransigent opponents, willing to stall the machinery of government for their own policy objectives.

Debate over mobilization intensified after the declaration of war. Conservative Republican senators were frustrated by the difficulties of preparing an expeditionary force. Poor construction of the cantonments, combined with inadequate supplies, led to significant levels of disease among army recruits. Shortages of cotton, grain, coal, and other commodities made war preparations difficult and created a restive civilian population. The Republicans denied any congressional liability for these problems, placing all blame on the steps of the White House. Conflict between Republicans and Democrats extended to the method of paying for the war. Wilson wanted to limit the national debt and so advocated high taxes over bond issues. Conservative Republicans feared that high taxes would generate inflation and undermine business stability.

Republicans recognized that the executive had extraordinary power over policy making when the nation was at war. In an effort to promote a policy of consensus, they called for a bipartisan war cabinet. Wilson, however, was not moved. Citing the difficulties of the Lincoln administration during the Civil War, he insisted that members of the cabinet remain loyal agents of the president.[37]

The insurgent approach to the war differed from that of conservative Republicans, but still was not supportive of the Wilson position. Unlike the aggressive interventionist Republicans under Lodge, they stressed issues of civil liberties and fought against the growth of corporate strength during the war. They attacked the Espionage Act because it threatened freedom of speech. They opposed the draft as an ultimate violation of human liberty. They favored Wilson's nationalization of the railway system, but argued that his war profits tax was insufficiently stringent.[38] The insurgents would not be reliable allies of Woodrow Wilson.

Differences between the Wilson administration and the Republicans occurred at every level during the debates over the war. Disagreements were not limited to specific issues of the war's prosecution, but extended to debates over the fundamental purpose of U.S. intervention. Wilson sought a new international order. This became clear before the entry of the United States into the war. In January 1917 Wilson made his "peace without victory" address. In it he urged that nationalism be checked and called for a peace treaty that "will win the approval of mankind, not merely a peace that will serve the several interests and immediate aims of the nations engaged." This concept of placing limits on national power was expanded a year later in Wilson's "Fourteen Points" address. The Fourteen Points did not disavow nationalism, but did condemn the aggression that had been generated by nationalism. National borders were no longer to be determined by military conquest; international trade would not be manipulated for the benefit of powerful nations. The key to this new international altruism was the creation of an association of nations that would impartially serve both great and small states. Wilson's advocacy of a League of Nations would soon become the focus of Republican opposition.

Support for international government had been growing since the turn of the century. In fact, Republican administrations had advocated an increased use of the International Court at the Hague to solve diplomatic disputes. In the context of judicial arbitration, the sovereignty of nations would be preserved. Republican congressmen consistently stopped short of allowing an international organization

---

[37] For a detailed analysis of the reaction of the Republicans in Congress to Wilson's European policy, see Livermore, *Woodrow Wilson and the War Congress, 1916–1918* and Ambrosius, *Woodrow Wilson and the American Diplomatic Tradition.*

[38] Robert Johnson's examination of "peace progressives" includes both these Republican insurgents and like-minded Democrats. Johnson viewed the war period as a prelude to the coalescing of the group in 1919, during the debates concerning the Webb-Pomerene Act (to bar antitrust prosecutions in regulating international trade) and American intervention in Russia; see Robert D. Johnson, *The Peace Progressives and American Foreign Relations* (Cambridge: Harvard University Press, 1995). For a treatment of isolationist sentiment within the insurgent movement, see Thomas Ryley, *A Little Group of Willful Men* (Port Washington: Kennikat Press, 1966) and Ray Billington, "The Origins of Middle Western Isolationism," *Political Science Quarterly* 60 (March 1945): 44–59.

to intervene in cases where the issues concerned the vital interests or the national honor of the United States. It was this very point that had led to the failure of the Anglo-American Arbitration Treaty of 1911. Some Republicans outside of government, such as Elihu Root, William Howard Taft, and Charles Evans Hughes, were willing to trust Wilson to protect American interests in a new League of Nations, believing that the sovereignty of member states would be preserved.[39] However, the attitudes of Republicans in the Senate were different. The partisan disputes over the prosecution of the war had embittered relations between Wilson and Republicans in Congress. The party's leader in the Senate, Henry Cabot Lodge, simply did not trust the president's judgment.

The insurgency movement in the Republican party changed dramatically under Wilson's presidency. Although domestic issues continued to dominate their thinking, insurgents no longer dismissed foreign policy questions as being of secondary consequence. They felt that an incorrect response to the European war could expand corporate power, create a dictatorial president, and ultimately undermine American democracy. By 1918 the insurgents shared in Henry Cabot Lodge's concern with foreign policy questions. While Republicans could not agree on what was wrong with the president's leadership during the war, they believed that their own party would have done much better.

During the second Wilson administration, the Republican party in the Senate was still divided by ideology. However, the leadership of the party was dedicated to reunification. Reforms in legislative procedure had been generated before the 1912 election. The defeated party then set about to restructure the national committee rules. The national party developed a systematic means of supporting Republican candidates in state and national elections. Procedural rules for the national convention were altered to encourage debate and consensus building. The primary qualification for an appointment to the national committee was now dedication to party harmony. Although the ideological divisions within the party remained, much of the animosity had left intraparty politics. After 1917 Woodrow Wilson would face a much more formidable enemy in the Senate.

---

[39] As Thomas J. Knock demonstrated, the League to Enforce Peace (LEP) was dominated by these Republican supporters of the League. They did support Wilson in the early months of the League debates, but LEP support of the president began to erode in the summer of 1919. See his *To End All Wars: Woodrow Wilson and the Quest for a New World Order* (New York: Oxford University Press, 1992), 192 and 258.

2

Negotiating the End of Armageddon

> This is an added obligation upon us who make peace. We cannot
> merely sign a treaty of peace and go home with a clear conscience. We
> must do something more. We must add, so far as we can, the security
> which suffering men everywhere demand.
>
> —Woodrow Wilson

The insurgency was still a dynamic political movement within the Republican party
after the election of 1912. After the Roosevelt bolt the nature of the movement had
changed considerably. Joe Cannon (R, Illinois) and Nelson Aldrich (R, Rhode
Island) were no longer in Congress. The new Republican leadership adopted a
policy of negotiating differences between the progressive and conservative poles
of the party. The insurgents had demonstrated that they could not be removed from
American politics. Although they proved to be difficult allies, the insurgents
clearly were dangerous enemies. As a result, party unity became the preeminent
goal for the Republican leadership. Government under Woodrow Wilson and the
Democrats had been unsatisfactory to conservative and progressive Republicans
alike. The common enemy—Woodrow Wilson—served to hold the party together.
Tensions occasionally erupted between the different factions of the Republican
party, but the open hostility of the Taft years was ended.

Changes in international politics had also affected the insurgency. Defense of
American interests abroad, the preparedness of the American military, and the
outbreak of the European war had forced the insurgents to deal with foreign policy
issues. In its political strategy the insurgency was less bellicose; in its political
ideology it was more complex. The behavior of this new insurgency would be
critically important to the development of American foreign policy after the First
World War.

DIFFERING INTERPRETATIONS OF ADVICE AND CONSENT

The process of consolidation within the Republican party had provided some electoral success. Between 1910 and 1916 Republican voters did not abandon their party to become Democrats. They might vote for a Democratic candidate, but were just as likely to vote for a third party candidate or abstain from voting altogether. As the infighting between progressive and conservative Republicans subsided, these disaffected voters trickled back to their party. Although it did not regain the White House in 1916, the Republican party did erode the Democratic majority in both houses of Congress. Henry Cabot Lodge hoped to seize control of the Senate in 1918 as a prelude to a complete Republican victory in 1920.[1] Republicans were united in their commitment to curb Wilson's control over government and would be vigorous in their assault on the Democratic party in Congress.

The conflict between Wilson and the Republicans came to a climax in the 1918 congressional elections. Fearing the loss of his majority, on October 25, 1918, Wilson called on the American people to elect a Democratic Congress. He argued, "I need not tell you, my fellow countrymen, that I am asking your support not for my own sake or for the sake of a political party, but for the sake of the nation itself in order that its inward duty of purpose may be evident to all the world." Republican politicians immediately made the Wilson speech a campaign issue. Despite Wilson's claims to the contrary, Republican politicians—conservative and insurgent alike—accused the president of being unduly partisan, having attacked the patriotism of Republicans and the concept of loyal opposition. Already disgruntled with Democratic leadership during the war, many Republican voters felt that Wilson's speech confirmed their doubts. Key congressional contests fell to Republican candidates. For the first time since 1913, the Republicans controlled the Senate.[2]

The most significant change of the election occurred in the agricultural areas of the Midwest and Plains States. These areas had been dominated by the Republican party from the Civil War until the Taft presidency. This old dominance had been undermined as conservatives and progressives fought to control state party machines. Frustrated by the political infighting of Republicans, voters in these states had elected populist Democrats in 1910 and 1912. However, by 1918 voters were becoming disenchanted with Democratic politics as well. The Democratic party experienced increasing difficulty portraying itself as the defender of farming interests during the first administration of Woodrow Wilson. Under Wilson, the impetus for reform shifted from the populists of the party to those who shared Wilson's orientation to middle-class professionals. The resignation of Secretary of State William Jennings Bryan in 1915 had been a blow to the symbolic power of

---

[1] For an examination of the coordination of Lodge's activities with those of the chairman of the Republican National Committee, see Knock, *To End All Wars*, 168–171.

[2] See Livermore, *Woodrow Wilson*, 206–247.

agrarian reform in the Wilson cabinet. The Democratic party's relationship with these regions was further complicated by the presence of important German-American communities, which opposed the declaration of war in 1917. Certain wartime economic measures, such as the regulation of grain prices, antagonized voters from the Midwest and Plains. Conservative Republicans and supporters of insurgent reform reunited in 1918 and returned the old strongholds of populist reform to the Republican party.[3] The Senate passed into the hands of a group that had not supported Wilson's conduct of the war, was not confident in the president's judgment regarding the peace, and suspected Wilson would try to exceed his constitutional limits in the direction of American foreign policy.

The president's position was further complicated by the problems of negotiating the European peace. Only a few days after the election, the Germans surrendered and the horror of World War I was over. The diplomatic problems involved went far beyond the simple question of armistice. World War I brought about the collapse of the nineteenth-century balance of power. It was clear that the peace settlement would restructure the international system, just as the Congress of Vienna had done a century earlier. Much of Wilson's justification for U.S. entry into the war had been based on the importance of the postwar settlement. He hoped that an American presence at the peace conference would generate a new international system based on Wilsonian ideals.

Wilson's war aims were rooted in his own liberal ideology. These liberal ideals were reinforced by the Inquiry, his panel of advisors on the postwar settlement. The Inquiry encouraged Wilson's efforts to bring about free trade and create open competition in the world's markets. It declared that all sovereign nations were equal in international law. These positions were taken in the context of various European efforts over the previous 50 years to construct hegemonies. The Inquiry's new world order would be marked by an emphasis on democratic government and national self-determination.[4]

Wilson and the Inquiry hoped to use this set of objectives to unite liberal politicians in all the nations of the postwar world. The objectives stated the Fourteen Points constituted a package of reforms to the international system that would appeal to political moderates in all the belligerent nations involved in World War I. The rising power of political parties on the left, such as the Bolsheviks in Russia and the Spartacists in Germany, needed to be counterbalanced by a liberal

---

[3] Selig Adler, "The Congressional Elections of 1918," *The South Atlantic Quarterly* 36 (October 1937): 450–451, 460–463 and Seward Livermore, "The Sectional Issue in the 1918 Congressional Elections," *Mississippi Valley Historical Review* 35 (June 1948): 29–60.

[4] Klaus Schwabe, *Woodrow Wilson, Revolutionary Germany, and Peacemaking, 1918–1919* (Chapel Hill: University of North Carolina Press, 1985), 14–22. See also Lawrence E. Gelfand, *The Inquiry: American Preparations for Peace, 1917–1919* (New Haven: Yale University Press, 1963) and Arthur Link, ed., *The Papers of Woodrow Wilson*, vol. 53 (Princeton: Princeton University Press, 1986), 350–357.

reform ethic. In addition, the conservative calls to ardent nationalism that had risen during the war needed to be mitigated. Wilson's Fourteen Points were designed as the liberal solution to extremism on the left and right.

The allies agreed that the Fourteen Points furnished a sound starting point for diplomatic negotiation. However, they argued that the problems of the postwar peace required complex negotiations that would go far beyond this starting point. The European Allies had their own political priorities. The more conservative European leaders emphasized the issues of political and economic security. The Europeans would abandon the objectives of the Fourteen Points if they ran counter to these concerns. The complexity of the issues at the peace talks would require skilled and committed negotiation on the part of the American delegation.

Great Britain's prime minister, David Lloyd George, had suggested in 1917 that the gravity of the decisions to be made at the Paris peace talks required that Wilson lead the American diplomatic delegation.[5] The president decided that Lloyd George's assessment of the situation was correct. Woodrow Wilson would be the first president to head an American diplomatic delegation. This decision was unprecedented and, as a result, risky. Partisan differences were likely to complicate the ratification process of the peace settlement. Furthermore, there was evidence that severe tensions between the executive and legislative branches would erupt.

Wilson was confronted with a fundamental dispute over the definition of the Senate's role of advice and consent. He asserted that the executive branch held the primary authority in defining policy objectives; this authority was almost unfettered in the area of foreign policy. He came to this idea before his political career began, first advocating it in 1908 with his study of American politics, *Constitutional Government in the United States*. The president independently negotiated treaties and the Senate approved them, only exercising its opposition to ratification in extreme cases of executive dereliction.

Republicans felt differently about foreign policy making. Because of the long-standing power of congressmen in the party, Republican presidents had to confer with members of the Senate at all stages of treaty negotiation. If a Republican president failed to defer to the wishes of key senators, he would face a hazardous ratification process. This relationship between Republican presidents and the Senate had been reaffirmed several times in the twentieth century, the most recent occasion having been the failure of William Howard Taft's Anglo-American General Arbitration Treaty in 1911. Taft had failed to consult with Republican members of the Senate Foreign Relations Committee during the negotiation process. The committee responded by refusing to consent to the treaty without crippling amendments.[6] This separation over the definition of advice and consent

---

[5] U.S. Department of State, *Foreign Relations of the United States, 1917, Supplement 1*, Page to Lansing, February 11, 1917, pp. 41–44.

[6] Despite the fact that internal State Department correspondence indicates that Secretary of State Philander Knox's primary concern with the treaty was its acceptability to the Senate, Knox failed to discuss the treaty with any members of the Senate Foreign

would create different expectations of the American diplomatic delegation to Paris and of the treaties ending the world war.

In terms of international politics, Wilson's decision to head the American delegation was sound. Prime Minister David Lloyd George and President Georges Clemenceau headed the British and French delegations. Wilson's position on the American delegation had enormous advantages in terms of diplomatic protocol. Not only did foreign diplomats support the decision, Wilson's presence at the conference received massive popular support in Europe. However, domestic political limitations demanded another course. The political debates between Republicans and Democrats during the war had already indicated that Wilson's foreign policy goals did not have bipartisan support.

Lodge and Wilson differed greatly in their political outlooks. Controversies during the war had set these men into bitter opposition. By 1918 their disputes were no longer about ideas or programs; they had degenerated into invective. Conflict over the ratification of the peace treaty was certain.

As leader of the American delegation at the peace conference, Wilson controlled the negotiating strategy. The American negotiating position reflected Wilson's goals, not the complexity of opinion on Capitol Hill. By 1919 Wilson's primary objective had become the creation of a League of Nations. This new international organization would exist to prevent the sort of state-sponsored aggression against neighbors that had led to the world war. Wilson's vision of a postwar international order was idealistic, a system that would be governed by vaguely defined Christian principles of morality. The president promised that the League of Nations would end the power politics of the prewar era. Republican nationalists were skeptical of this vision. Curbs on national power would also affect the traditional diplomatic interests of the United States. Lodge, one of the leading adherents of American nationalism, was not willing to stand by and permit the death of Republican progressive diplomacy.[7] The man who was both Senate majority leader and chairman of the committee that would begin consideration of the peace treaty would certainly engage in concerted opposition to Wilson's foreign policy revolution.

Facing opposition from the majority leader, Wilson had to construct a strategy to undercut Lodge's power in the Senate. The insurgents could provide a powerful wedge to divide the opposition. If they could be absorbed into the president's camp, Lodge's power would be critically limited. However, Wilson faced nearly insurmountable problems in his dealings with this group. The ideological basis of the insurgency was rooted in the populism of the nineteenth century. The

---

Relations Committee until after it was presented to the Senate. Both Henry Cabot Lodge and former Secretary of State Elihu Root were serving on the committee at the time and anticipated a request from Knox for consultation. This breach of political etiquette was a major factor in the Senate's opposition to the treaty.

[7] Widenor, *Henry Cabot Lodge*, 266–299.

insurgents had adopted the assumption that the power brokers of Wall Street were engaged in an attempt to deny the common man his share in America's prosperity. They also reckoned that the ultimate villain was not the banking community of Wall Street, but the English financiers who controlled New York. Insurgent Republicans suspected British influence in Wilsonian internationalism. They reasoned that if such internationalism was actually inspired by Great Britain, then it was surely a weapon designed to destroy American democracy.[8] Their relationship was further complicated by Wilson's desire to maintain total control over foreign policy. The president's concept was reminiscent of the attitudes of the congressional leadership during the Taft administration. Insurgents began using the term "Aldrichism" when referring to Wilson's direction of policy making. They felt they were faced with the critical problem of an executive who assumed too much authority in policy making while that same executive was falling under the influence of a foreign government whose commitment to democracy was questionable.

Wilson did possess some potential advantages. The reunification of the Republican party was not complete. Lodge's authority over the wings of the party was not secure in the winter of 1918–1919. By sharing power with elements of the Republican party, Wilson could capitalize on Lodge's limited authority. This political strategy would require a departure from the policy-making process developed by the Democratic party over the previous six years. It was an adjustment Wilson was not willing to make. He insisted on executive leadership of foreign policy making, and took the principle of caucus homogeneity and applied it to the creation of the American delegation to the peace conference.[9] His actions—the abandonment of Republican foreign policy goals and the creation of an executive-centered policy-making apparatus—only served to unite the Republican party.

Wilson could have promoted an alliance with Republican insurgents by including

---

[8] For a detailed examination of the ideological foundations of insurgent foreign policy objectives, see Johnson, *The Peace Progressives*, 34–70. See also David A. Horowitz, *Beyond Left and Right: Insurgency and the Establishment* (Urbana: University of Illinois Press, 1997), 30–35.

[9] See A. J. Wann, "The Development of Woodrow Wilson's Theory of the Presidency: Continuity and Change," in *The Philosophy and Policies of Woodrow Wilson*, ed. Earl Latham (Chicago: University of Chicago Press, 1958), 62, and Louis Fisher, *Constitutional Conflicts between Congress and the President* (Princeton: Princeton University Press, 1985), 255–256. Arthur Link noted that Wilson considered the appointment of the ranking Democrat on the Senate Foreign Relations Committee, but protocol would require the additional inclusion of Henry Cabot Lodge, whom Wilson refused to consider. See Link, *Woodrow Wilson*, 105. August Heckscher argued that Wilson was also acting under considerations of health. Chary of personal confrontations, Wilson preferred to avoid the stress of protracted negotiations within the American delegation. See Heckscher, *Woodrow Wilson*, 490–493.

them in the American delegation to the peace talks. This technique had been used at the turn of the century when Secretary of State John Hay exploited political splits by using senators as delegates to major diplomatic conferences. This practice had not been used continuously by Republican presidents because some conservative members of the Senate perceived the technique as a mechanism for co-opting Senate consent.[10] However, Democratic senators, recognizing that Wilson would have to broaden the base of his domestic political support, thought that Wilson would do well to return to Hay's method of delegate selection. This would mean both Democratic and Republican members of the Senate Foreign Relations Committee taking an active part in the negotiation. Key Pittman was a Democratic member of the Foreign Relations Committee and an important figure in his party's western populist wing. Pittman strongly encouraged Wilson to include William Borah as a delegate to the peace conference, describing him as one who "represents the best thought in the Republican party."[11] Although he had major ideological differences with the president, Borah did admire Wilson's intellect. The idea of using him as a wedge in Senate politics was not sheer folly.

Nevertheless, Woodrow Wilson was committed to the concept of the executive's absolute control of foreign policy making. Undeterred by earlier conflicts between Republicans and Democrats over the American role in the European war, Wilson persisted in his position on executive domination of foreign policy making. Not only did he head the American delegation in Paris, but he also decided to make ideological homogeneity a criterion for the appointment of the other delegates. The principal American delegates to the Paris conference were President Woodrow Wilson, Secretary of State Robert Lansing, White House Advisor Colonel Edward House, General Tasker Bliss, and career diplomat Henry White. Although White was a Republican, his ties to the party were weak. The Republican party's reaction to Wilson's decision was negative. Henry Cabot Lodge later described the delegation by saying, "The four gentlemen who went with him were called delegates, but they were mere surplusage."[12]

---

[10] This practice was initiated in 1898 during the negotiations with Spain. Of the five principal negotiators, three were members of the Senate Foreign Relations Committee. Continued use of senators as diplomatic agents sparked protest over the confusion of executive and legislative roles in foreign policy making. This protest was led by George Hoar (R, Massachusetts), Eugene Hale (R, Maine), and Joseph Foraker (R, Ohio). Denna Frank Fleming, *The Treaty Veto of the American Senate* (New York: G. P. Putnam's Sons, 1930), 27–31.

[11] Fred L. Israel, *Nevada's Key Pittman* (Lincoln: University of Nebraska Press, 1963), 38, and Pittman to Wilson, November 15 and 27, 1918, Key Pittman Papers, Library of Congress.

[12] Henry Cabot Lodge, *The Senate and the League of Nations* (New York: Charles Scribner's Sons, 1925), 217. A detailed critique of Wilson's selection of delegates appears in Robert Ferrell, *Woodrow Wilson and World War I, 1917–1921* (New York: Harper and Row Publishers, 1985), 136–138.

Wilson's final selection of delegates ensured the homogeneity of the American negotiating position. However, when seen in conjunction with the Republican electoral success of 1918, it was perceived as a calculated slap in the face. Republican senators assumed an adversarial position and were ready to challenge the president on virtually every point. What had been Wilson's war would become Wilson's peace. The Treaty of Versailles and the League of Nations would be irreversibly linked to the person of Woodrow Wilson.[13]

During the winter of 1918–1919 the various delegations met in Paris, debated the basic guidelines of the treaty, and generated draft agreements. To facilitate negotiation, they decided that the work of the committees should be conducted in relative secrecy. Press releases were limited and delegates gave out little information regarding negotiating positions or the status of agreements. Because of this general silence and Wilson's physical separation from Congress, the Senate was effectively shut out of policy making. This isolation of the Senate conformed to Wilson's conception that the formulation of foreign policy rested with the executive. In the winter of 1918–1919 the supremacy of the executive's position was extended, however, as Woodrow Wilson began to argue that he could formally commit the U.S. government to a preliminary peace.

Wilson insisted that this arrangement, which included U.S. membership in the League of Nations, would be achieved through an executive agreement, and consent of the Senate was unnecessary.[14] This decision was made despite condemnations by leading Republicans in the Senate. Philander Knox (R, Pennsylvania), who had been secretary of state under William Howard Taft, submitted a resolution to Congress calling for the president only to negotiate the peace and leave questions of the League of Nations to a separate conference. Henry Cabot Lodge also attacked the merging of the League of Nations and peace issues and raised the specter of nonratification.[15]

The emphasis on foreign policy through executive agreement conformed to Woodrow Wilson's concept of executive leadership. Wilson used as his precedent the case of the Roosevelt *modus vivendi* with the Dominican Republic. In 1905 Theodore Roosevelt had attempted to ensure Dominican financial stability by taking control of its customs houses and providing a military guarantee to Dominican sovereignty. When Roosevelt was faced with Senate opposition to this arrangement, he set aside attempts to secure the relationship with a treaty. Instead

---

[13] See John McCook Roots, "The Treaty of Versailles in the United States Senate," honors thesis, Harvard University, 1925. Roots's thesis benefited from complete access to the papers of the Senate Foreign Relations Committee and interviews with most of the key committee members. These papers passed from Lodge to Borah upon Lodge's death. Most of these papers have since disappeared.

[14] Kurt Wimer, "Woodrow Wilson's Plans to Enter the League of Nations through an Executive Agreement," *The Western Political Quarterly* 11 (December 1958): 800–812.

[15] *Congressional Record*, 66th Congress, 2nd Session, December 3, 1919, p. 23, and December 21, 1919, p. 724.

he used an executive agreement to define the relationship between the United States and the Caribbean republic. However, when he decided to rely on an executive agreement, Roosevelt had been careful to secure the support of an important faction of senators led by John Coit Spooner.[16] Wilson failed to understand that Roosevelt had succeeded because he had a strong core of support in the majority party of the Senate. The Roosevelt *modus vivendi* was indicative of his working relationship with Republican senators and a capacity to outmaneuver the opposition within his own party.[17] It did not indicate the emergence of a foreign-policy-making procedure dictated by the executive. In the case of the League, Wilson had no such working relationship with a core of leading senators in the majority party. Senators Henry Cabot Lodge, Philander Knox, and William Borah were those Republican senators whose opinions regarding foreign policy were most respected. All of them questioned the very principle of international government as well as the legitimacy of the executive's domination of foreign policy making.

Wilson's argument for this use of the executive agreement was not even agreed to by the other members of the American negotiating team. Both House and Lansing feared domestic political problems over the League of Nations and did not want to complicate American entry into the League with a debate over the legitimacy of executive agreements. Wilson dropped his proposal to skirt Senate advice and consent, but continued to link the League of Nations to the general peace treaty. He felt that its importance to the preservation of world peace was self-evident, and as a result he could force senatorial support.

In the winter of 1918–1919 Woodrow Wilson was not yet willing to run a course of full opposition against the Republican majority in the Senate. He assumed that the Republican Senate would follow his lead in policy making as the Democratic Senate had before 1919. This was not an entirely unreasonable assumption. Before the Republican congressional victory, the Senate Foreign Relations Committee had been chaired by William J. Stone (D, Missouri). "Gumshoe Bill" Stone was a conservative Missouri politician. Even though he was philosophically

---

[16] Roosevelt did use executive agreements to bypass opposition in the Senate, but he was always mindful of Senate power. In the case of relations with the Dominican Republic, Roosevelt was faced with both a hostile Democratic party and Republican senatorial leadership jealous of its foreign policy prerogatives. The president, with Senators Knox, Spooner, and Lodge, determined that the best course of action was to indefinitely postpone the Senate vote on the treaty and allow the president to create a *modus vivendi* with the Dominican Republic. The Senate had not abdicated its strong position in treaty making and the president succeeded in developing a system of relations with the Dominican Republic that ensured executive latitude. See W. S. Holt, *Treaties Defeated by the Senate* (Baltimore: Johns Hopkins University Press, 1933), 218–229.

[17] In fact, Roosevelt was often criticized by the more radical insurgents for his cooperation with conservatives like Joe Cannon and Nelson Aldrich. See Robert LaFollette, *LaFollette's Autobiography* (Madison: The University of Wisconsin Press, 1913), 285–321.

opposed to most of Woodrow Wilson's foreign policy initiatives, he still consistently complied with the decisions of the president and the Democratic caucus. Differences between Stone and Wilson became greater and greater as the debate over German submarine warfare intensified. Although he supported the filibuster against the armed merchantmen bill, Stone never used his full powers as chairman to block Wilson's efforts. As the likelihood of war with Germany increased, Wilson was no longer certain of the compliance of Stone. To avoid an open conflict, Wilson and Stone agreed that Gilbert Hitchcock (D, Nebraska), the second-ranking Democrat on the committee, would shepherd the war resolution through committee. In this way disagreements between the president and the chairman of the Senate Foreign Relations Committee would not interfere with the smooth construction of American policy.[18]

Wilson's approach to the peace settlement ignored two key problems: Henry Cabot Lodge's contempt for the president's judgment in foreign affairs and the Republican party's search for campaign issues. As the leader of the Republicans in the Senate, Lodge's attitudes would be critical. Like Theodore Roosevelt, Lodge assumed that the international system was evolving toward dominance by the English-speaking peoples. The rise of American leadership was best served by the preservation of an international system where sovereignty extended only as far as the nation-state. America's commercial strength guaranteed its power; cooperation with the other great commercial power, Great Britain, was essential to continued American growth. While Borah feared the British would manipulate Wilson, Lodge feared Wilson was frittering away the good relations between the United States and Great Britain for the sake of internationalism.[19] Lodge maintained that Wilson's approach to the negotiations in Paris was not based on national self-interest, but on a dogged attraction to abstract and unproved political theory. The good that could be achieved at the close of the European war would be lost because of the vacuous idealism of the president. Lodge was confident that American interests were not being served during the negotiations, "Everything in Paris seems to be very confused. The President has managed to irritate Australia,

---

[18] See Ruth Warner Towne, *Senator William J. Stone and the Politics of Compromise* (Port Washington, N.Y.: Kennikat Press, 1979), 213–218 and Barbara Tuchman, *The Zimmermann Telegram* (New York: Macmillan, 1966), 174–175. By the time of his death in April 1918, Stone had become a strong supporter of the war effort and argued that the personal opinions of members of Congress needed to be subordinated to national policy goals. See *New York Times*, April 15, 1918, p. 15.

[19] Friction had already occurred between the British and Wilson. Lloyd George had opposed Wilson's idea of committing the United States to the League of Nations through an executive agreement. The British feared that a major fissure between the two branches of the American government would result in absolute deadlock and inaction. It was actually the pressure exerted by Lloyd George that caused Wilson to back away from his advocacy of an executive agreement, not that of House or Lansing. See Wimer, "Woodrow Wilson's Plans, " 805–807.

the Boers and South Africans, the English with Daniels' foolish talk about the navy, and I fear there has been some friction with France of a serious character."[20]

While still in Paris, Wilson arranged for a dinner meeting at the White House for members of Congress, including the membership of the Senate Foreign Relations Committee. This meeting was to be held on February 26 and would be Wilson's first public address upon his return to the United States. Wilson saw it as an opportunity to brief those congressmen directly related to the foreign policy process. He argued that this session was designed to foster cooperation between the White House and Capitol Hill. In such a spirit of cooperation, the president requested that the invitees refrain from making any public statements regarding the Paris Peace Conference until after matters had been explained to them by the chief of the American delegation. The impact of this gesture was ruined on the evening of February 25. While Wilson crossed the Atlantic, his secretary, Joseph Tumulty, arranged for a presidential address at Mechanics Hall in Boston. Although he objected to the symbolism of the venue, Wilson decided an abrupt cancellation would be more dangerous than the public address. The president's ship landed in Boston, and a few hours later Wilson made a major public address supporting his position on the peace conference. Republican senators considered this speech an affront to their commitment to silence; it was a particular blow to Henry Cabot Lodge, whose political base was in Boston.[21]

The Republicans who arrived at the White House meeting on February 26, 1919, were already suspicious of the president's intentions.[22] Many thought Wilson had acted in bad faith by asking them not to make public addresses regarding the European peace, and then delivering a major speech himself. Republican senators were uncomfortable with the negotiations. With both the president and the secretary of state absent from the country, the ability of the Senate to keep apprised of the negotiations was limited. The adversarial tone of the meeting was intensified by extensive questioning by Senators Philander Knox (R, Pennsylvania) and Frank Brandegee (R, Connecticut), who were unsympathetic to Wilson's concept of international government. By the end of the White House session, Republicans were attacking the president's seeming duplicity. They had hoped for details on the

---

[20] Lodge to J. D. Henley Luce, February 14, 1919, Lodge Papers.

[21] Link, ed., *The Papers of Woodrow Wilson*, vol. 55, 205–226. Some historians, most recently August Heckscher, have argued that Wilson agreed as a deliberate challenge to Henry Cabot Lodge. See Heckscher, *Woodrow Wilson*, 538.

[22] Wilson was spared the presence of some of his sharpest critics. William Borah declined Wilson's invitation, saying, "The differences between the President and myself on this question are fundamental, I am sure no suggestion of mine would modify in the slightest the views of the President and nothing could induce me to support this League as outlined in this proposed constitution or anything like it. I feel, therefore, that it would not be fair to the President to accept his confidence, or receive from him confidential information regarding the subject." Borah to Tumulty, February 17, 1919, William Borah Papers, Library of Congress.

negotiation process but received a generalized description and Wilson's request for patience. Lodge's darkest suspicions were confirmed. He described the session by saying, "We went away as wise as we came."[23]

The senators were facing the end of the lame-duck congressional session on March 4. Frank Brandegee, who was fundamentally opposed to the formation of a League of Nations, approached Lodge and suggested the Republicans make some public statement of their dissatisfaction with Wilson's League. After some consultation with the insurgent Albert Cummins, Lodge presented the draft of the "Round Robin Letter" to the Republican members of the next Congress. The Round Robin advocated the total separation of the question of peace with Germany from that of the League of Nations. The letter eventually gained thirty-eight signatures and was indicative of the difficulty Wilson would have in the Versailles Treaty ratification process.[24] Lodge knew that with the Democrats still in control of the Senate, the Round Robin could not pass as a resolution. He contented himself with reading it into the *Record* as a declaration of Republican intent. The Round Robin was the first blow in what would become a long and involved partisan battle between Wilson and the Republican Senate. Exchanges between the White House and the Senate tended to remain on this public level. Wilson continued to demand authority over foreign policy making and Republican senators became increasingly adamant in asserting their authority. There was no mechanism of private negotiation; compromises in the text of the peace treaty would be determined by the strict constitutional formulas of reservations, amendments, and ratification.

THE POLITICS OF CONSENSUS AND THE NEW REPUBLICAN MAJORITY

The election of 1918 marked a new plateau in the career of Henry Cabot Lodge. In the summer of 1918 he had been chosen minority leader of the Senate.

---

[23] Lodge, *The Senate,* 99–101. See also Ferrell, *Woodrow Wilson,* 166–167, and Ambrosius, *Woodrow Wilson and the American Diplomatic Tradition,* 82–83.

[24] The signatories of the "Round Robin" were: L. Heisler Ball, William Borah, William M. Calder, Albert B. Cummins, Charles Curtis, William P. Dillingham, Walter Edge, Davis Elkins, Albert Fall, Bert M. Fernald, Joseph Irwin France, J. S. Frelinghuysen, Asle Gronna, Frederick Hale, W. G. Harding, Henry Keyes, Hiram Johnson, Philander C. Knox, I. L. Lenroot, Henry Cabot Lodge, Medill McCormick, George P. McLean, George S. Moses, Harry S. New, Truman Newberry, Carroll S. Page, Boies Penrose, Lawrence C. Phipps, Miles Poindexter, Lawrence Y. Sherman, Reed Smoot, Selden P. Spencer, Thomas Sterling, Howard Sutherland, Charles E. Townsend, J. W. Wadsworth, F. E. Warren, and James E. Watson. *Congressional Record*, 65th Congress, 3rd Session, March 4, 1919, p. 4974. See also Lodge, *The Senate,* 119–120, and Ralph Stone, *The Irreconcilables: The Fight against the League of Nations* (Lexington: University of Kentucky Press, 1970), 70–75.

Although the reforms of 1909–1911 had placed some limitations on the power of the floor leaders, Lodge maintained a high level of authority over his colleagues through the strength of his personality. Despite his slight stature, Lodge was a man of great presence. His wit could be vicious, and he readily used ridicule as a weapon. He stood out in the Senate as both an extraordinary politician and as a great intellect. His continual push for compromise within the Republican party, his efforts to hold the insurgents in the party structure and reincorporate the Progressive bolters had led to the congressional victories of 1918. The Republicans would formally take control of the Senate at the beginning of the next congressional session, in May 1919. Lodge, in his dual role of Senate majority leader and chairman of the Foreign Relations Committee, determined that the first Republican objective would be a foreign policy victory over Woodrow Wilson. This victory would provide the foundation for a successful Republican presidential campaign in 1920.

The Republican victory in 1918 had not been overwhelming. They gained seven seats in the Senate, but their margin of majority was only two votes. One Republican seat was held by Truman Newberry, whose election was being contested over issues of campaign ethics.[25] The strength of the majority was further compromised by the political position of Robert LaFollette. It was LaFollette's opposition to the armed merchantmen bill that had triggered the outburst of wrath from Wilson; the Republican leadership, confronted with sniping and obstructionism from LaFollette since 1909, felt something much deeper. LaFollette had been the one insurgent to continue vitriolic attacks against the party hierarchy after the retirement of Nelson Aldrich. His attacks on conservative Republicans were always vocal and often personal. This style of political confrontation alienated even those Republicans who were sympathetic to his ideals. LaFollette's filibuster of the armed merchantmen bill also blocked a number of Republican-sponsored bills slated for consideration at the end of the congressional session. Frank Kellogg (R, Minnesota) and other moderate Republicans moved to censure LaFollette. The original move to censure did not succeed, but throughout the war LaFollette's Republican enemies threatened to resume their efforts.[26]

---

[25] Newberry's victory was being contested by his opponent, Henry Ford. The state of Michigan had officially recognized Newberry as the winner, but during the process of the recount, questions had been raised about the free spending of Newberry supporters. The questions of campaign financing and expenditure raised concerns among Republican insurgents who feared the involvement of special interests in Michigan politics. Democratic senators hoped to split the Republican vote and deny Newberry his seat. This attempt in the late spring of 1919 failed, but the debate over the ethical standards of Newberry's campaign continued well into the 1920s. See Spencer Ervin, *Henry Ford vs. Truman H. Newberry, the Famous Senate Election Contest: A Study in American Politics, Legislation, and Justice* (New York: Richard R. Smith, 1935) and *Congressional Record*, 66th Congress, 1st Session, May 20, 1919, pp. 33–40 and 62–63.

[26] Livermore, *Woodrow Wilson and the War Congress*, 115.

However, even this sort of inconclusive attack on renegade Republicans was curtailed after the election of 1918. With a majority of only two votes, the party focused on smoothing over party divisions and stifled intraparty disputes.

Relationships among the factions of the Republican party continued to be tense in the aftermath of the election. The Democratic Speaker of the House, Champ Clark, described insurgents as "few in number, [but they] are mighty in declamation and threats."[27] Despite earlier political posturing, all Republicans understood the advantage of unity. Henry Cabot Lodge was unanimously elected Senate majority leader as a show of solidarity in the face of Democratic opposition. Members of the party hoped that somehow reality would come to resemble the pose. The political decisions that were made in this atmosphere of compromise greatly affected the foreign policy goals of the Republican party and the peace in Europe.

The Republican party was guided by the lessons of 1912. It was politically unwise to drive straying Republicans out of the fold; insurgents would be incorporated into the party structure as a means of guaranteeing their loyalty. The goal was to bring them into the party hierarchy while maintaining the control of the established leadership. Lodge argued that all Republicans should be treated alike but "with full recognition of what has happened in the past."[28]

The immediate consequence of this position was political tension. LaFollette had provided the most extreme case of intraparty conflict in the previous session of Congress, but he was not alone in being out of step with his party's leadership. Taft insurgents—senators like William Borah and Albert Cummins—were still serving in Congress. They had continued their drive for domestic reform, and were comfortable in attaining that reform through confrontation. It was, after all, confrontation that had first defined the insurgency movement during the Taft administration. Opposed to the institutional power of the Democratic caucus as well as the conservative leadership of the Republican party, the insurgents had spent six years outside the channels of policy making. During this time they had promoted their own rebuttal to Wilsonian policies. In this effort they had been joined by new members of the Senate, several of whom had participated in the Progressive party bolt of 1912. If the insurgents were not handled correctly, they could attack the Republican leadership and drag the party into chaos.

Between March and May 1919 Congress was not in session. Henry Cabot Lodge had two months in which to reorganize the floor leadership and determine committee assignments in the Senate. This new institutional balance of the party would have to encourage stability and compromise in the next critical months. Lodge was determined to pull key members of the potentially dangerous insurgent

---

[27] *Washington Evening Star*, March 16, 1919, Section 2, p. 1.

[28] James Oliver Robertson, *No Third Choice: Progressives in Republican Politics, 1916–1921* (New York: Garland Publishing, 1983), and Lodge to McMurtie, November 19, 1918, Lodge Papers.

wing into the party's hierarchy. This included the appointment of insurgent progressives to high-profile positions of little power and to major committees where their basic reform ethic would not be translated into political action. The second most influential position in the Senate was the Majority Whip. However, this post required selfless devotion to party policy. The moderate, Charles Curtis (R, Kansas) was selected.[29]

The primary position for insurgent representation was to be the president pro tempore of the Senate. The Republican party leadership wanted the position to go to Hiram Johnson, who had risen to national prominence as the reform governor of California. Johnson's political career rested on an opposition to the influence of the Southern Pacific Railway over California's economy. He sought to end corporate influence over legislation by rationalizing the process of government. Under his leadership, California had implemented a state budget and had begun to require competitive bidding for state contracts. These revolutionary changes in state government conformed perfectly to the general spirit of progressive reform. As a consequence, Johnson not only had a strong base of support with California voters but also national recognition as a reformer. As Roosevelt's running mate in 1912, he had personified the western revolt against the Republican party. Making a nationally respected progressive the president pro tempore would be of symbolic importance. At the same time Johnson would not have so much power that he could present a threat to Lodge's leadership. However, Johnson would not accept the position. He was interested in the Republican presidential nomination in 1920 and felt it would be better to remain detached from the party leadership. He understood that the leadership of the Republican party would not be interested in encouraging his candidacy, and that his chances for the nomination were stronger as an outsider who could continue to cultivate a public image as a reformer.

Johnson's decision not to serve as the president pro tempore did not end the efforts to use the office to absorb insurgents into the party leadership. The position ultimately fell to Albert Cummins as a reward for the senator's willingness to work with party conservatives. Cummins was one of the original Taft insurgents. He had a strong record of reform as the governor of Iowa and had been a leading progressive in the Senate since 1909. As an opponent of the Payne-Aldrich Tariff, a supporter of the federal income tax, and an architect of the Federal Trade

---

[29] When the Senate discussion of the Versailles Treaty began, Lodge decided Curtis would not be a suitable figure for maintaining the Republican opposition to Wilson's treaty. He asked James Watson to become the special Whip for the League of Nations fight, with Curtis retaining his Whip position for all other questions of debate. Watson was to report only to Lodge and keep the arrangement a secret. While Watson was relatively new to the Senate, he had served in the House of Representatives and had been a protégé of Joe Cannon. The Versailles debate was not the first time Watson served as a special Whip; Cannon had assigned him the task of blocking the Norris proposals to alter the structure of the Committee on Rules. James Watson, *As I Knew Them: The Memoirs of James Watson* (Indianapolis: The Bobbs-Merrill Company, 1936), 190–191.

Commission, Cummins had solid progressive credentials. He was also a pragmatist and willing to work with conservative members of his party. Cummins's position as president pro tempore gave legitimacy to the Republican claim that insurgents were being welcomed back into the party as equals.

In the same vein, Henry Cabot Lodge worked to assign two members of the insurgent group to the Committee on Committees. Committee assignments would be made by a politically diverse group and would seem to be determined more equitably. Progressive insurgents immediately recognized that the suggested two votes provided them with a forum for debate on assignments, without giving them a chance to alter the Committee's decisions. Tradition bound members of the Committee on Committees to discontinue debate over assignments in the more public forum of the Senate floor. In effect, an assignment to the Committee on Committees would be used to stifle debate, not encourage it.

The most important question before the Committee on Committees concerned the chairmanship of the Senate Committee on Finance. The traditions of seniority rule would make the arch-conservative Boies Penrose (R, Pennsylvania) the chairman of the committee. Penrose was one of the remaining members of the Old Guard. He had been a devoted protégé of Nelson Aldrich, and had bitterly opposed even the mildest progressive reforms. The Penrose chairmanship would thwart the influence of progressives in finance legislation. Continued reform in taxation and banking would be difficult; even some of the gains that had occurred might be lost. Former Progressive party leader, Gifford Pinchot, described Penrose's appointment as utterly unacceptable, maintaining that he was "incapable of writing a tariff bill free from the influence of the corporations and monopolies which in politics he has always served."[30] Politicians who wished to be viewed as progressive reformers would not serve on the Committee on Committees, knowing they would be placed in a position where they could not attack the chairmanship of Penrose. While it was the subject of less notoriety, the rise of Francis Warren (R, Wyoming) to the chairmanship of the Senate Appropriations Committee was also opposed by insurgent Republicans. Like Penrose, Warren was a staunch conservative and would use his chairmanship to block progressive reform.

Lodge first asked Hiram Johnson and William Borah to serve on the Committee on Committees; they refused. William Kenyon (R, Iowa) and Wesley Jones (R, Washington) were asked and they refused. Finally, Asle Gronna (R, North Dakota) and Charles McNary (R, Oregon) agreed to serve.[31] Penrose would eventually become chairman of the Finance Committee, but not without strident opposition throughout April 1919.

Lodge feared that an open debate on the suitability of Penrose as chairman would be disastrous to party unity. He felt that the issues concerning expenditures,

---

[30] Gifford Pinchot to Lodge, February 7, 1919, Lodge Papers.
[31] Robertson, *No Third Choice*, 173—174. See also Borah to Lodge and Johnson to Lodge, May 19, 1919, Lodge Papers.

bonds, and taxes would fail to capture the public imagination; Senate debate regarding the conservatism of Penrose would do no more than raise public curiosity for a few days, and then be forgotten. This debate would distract the public from the crucial issues of the European peace, and more important, undermine the fragile unity of the Republican party. Henry Cabot Lodge encouraged J. T. Williams of the *Boston Evening Transcript* to use his friendship with William Borah to pressure the senator to compromise on the Penrose issue. He argued, "If they once get it to the floor and make a series of bitter personal attacks, Penrose and the others will retaliate. The attack will run on down the list and we shall lose control of the committees."[32]

When the Senate returned to session in May 1919, the Republican commitment to unity was still ambiguous. Democrats, realizing the tentative loyalty of the insurgent wing, hoped to spark a full separation of the two elements. The first challenge to Lodge's control over all the members of the Republican party came with the election of the president pro tempore of the Senate. Gilbert Hitchcock challenged the Republican sponsored candidate, Albert Cummins, and proposed that the Democrat Key Pittman be elected in his place. Pittman was from Nevada and had maintained good relations with western insurgents like William Borah and George Norris. Nonetheless, the Lodge strategy worked; the insurgents held with their party and Cummins was elected in a vote that followed strict party lines.[33]

A more serious challenge to Lodge's control came with the appointment of senators to committees. By tradition the resolution for committee membership was held under one vote, and then each existing committee elected its own chairman—routinely the most senior member of the majority party. Lodge insisted that the resolution not only serve to define committee appointments, but that it designate the chairmen of the major committees at the same time. The chairmanship of the major committees would then fall not to the committee membership, but to the membership of the Senate as a whole. Such a process would so widen the scope of debate—simultaneously throwing into question all of the memberships and all of the chairmanships—that it would serve to discourage attacks on specific positions. The Democrats bitterly accused Lodge of attempting to violate the rules of the Senate. After lengthy debate, it was determined Lodge was acting within the rules by introducing this sort of resolution. The vote on the committee assignments followed party lines; the insurgents had swallowed the Penrose and Warren chairmanships in exchange for Albert Cummins's chairmanship of the Committee on Interstate Commerce, William Kenyon's chairmanship of the Committee on Elections, and the guarantee of insurgent seats on all the major committees. The Democrats had once again failed to divide the Republican majority.[34]

---

[32] Lodge to J. T. Williams, May 19, 1919, Lodge Papers.

[33]*Congressional Record,* 66th Congress, 1st Session, May 19, 1919, p. 4.

[34]*Congressional Record,* 66th Congress, 1st Session, May 28, 1919, pp. 314–315.

While the insurgent element was in the party, it was not of the party. The Penrose issue still separated these progressives from the party hierarchy, and another issue was needed to secure party solidarity. At this point the intraparty political conflict began to have a direct bearing on the Republican foreign policy position. The role of the United States in the European war and the treaty-making process was clearly going to be a major campaign issue in 1920. It was a relatively safe issue in terms of intraparty politics in that it skirted the basic controversies of progressive reform. A tactical emphasis on the European peace would also serve to reinforce the authority of Majority Leader Henry Cabot Lodge. Lodge's authority in Republican foreign policy making was derived not only from his party leadership, but from his seniority on the Foreign Relations Committee. He had served on the committee since 1895, and had more seniority than all the other Republican members combined. Not only was Lodge principally concerned with issues of foreign policy, in this sphere he could exercise his greatest authority. Lodge understood that the selection of members of the Senate Foreign Relations Committee would be extremely important for the future of his party.

Henry Cabot Lodge saw the Foreign Relations Committee as a device for binding the party together. It was the most prestigious committee of the Senate, and appointment to it would be construed as a political favor. The subjects of committee discussion would allow progressives to adhere to the party position with limited liability. Lodge considered it essential to mitigate the power of the insurgents on this committee, and on the other major committees of the Senate. In the initial determination of committee composition, Lodge insisted on a margin of three votes on the Interstate Commerce, Elections, Finance, and Foreign Relations committees, staffing each with ten Republicans and seven Democrats. The Democrats objected that the ratio of votes in these major committees did not reflect the balance of power in the Senate. Lodge reminded the members that Democrats of the previous three Congresses had constructed committees to the political advantage of Woodrow Wilson. He defended his decision on the floor of the Senate by arguing, "We feel that the makeup of your committees is your business and your responsibility, and that the makeup of our committees is our business and our responsibility."[35] Lodge had guaranteed that dissenting voices would be heard in the major committees, but that dissent would not threaten the Republican leadership.

Henry Cabot Lodge wanted to consolidate the Republican position regarding the European peace. By generating a united front within the Senate Foreign Relations Committee, the Republican party could launch a sustained and effective attack against administration policies. The questions discussed by this committee would be the least likely to precipitate factionalism. It would be possible to include

---

[35] *Congressional Record*, 66th Congress, 1st Session, May 28, 1919, pp. 314–321. See also George Haynes, *The Senate of the United States* (New York: Russell & Russell, 1938), 290.

insurgent progressives on this committee and tie them to the mainstream of the party without risking schism.

Four new Republican members were to be added to the Senate Foreign Relations Committee; all would be chosen on the basis of their opposition to Wilson's foreign policy. The most clear-cut case of exclusion was Lodge's opposition to the appointment of Frank Kellogg (R, Minnesota), who was a supporter of Wilson's concept of the League of Nations. Despite Kellogg's interest in foreign affairs, his eagerness to serve on the committee, and his seniority, he was passed over in favor of George Moses (R, New Hampshire).[36] While the evidence is less obvious, it is likely that Albert Cummins was also passed over because his stand against the League was insufficiently vigorous.[37]

The Republicans added to the committee in 1919 were Warren Harding (R, Ohio), Hiram Johnson (R, California), Harry New (R, Indiana), and George Moses (R, New Hampshire).[38] All had signed the Round Robin Letter, which opposed the League of Nations as negotiated by Woodrow Wilson. The text of the resolution stated that "it is the sense of the Senate that while it is their sincere desire that the nations of the world should unite to promote peace and general disarmament the constitution of the league of nations in the form now proposed to the peace conference should not be accepted by the United States."[39] The appointment of Hiram Johnson marked a particular victory for Lodge. His membership on such a major committee constituted a public recognition of his importance, as well as assured his final cooperation with the party leadership. For Johnson, it meant a prestigious committee appointment without any real constraints on his image as a progressive reformer. His membership also marked a concession to William Borah, who had been seeking an ally on the committee.[40]

The Republicans on the Senate Foreign Relations Committee were now solidly

---

[36] Eleanor Dennison, *The Senate Foreign Relations Committee* (Stanford: Stanford University Press, 1942), 9–10. See also Kellogg to Lodge, May 31, 1919, Lodge Papers, and *Congressional Record*, 66th Congress, 1st Session, "Taft Urges Republicans to Oppose Knox Resolution and Save Party's Prestige," June 20, 1919, pp. 1430–1431.

[37] This issue is clouded in that Cummins was already tied to the party organization through his position as president pro tempore and Lodge clearly had a motive to use the Senate Foreign Relations Committee as a means of pulling other insurgent progressives into the party organization.

[38] The full membership of the Senate Foreign Relations committee for the Sixty-sixth Congress was as follows: Henry Cabot Lodge, Porter J. McCumber, William E. Borah, Frank B. Brandegee, Albert B. Fall, Philander C. Knox, Warren G. Harding, Hiram Johnson, Harry S. New, George H. Moses, Gilbert M. Hitchcock, John Sharp Williams, Claude A. Swanson, Atlee Pomerene, Marcus A. Smith, Key Pittman, and John K. Shields.

[39] *Congressional Record*, 66th Congress, 1st Session, March 4, 1919, p. 4974.

[40] Borah's move to get a political ally had consistently failed under the Republican minority. During the war Senator Kenyon sought a position on the committee, but failed, most likely because of his position on the embargo. See Holt, *Congressional Insurgents*, 126, and the *New York Times*, December 12, 1915.

against the League of Nations. Only one of the ten, Porter McCumber (R, North Dakota) had not signed the Round Robin. Although he was from an area dominated by insurgent politics, McCumber was not a member of the insurgent movement. He had distinguished himself by being one of the few Republicans in Congress to support wholeheartedly Wilson's concept of the League. As the second-ranking Republican on the Committee, McCumber could not be removed from the committee without dire political consequences. Lodge had to content himself with isolating the North Dakota Republican.

Not only was the Republican representation on the Committee solidly opposed to Wilson's version of the League, a significant minority was opposed to any version of international government. With the new additions to the committee, there were now four Republican members who were irreconcilably opposed to the League of Nations—William Borah, Frank Brandegee, Hiram Johnson, and George Moses. Under no circumstances would any of these men support U.S. entry into the League of Nations.

The selection of the new committee members had several effects. It created a unified, committed opposition to Wilson's League within the Senate Foreign Relations Committee. It widened the political base of Republican opposition by including both mainstream and insurgent elements. It provided political compensation to Borah and Johnson for their defeated attempt to block Boies Penrose's chairmanship of the Senate Finance Committee. It also meant that the full spectrum of opposition to Wilson's League was represented on the committee. Irreconcilables had been joined to those Republicans who would only support the conditional participation of the United States in the League of Nations.

THE ORGANIZATION OF REPUBLICAN RESISTANCE TO THE WILSON PEACE

Despite the fact that the treaty was still being negotiated and the League covenant was not complete, Republicans began forming into camps over the issue of the League of Nations in the spring of 1919. Three groups began to emerge—those who supported the president's plan, those who would accept a League of Nations if its power was circumscribed, and those who were irreconcilably opposed to any American entry into the League.

Supporters of the president comprised the smallest group within the Republican party and gravitated toward a reservationist sentiment as pressure against the Versailles Treaty mounted in the summer of 1919. The leadership of this group tended to come from senators with an interest in international law, such as Frank Kellogg. To compensate for their small numbers, they sought support outside the Senate by making ties to established Republican leaders involved in the League to Enforce Peace, including William Howard Taft and Charles Evans Hughes.

Fourteen Republicans in the Senate were irreconcilably opposed to the treaty. This group remained essentially static in membership, but was important because its commitment was intense and vocal. This group was unusual in that it resulted from cooperation between arch-conservatives and insurgent Republicans.[41] They were united by their fear that under a League of Nations, American foreign policy making would be subject to interference by other nations. Leadership of this group rested in the hands of William Borah and Hiram Johnson. As a result, the political style that governed the irreconcilable faction was one of insurgency.

The reservationist group was clearly the largest and ideologically the most diverse in the Republican party. Its members were not opposed to international organizations, but were chary of granting the League of Nations extraordinary power. They were willing to accept American entry into the League if they were certain U.S. interests were not jeopardized. The group's strength was determined by the fact that the undisputed leader of the faction was Henry Cabot Lodge. The reservationist position quickly became the de facto position of the Republican party. The group was further strengthened in the summer of 1919 as Lodge began to bridge the differences between reservationists and supporters of the League. Lodge was able to persuade the League supporters to accept reservations to the treaty that would define the limitations of the League's authority over the U.S. government. Republicans who supported the League believed that mild reservations that merely restated customary interpretation of international law would not undermine the fundamental characteristics of Wilson's proposal.

Before the Versailles Treaty negotiations were complete, the Senate Republicans were coalescing around an anti-League position. After the Round Robin, the Republican party prepared for a major confrontation when Wilson presented the treaty for the Senate's advice and consent. Henry White, the one Republican in the American delegation, recognized the threat to the League of Nations. He appealed to Lodge to cooperate with Wilson and suggested that Republican opponents work with the American delegation to create a treaty text that could be ratified without controversey. However, Wilson's February speech in Mechanics Hall had destroyed any sense of trust that had remained between the president and Senate Republicans. White's attempts to mediate between the executive and legislative branches failed.[42] The Republican position would be defined by its opposition to Woodrow Wilson.

---

[41] Those senators who were irreconcilably opposed to American entry into the League of Nations were William Borah (R, Idaho), Frank Brandegee (R, Connecticut), Albert Fall (R, New Mexico), Bert Fernald (R, Maine), Joseph France (R, Maryland), Asle Gronna (R, North Dakota), Hiram Johnson (R, California), Philander Knox (R, Pennsylvania), Robert LaFollette (R, Wisconsin), Medill McCormick (R, Illinois), George Moses (R, New Hampshire), George Norris (R, Nebraska), Miles Poindexter (R, Washington), James Reed (D, Missouri), Lawrence Sherman (R, Illinois), and Charles Thomas (D, Colorado).

[42] John Chalmers Vinson, *Referendum for Isolation: Defeat of Article Ten of the League of Nations Covenant* (Athens: University of Georgia Press, 1961), 67. See also Allan Nevins, *Henry White: Thirty Years of American Diplomacy* (New York: Harper & Brothers, Publishers, 1930), 397–402.

The party as a whole was to remain cohesive in the face of the Versailles Treaty. Both Republican reservationists and irreconcilables were careful to coordinate their efforts to stop the Wilson treaty. This cooperation existed in regard to procedural strategy. The two groups consulted over the presentation of amendments and reservations. They developed a joint strategy in committee hearings and during floor debates. They even made joint plans in their efforts outside the Senate in terms of rallying public support for their resistance to Wilson.

As he was establishing the Republican strategy against the Versailles Treaty ratification, Lodge solicited aid from William Borah. Borah was a man of considerable stature in the Senate. He had entered national politics in 1908 as a Roosevelt protégé. Borah had been a vocal advocate of progressive reform, and had been an articulate supporter of limitations on Senate Majority Leader Nelson Aldrich. He had refused to bolt in 1912 and so held the respect of loyal party men; he was an advocate of reform that followed basic rural progressive guidelines and so was respected by the other western progressives. He had continued his crusades for a downward revision of the tariff and federal regulation of large corporations. After his appointment to the Foreign Relations Committee during the Sixty-third Congress, he developed a strong position on American foreign policy. Borah had disapproved of Wilson's policy toward Mexico. He opposed the occupation of Veracruz in 1914, arguing it did little to support American national interests or Mexican political stability. He questioned Wilson's shifting support from one revolutionary leader to another, accusing the president of "meddling" in Mexican politics. He had joined Roosevelt and Lodge in their condemnations of the levels of military preparedness during the Pershing Expedition. Borah argued that the military had to be sufficiently equipped and trained to defend American citizens from border attacks. He supported U.S. participation in the war effort, but resisted attempts to equate patriotism with support for the war. During the war he was one of the most vocal advocates of civil rights, concentrating much of his energy against the Espionage Act and the efforts of the Department of Justice to curb public criticism of Wilson's war effort. Borah, one of the best orators of the Senate, had a fascinating ability: he could doggedly attack the actions of other senators without incurring personal animosity. Most important, because Porter McCumber (R, North Dakota) was an internationalist, Borah's rank as the third most senior Republican on the Foreign Relations Committee was critical in consolidating opposition against the Democrats. A political alliance between Lodge and Borah would effectively isolate McCumber and solidify the senior Republicans of the party. It was this alliance with Borah that made Lodge confident of his strategy to defeat the Democrats in the Versailles Treaty battle.[43]

The irreconcilable Republicans who followed Borah were an odd assortment of insurgents and archconservatives. The insurgents—Gronna, Johnson, LaFollette, McCormick, Norris, and Poindexter—all quickly acceded to his leadership.

---

[43] Lodge, *The Senate*, 148.

However, there were other members of the movement who were not so naturally inclined to participate in the politics of insurgency. The conservatives of the movement linked themselves to Borah's leadership for different reasons. The Republican position regarding the Versailles Treaty was going to be defined by Henry Cabot Lodge; any alterations in that policy would be made only by bringing considerable pressure to bear on the majority leader. The conservatives George Moses and Frank Brandegee were both friends of Lodge; but the importance of their opinions was measured by their link to a larger political movement, not by personal relations. As a former secretary of state, Philander Knox had a great deal of prestige; nonetheless, his opinions meant little to Lodge, who considered Knox a newcomer to the foreign policy debate. Conservative opponents of the treaty could best sway Lodge if they could throw party unity into question.[44] The arguments of an individual senator, no matter how articulate or impassioned, did not have the same force as the threat of a bolt. As a result, conservatives deferred to the leadership of Borah. He would define the irreconcilable attack and that attack would bear marked insurgent qualities.

In March 1919 Lodge and Borah developed the basic Republican strategy. Those senators who were irreconcilably opposed to the treaty would support all Republican-sponsored amendments and reservations. Borah was willing to accept even weak attempts to defend what he saw as the traditions of an independent American diplomacy. The Monroe Doctrine, which was designed to separate the Western Hemisphere from the political intrigues of Europe, had to be guaranteed. The United States could only maintain its independence from Europe if Congress's role in war powers was preserved. Such alterations of the treaty would help to "Americanize" the document and make it less dangerous.[45] It was understood that the Republicans would offer a unified front in regard to limiting the provisions of the Treaty of Versailles, but that on the final vote, reservationists and irreconcilables would not be bound by party instructions. Lodge assumed that this gave the reservationists the right to negotiate a compromise settlement with Senate Democrats and Republican internationalists. This was not an assumption shared by Borah, and this difference would eventually lead to controversy in the winter of 1919–1920.

Because the Republicans mounted their attack before the treaty text was negotiated, their criticisms began as a debate over general principles of American diplomacy. Not only did the early Republican critiques fail to examine specific

---

[44] Lodge, *The Senate*, 146–147 and Robert Maddox, *William E. Borah and American Foreign Policy* (Baton Rouge: Louisiana State University Press, 1969), 57–58.

[45] A major irreconcilable objection to the treaty—particularly true in the case of Borah—was the fear that the League of Nations would be dominated by the English and the French. The enforcement clause in Article X could be used to promote European colonial interests and deny American enforcement of the Monroe Doctrine. See Claudius Johnson, *Borah of Idaho* (Seattle: University of Washington Press, 1936), 239–240 and Maddox, *William E. Borah*, 50–68.

points of the treaty, they were not based on a single ideological framework. Lodge's decision to incorporate both reservationist and irreconcilable factions resulted in a continuous assault on Wilson from a variety of directions. Although it was effective in confrontations with Wilson, this diversity in the Republican party made it difficult for Lodge to generate a cohesive response to the treaty.

The Republican attack centered on the issue of sovereignty. It was believed that the new League of Nations covenant would contain provisions that could require U.S. military intervention on behalf of the League. This was seen as a violation of congressional control over declarations of war. Congress could be forced to act, regardless of domestic political considerations. Irreconcilables, in particular, feared that American military force would be used to defend European colonial interests. This potential misuse of American military force was seen to be particularly dangerous in Latin American disputes. In that region the cornerstone of American foreign policy, the Monroe Doctrine, was jeopardized. Throughout the Versailles Treaty debates, Republicans would maintain a solid defense of congressional prerogatives in foreign policy making. However, they would not be able to come to any compromise in defining acceptable American participation in the League.

This defense of the ability of the United States to act independently was accentuated by the Republican concern over the issue of secrecy. As early as February, the negotiators in Paris had a draft of the peace treaty; however, commitments to secrecy, combined with Wilson's notions of the independence of the executive branch in foreign policy making, led the president to deny members of the Senate access to the unfinished document. Denied access to treaty drafts and uninformed despite Wilson's February 26 meeting with members of Congress, Senate Republicans searched for some means to control the substance of the peace settlement. Frustrated by their lack of information, the Republicans simply made secrecy another point in their debate with Wilson. Once established as a legitimate subject of controversy, secrecy remained an important issue in the Versailles Treaty debates. Republicans defined the issue broadly, applying their attack to the absence of information pertaining to the current treaty negotiations and to earlier secret treaty commitments that had helped to form the wartime alliance.

Concern over secret diplomacy was not new in 1919. Secret treaties had been a major focal point of American diplomatic theory during the Progressive Era. The constitutional requirements of Senate support of ratification, combined with the public nature of Senate debate, effectively forced the U.S. government to make all its international commitments public. European nations were not so restricted and their heads of state regularly made commitments, often security arrangements, which were not announced until they were suddenly put into effect. American politicians, Republican and Democrat alike, had steadily attacked specific provisions of various European secret treaties. The American public became more concerned with this issue after the Russian Revolution in 1917. The new Russian government denounced the czarist claims to Constantinople in an effort to spur a negotiated peace. Trying to discredit Western liberalism's drive for total victory, they also made public the demands of Great Britain and France for the transfer of colonial areas in the Levant, Africa, and Asia. By 1919 the question of territorial claims in the secret treaties had clouded the discussion of the general peace. The sense of suspicion that permeated Capitol Hill was not allayed by Wilson. In an interview with the president, both Borah and Johnson asked about his knowledge of the secret treaties the Europeans had signed regarding postwar territorial disposition. He insisted he had no knowledge of the agreements prior to his arrival in Paris; he complicated the situation by suggesting that the State Department might have known of the treaties, but not forwarded the information. This simply confirmed insurgents' suspicions of manipulation by the Europeans. It also threw into question the role of the State Department in protecting American interests.[46]

Although Borah and Johnson first raised the issue, concern for secret diplomacy was not limited to the insurgent wing of the party. The party as a whole questioned Britain's use of the secret treaties that gained it territory in the Middle East and sub-Saharan Africa at the end of the war. Senator James Watson, the Republicans' special Whip for the Versailles Treaty debates, was vehement in his denunciation of the British. He reserved particular venom for Lord Balfour, who "spoke in most rapturous terms of the work we were doing in coming to the defense of human right, human liberties, and the 'democracy of the world.' And at the same time his pockets were bulging with secret treaties that had been made by the Allies to divide up the possessions of Germany."[47]

The criticism of secret diplomacy became intertwined with the issue of secret negotiation. Inability to secure detailed information regarding the discussions at Versailles simply reinforced the suspicion that the American negotiators were being manipulated by the British and French. This suspicion increased as General Jan C. Smuts, prime minister of the Union of South Africa, became closely identified with the covenant of the League of Nations. Irreconcilables were quick to point to the role of General Smuts in British imperial politics. In an address to the Senate, William Borah suggested that the prime minister was part of a British conspiracy to control the League of Nations.[48]

Lodge, Brandegee, and Borah complained that information regarding the negotiation process was being withheld from the Senate. Statements of negotiating positions, records of discussion, and working drafts were denied to the members. The tension that this situation generated was periodically intensified as senators discovered press accounts that included information that had been denied to the Senate Foreign Relations Committee. Brandegee complained that "the official records, as finally made up, reflect not what was actually said and done but what

---

[46] See Carton 4, Part III, Hiram Johnson Papers, and "The Innocent Abroad," *The Nation* 109 (August 30, 1919): 272–274.

[47] Watson, *As I Knew Them,* 204.

[48] *Congressional Record,* 65th Congress, 3rd Session, February 21, 1919, pp. 3911–3915.

it is deemed advisable to record."[49]

The lack of information regarding the negotiation of the treaty came to a climax in June. In the spring, the four major Allied delegations had agreed that the delicacy of negotiations demanded that some issues be held from public scrutiny until a compromise could be attained. In an effort to comply with this policy, Wilson had consistently argued that the Senate could not have a text of the treaty until it had been finalized and signed. He held to this position despite the fact that the German delegation had already distributed copies of the treaty draft to the European press. This problem of access to the treaty text was further complicated by the fact that the Allies had decided to limit public knowledge of the negotiations after several sessions had taken place. Before Wilson had agreed to keep the progress of negotiations secret, American businessmen had been consulted on the potential economic impact of the treaty; as a result some copies of the treaty were held by individuals who were not members of the American delegation. Rumors of these copies were particularly irritating to William Borah. The senator was able to procure one of "Wall Street's copies" through an intermediary at the *Chicago Tribune* and proceeded to read the text of the unsigned treaty into the *Congressional Record*.[50]

This unofficial text of the treaty confirmed the suspicions of Republican critics. The irreconcilables were particularly concerned that territorial adjustments at the end of the war reflected the goals of the secret treaties. The transfer of Alsace-Lorraine to the French and the demilitarization of the Rhineland were not criticized extensively in the United States. The transfer of Fiume to Italy was also seen as acceptable, if not desired. This city in the northern Adriatic had strong ethnic ties to Italy and had been the subject of a long-standing controversy between Italy and the Austro-Hungarian Empire. Attacks on the disposition of territory did not focus on these European questions, but rather on the control of colonial areas.

Colonial empires were going to be changed dramatically by the Versailles Treaty. Germany lost its entire empire at the end of the war. Its African colonies were divided between the French and British. Its Pacific colonies were mandated to the Japanese, British, and Americans. The Ottoman colonial empire was also affected by the peace settlement. Turkish government in the Levant was ended and the region was divided into spheres of French and British control. However, this transfer of territory was not limited to the defeated; although China had allied itself to Great Britain and France, it was powerless to prevent recognition of the Japanese seizure of the Shantung Peninsula.

The question of political control in Africa and Asia became a volatile topic as a consequence of Wilson's rhetoric regarding national self-determination. The public

---

[49] Brandegee to Lodge (copy of Conwell to Brandegee), undated—spring 1919, Lodge Papers.

[50] Johnson, *Borah of Idaho*, 237. The *Chicago Tribune* was controlled by the family of the irreconcilable, Medill McCormick.

had become inspired by the ideal of governments defined by ethnicity.[51] French control of Alsace-Lorraine and Italian control of Fiume reflected this logic of self-determination. This desire also provided the basis of the dissolution of the Austro-Hungarian Empire. However, Republicans, particularly those with Irish-American constituencies, pointed out that British rule over Ireland was left unquestioned.

The most liberal aspect of the Versailles Treaty, the covenant of the League of Nations, provided material for Republican attack. Provisions for enforcement of League decisions were defined under Article X, which stated, "The Members of the League undertake to respect and preserve as against external aggression the territorial integrity and existing political independence of all Members of the League. In case of any such aggression or in case of any threat or danger of such aggression the Council shall advise upon the means by which this obligation shall be fulfilled." Republicans feared this article would limit American sovereignty. A decision by the League could require the United States to wage war without a declaration by Congress.

Once provided with a document, Republican critics of the president could be more specific in their attacks. Article X of the League covenant provided an excellent target. The language of the article was vague. The full meaning of the League Council's ability to "advise" action was to be derived from established international law; it was not explicitly stated. Opponents of the League assumed that the power of the Council would infringe on the power of Congress. Furthermore, the League's critics could expand their attacks on Article X and condemn hypothetical wars to defend the territories transferred at the end of the war. Republicans used the term "Article X" to encompass all their objections to Wilsonian foreign policy.

When Woodrow Wilson returned from Paris with the final version of the treaty, he knew he faced stiff opposition from members of the Republican party. Nonetheless, he was convinced that the League of Nations was crucial to future stability, and that Republicans would cross party lines to support a peace treaty that contained the League covenant. Wilson had two options in his course of action. He could take up negotiations with members of the Senate in the hopes of settling the problem in a more confined arena. Alternately, he could appeal directly to the public, and hope that popular pressure would be enough to break up Republican resistance.

Wilson decided that an appeal to senators would be more successful, and in any event popular support could be marshaled if this direction proved to be fruitless.

---

[51] In fact, Woodrow Wilson's views regarding self-determination were limited. Betty Uterberger has demonstrated that Wilson viewed self-determination as a complex problem where ethnicity was only one of several factors in determining national boundaries. Nonetheless, the public perceived Wilson's call for self-determination as a sweeping defense of ethnic-based government. See "The United States and National Self-Determination: A Wilsonian Perspective," *Presidential Studies Quarterly* 26 (Fall 1996): 926–941.

Both Gilbert Hitchcock, the ranking Democrat on the Foreign Relations Committee, and Herman H. Kohlsat, a Republican advisor to the president, encouraged Wilson to concentrate his political efforts in Washington. They argued that the public was already supportive of the League and that senators could be more easily persuaded by quiet, direct pressure.[52] In July, Wilson announced that he would discuss the Versailles Treaty with any senator who wished to come to the White House. He continued this policy by specifically inviting senators to the White House for consultations.[53] This was an ideologically varied group, containing irreconcilables, reservationists, and internationalists. It served as a potential rapprochement between the Senate and the president. However, this effort had a limited effect. Not all who were invited to the White House accepted Wilson's arguments. Those Republicans who did take advantage of Wilson's overtures were already in his camp of supporters; these internationalist Republicans had already been effectively eliminated from a position of power by Henry Cabot Lodge.

The two Republican senators who were most willing to cooperate with Wilson were Frank Kellogg and Porter McCumber. Kellogg's stature as a lawyer familiar with questions of international law was undercut by Lodge's resistance to his counsel. McCumber's position on the Foreign Relations Committee was weakened after he was effectively isolated by Lodge. Furthermore, Wilson initially opposed even the internationalist Republicans' tactic of proposing mild reservations. These supporters of the League believed that mild reservations attached to the treaty would pull some Republicans into Wilson's camp. These mild reservations would do nothing more than reiterate standard interpretations of international law that defended the independence of sovereign nations. They asserted that Congress would retain its control over the declaration of war. In addition, Congress would preserve its influence over foreign policy through budgeting and appropriation. Established policies such as the Monroe Doctrine would not be affected by the decisions of the League Council.[54]

---

[52] See Kurt Wimer, "Woodrow Wilson Tries Conciliation: An Effort that Failed," *The Historian* 25 (August 1963): 419–438.

[53] Those specifically invited included Senators Porter McCumber (R, North Dakota), LeBaron Colt (R, Rhode Island), Knute Nelson (R, Minnesota), Arthur Capper (R, Kansas), Charles McNary (R, Oregon), Carroll Page (R, Vermont), Thomas Sterling (R, South Dakota), George McLean (R, Connecticut), Truman Newberry (R, Michigan), William Dillingham (R, Vermont), Bert Fernald (R, Maine), Warren Harding (R, Ohio), and Irvin Lenroot (R, Wisconsin).

[54] Wilson's efforts to attract the support of the Republican mild reservationists were supplemented by Senator Claude Swanson (D, Virginia). Swanson also courted Republicans who supported the League; unlike Wilson, Swanson encouraged the attachment of mild reservations to cement the alliance. See Jack E. Kendrick, "The League of Nations and the Republican Senate, 1918–1921" (Ph.D. dissertation, University of North Carolina, 1952), 204–205.

Despite the fact that he agreed with the soundness of many of the reservations, Wilson objected to their adoption for fear they would undermine the language of the negotiated treaty. He insisted that the League had no legal ability to compel the United States to act, and argued that the League possessed only the force of moral suasion. Wilson's explanation for opposing alterations of the treaty text was incomprehensible to most Republicans. Because they could not see his distinction between moral and legal compulsion, Republicans could not understand Wilson's objection to treaty reservations. The president's position was viewed as unreasonably recalcitrant.[55] This image of recalcitrance undermined his ability to split the vote of the Republican senators. Because Wilson did not recognize and address the Republican opposition to his claim on executive control in the determination of foreign policy direction, his overtures were badly targeted.

Woodrow Wilson faced an enormous problem in the summer of 1919. The partisan hostility that had marked the policy making during the prosecution of the war escalated during the peace negotiations. Ideological differences between the president and Republican senators were heightened as the 1920 presidential election drew near.

Although the Republicans in the Senate were divided, nearly all shared a common desire to see Wilson's Versailles Treaty defeated. Before they even had a copy of the treaty, Henry Cabot Lodge and William Borah had formed a unified Republican position and had charted a strategy for the Versailles Treaty debates. To see his treaty ratified, Wilson had to create a responding strategy that would undermine the authority of Lodge, divide the Republican majority, and pull straying Republicans into the Democratic camp. This task would have to be done in the short time between the commencement of the Senate Foreign Relations Committee hearings and closing arguments of the Senate floor debate, the very period when Henry Cabot Lodge set the agenda for discussion.

---

[55] Older accounts of Wilson's reaction to proposed reservations emphasize a lack of flexibility; see Vinson, *Referendum for Isolation*. The more recent Wilson biographers have been more charitable. Arthur Link noted Wilson's consistent attempts to persuade mild reservationists into his camp. See Link, *Woodrow Wilson*, 112–113 and 122–124. August Hecksher pointed to Wilson's willingness to accept the Republican reservations, except those concerning Article X. See Heckscher, *Woodrow Wilson*, 586–590. Nonetheless, the Republicans of the Senate consistently portrayed (and in all likelihood perceived) Wilson to be obdurately opposed to any reservations.

3

The Republican Party
and the League of Nations

A diplomatic affair with the United States is like a two volume novel in
which the hero marries the heroine at the end of the first volume and
divorces her triumphantly at the end of the second.
                                                    —Walter Lippmann

Woodrow Wilson faced a complex political task in the summer of 1919. He had
successfully completed the negotiation of the Versailles Treaty text, but at
considerable expense. His call for a peace without acrimony, designed to construct
a new and rational world order, was met with popular support in both America and
Europe. Cheering throngs had welcomed his arrival in Europe and newspaper
editorials lauded his efforts for a just and lasting peace. However, this public
acclaim for Wilsonian liberalism did not translate into a consensus among
politicians. The negotiation of the peace settlement forced compromises between
legitimate concerns. The Versailles Treaty, the cornerstone of the new world order,
had produced political division and disappointment.

It was in this context that Henry Cabot Lodge would be constructing a partisan
assault on Wilson's treaty. Most Republicans in the Senate were disappointed in
the treaty, both in the manner of its negotiation and in its substance. Lodge could
appeal to this disappointment and forge a Republican opposition to the Versailles
Treaty. The treaty debates could be absorbed into the process of forming a
Republican consensus; as such, they could provide the conclusive step in healing
the wounds of the 1912 election.

Wilson faced a more delicate task. Without the tools of party discipline or
political trust, he would have to convince Republicans to set aside their
disappointments. He would have to persuade them that the future of world stability
rested with the League of Nations, an organization that had received bipartisan
support as an abstract concept, but had never existed in any concrete form until
1919. This had to be achieved in the context of a presidential election campaign.

THE VERSAILLES TREATY AND THE APPEAL FOR PUBLIC SUPPORT

The treaty passed into the hands of the Senate on July 10, 1919, and was in the Committee on Foreign Relations within four days. Lodge feared accusations of dilatory activity in the Senate. He encouraged the immediate printing of the treaty and began preparations for committee hearings. Shortly after Wilson presented the text of the treaty to the Senate, the irreconcilable Medill McCormick (R, Illinois) began to push the Foreign Relations Committee to make public the debate on the treaty. McCormick feared the Republican position was being misrepresented by the president's supporters. To secure public confidence, McCormick urged the Republican leadership to invite extensive press coverage.[1] Lodge concurred with McCormick's analysis. The committee sessions were not only public, but highly publicized.

The hearings before the committee were extensive; their purpose was not to develop a fuller understanding of the treaty, but to inflame opinion against the peace settlement. The majority of witnesses testified on issues of postwar boundary settlements, where the influence of the secret treaties was strongest. The senators' queries concerned both the political balance within Europe and the dominance of international relations by the major powers. The testimony concentrated on the control of Ireland and the Shantung Peninsula, political questions that would inevitably prompt public disillusionment. Because the nature of the testimony taken by the Foreign Relations Committee was clearly anti-administration, both Wilson and Gilbert Hitchcock (D, Nebraska) began to pressure Lodge to draw the hearings to a close and move the treaty to the floor of the Senate. However, the Senate Foreign Relations Committee hearings were not the only venue for public attacks on the Versailles Treaty. Wilson and Hitchcock faced a series of Republican assaults staged in every region of the country.

American politics of the previous fifteen years had witnessed an increasing tendency toward the publicizing of political debate. This was a characteristic of progressive politics of both parties. Republican resistance to the Versailles Treaty would be marked by coordinated efforts to raise public support. The party's strategy was based on the Lodge/Borah plan to defeat the treaty through extensive debate and modification. However, the insurgents were not content to confine their activity to parliamentary politics and had supplemented the process of legislative resistance with a public appeal campaign in the spring and summer of 1919.

As early as March of 1919 William Borah had begun to put the insurgent stamp on the irreconcilable movement. Drawing from the old progressive practice of going directly to the people, he pushed for Republicans to appear at rallies in an effort to consolidate public opposition to Wilson's peace. He made a series of speeches in New York City, Boston, and Rochester. His attacks centered on the

---

[1] Johnson to Lodge, July 19, 1919, Lodge Papers, (copy of McCormick to Johnson, July 18, 1919).

issue of American independence of action and the suspicion that the League of Nations would be dominated by British interests.

The party leadership did not initially support these outright public attacks on Wilson and the League. During the treaty negotiations, President Wilson had been extraordinarily successful in catching the imagination of the American people. He had high levels of support within the church organizations, the academic community, and the press. Lodge was skeptical of Borah's ability to overwhelm such widespread support. The Republican party of Massachusetts absolutely opposed Borah's drive to build public sentiment against Wilson's peace. Calvin Coolidge was adamant on this issue. He tried to persuade Lodge that Massachusetts was already lost to the president, and refused to appear on the dais during Borah's Boston speech. However, Borah's first wave of speech making in March 1919 was marked by responsive crowds and laudatory press accounts. He was able to take advantage of nationalistic sentiments that existed in the general public. The success of this first trip convinced other Republicans of the usefulness of a direct appeal for popular support.[2]

Borah's successful speaking appearances encouraged the leadership to take the offensive in the battle for public opinion. In the spring of 1919, Louis Coolidge, a conservative Massachusetts party figure, built a cover organization that would provide support for anti-League politicians. This organization, the League for the Preservation of American Independence, did most of the groundwork for the speaking tours of the anti-League senators. The group initially targeted New England and California, areas where liberal internationalism was strong. The League for the Preservation of American Independence used Henry Cabot Lodge, William Borah, and Hiram Johnson as its primary speakers. Borah and Johnson found this duty appealing. Their political background as insurgent progressives inclined them to include the public in the debate over Wilson's League. Both were skilled orators and enjoyed the tumult of public appearances. Johnson, in particular was less comfortable in the Senate chamber than on the hustings. He recorded in his diary that "I really feel after my experience in New England I can do more in talking to our people than in talking to the Senate. I will take one more blast in the Senate before my departure then go upon the road."[3]

The first round of anti-League speeches sponsored by the Coolidge group was set for New England, a region marked by strong support for the League. University communities and the leadership of the established Protestant churches in New England tended to favor Wilsonian internationalism. Wilson's political supporters were effectively using sympathy from these two groups to gain popular support for the League of Nations. A successful speaking tour in New England was essential for undercutting the authority of these pro-Wilson religious and intellectual leaders. Counterbalancing this situation was a cohesive Republican party structure in these states. Lodge's influence in Massachusetts politics ensured

---

[2] Johnson, *Borah*, 233–235.
[3] Diary Letters, August 15, 1919, Johnson Papers.

good audiences, favorable press coverage, and complete logistical support. The local party leadership was kept abreast of daily arrangements throughout the tour. The impassioned oratory of Johnson, Borah, and Lodge resonated in halls filled with enthusiastic supporters. The plan to shift the political momentum to the favor of League opponents could become an effective strategy.

Public appearances in New England were continuous. Borah and Johnson tended to deliver conventional public addresses. The basic points of opposition centered on the independence of American foreign policy and the defense against a rising Anglo-French hegemony. Specific complaints concerned the defense of the 100-year-old Monroe Doctrine from League interference; the role of the Congress in armament, war making, and treaty ratification; and the Senate's reluctance to support the legitimization of secret treaty agreements through boundary changes and mandate decisions. The League was portrayed as an institution designed to consolidate British and French colonial positions. As evidence, the speakers pointed to the mandate decisions, the voting rights of British dominions, and the economic subjugation of the principal European rival—Germany.

The themes developed during this first phase of speeches formed the basic arguments used by Borah and Johnson throughout the anti-League campaign. Because of the dominance of Borah and Johnson in the irreconcilable movement, these themes would also be the heart of the irreconcilable attack on the Versailles Treaty. Their arguments were heavily infused with old-style progressive rhetoric and calls for ardent nationalism. In September 1919 Johnson summarized his attack, "Naively the President remarks that secret treaties hampered him at the Peace Conference and embarrassed the whole settlement. Inferentially, he concedes the wickedness of these secret treaties, but he was neither hampered nor embarrassed to such a degree as to cause him to stand manfully and courageously for his oft-expressed principles."[4]

At this early stage the irreconcilable movement borrowed heavily from progressive nationalist rhetoric. The League was seen as part of a generalized duplicitous plot that the progressives had been fighting since the turn of the century. Wall Street had foisted the peace treaty on an unsuspecting American public. These financial interests were served by weak and vacillating politicians who dominated both parties. Despite the opposition of the insurgents, Johnson predicted a victory for Wall Street, lamenting that "soon the President will accept the reservations, the League of Nations will be accepted with them, and the Republicans will claim a great victory with their reservations. The President [will claim] a greater victory with his League, and the International Bankers will chuckle as they take receivership of the world through any kind of League of Nations and make billions of profit."[5]

The broader circumstances of American politics increasingly favored the Republicans in the summer of 1919. War-induced inflation combined with the

---

[4] Speech delivered in September 1919, Johnson Papers.
[5] Diary Letters, July 24, 1919, Johnson Papers.

specter of postwar unemployment was generating unrest in the ranks of labor. Ethnic tensions, which had been heightened by the war, continued to divide American society. In addition, Attorney General Mitchell Palmer's efforts to eliminate socialist elements from American politics sparked complaints from civil libertarians and radical labor leaders. Wilson's popularity was not secure, a situation that clearly benefited the Republican critics of the Versailles Treaty. The Republicans had the opportunity to defeat Wilson's treaty; more important, they had an opportunity to defeat Wilson in the next presidential election.

The Republicans continued their public attacks against Wilson's League throughout the summer of 1919. They would not permit any statement on behalf of the League to go unanswered. When the supporters of Wilson's League delivered a well-received speech, the League for the Preservation of American Independence arranged for a response shortly thereafter.

The extensive hearings conducted by the Committee on Foreign Relations became intertwined in this publicity effort. Lodge's avowed reasons for insisting on such detailed hearings were to gain specific information regarding the negotiation process at Paris and to pull pro-League Republicans into the reservationist camp. However, Lodge was also buying the allegiance of Borah and Johnson by giving them the opportunity to continue their public-speaking campaign. As a result of this pact, the insurgents took on an increasingly powerful role in defining the public discourse surrounding the League of Nations.

In general, members of the irreconcilable movement were unhappy with the moderation of the party position in the summer of 1919. Lodge's desire to build consensus in the Republican party, combined with his willingness to accept a modified version of the League of Nations, troubled those who were irreconcilably opposed to the treaty. The insurgent members of the irreconcilable movement saw themselves as saving not only American nationalism, but American democracy. Although his complaints were private, Hiram Johnson was dismayed by the lack of drama in Lodge's opposition to the Versailles Treaty. He interpreted Lodge's demeanor as a lack of will and questioned the Majority Leader's commitment to the defeat of Wilson's treaty.[6] However, Johnson and the other insurgent irreconcilables were not totally alienated by Lodge's leadership.

Despite differences in outlook Republicans of both reservationist and irreconcilable factions could still be unified in their opposition to the Democrats. Woodrow Wilson's administration still presented an even greater threat to the insurgents' vision of American democracy. Johnson vehemently criticized the secretary of state, saying, "When I finished with Lansing, I walked over to the office saddened and humiliated, because my country was in the hands of such men, and at the mercy of their dullness, stupidity and worse."[7]

Lodge was still committed to the idea that the irreconcilables had to be held to the Republican party. This required some concessions to Borah and Johnson.

---

[6] August 23, 1919, Diary Letters, Johnson Papers.
[7] August 23, 1919, Diary Letters, Johnson Papers.

These senators wanted to cement public opposition to the League before the Senate floor debates began. By prolonging hearings in the Senate Foreign Relations Committee, anti-League speakers would have time to make public appearances. Borah, Johnson, and other irreconcilables periodically absented themselves from the wide-ranging committee hearings to make anti-League speaking tours.[8]

The success of these tours prompted Woodrow Wilson to adjust his ratification strategy. By August he was becoming aware that his efforts to sway Republican senators were not successful. Despite Hitchcock's assurances that the Republicans were in disarray, Wilson found the Republican leadership to be confident. Relations between the president and Lodge had deteriorated to the point where Wilson was no longer dealing with the majority leader, but with the Republican Whip, James Watson. Watson was confident Wilson had lost control of the treaty and described the situation, "You are like a man in quicksand now and every struggle you make will only sink you the deeper."[9] As a final attempt to subdue a confident opposition, Wilson embarked on a national speaking tour to defend the League.

Henry Cabot Lodge understood the risk of continuing to hold the Versailles Treaty in the Senate Foreign Relations Committee. Wilson could accuse him of dilatory behavior and charge that the hearings were an obstructionist effort designed for partisan ends. Fearing public reaction against the Republicans, Lodge passed the Versailles Treaty onto the floor of the Senate on September 10. However, he was careful to defend the prerogatives of the Foreign Relations Committee. He pointed to the complexity of the treaty text and to its implications for a new international order. In an effort to turn the political onus on the administration, Lodge argued that the Senate "cannot dispose of this momentous document with the light-hearted indifference desired by those who were pressing for hasty and thoughtless action upon it."[10]

After Wilson's announcement of the presidential speaking tour in September 1919, Louis Coolidge began arrangements for a series of rebuttals. The Coolidge group hired a private railroad car to transport anti-League speakers. This group included Philadelphia lawyer James Beck; former senator Albert Beveridge; diplomat David Jayne Hill; and Senators George Pepper, William Borah, Hiram Johnson, and James Reed. The estimated cost of maintaining this stable of orators was $15,000, one-third of which was immediately furnished by James Beck.[11]

When Wilson decided to make his appeal to the nation, the Republicans had already made substantial gains in swinging public opinion to the anti-League position. The League for the Preservation of American Independence had established an infrastructure to aid Republicans in their efforts to deliver major speeches against the League of Nations and the Versailles Treaty. Senators Borah

---

[8] Roots, "The Treaty of Versailles."

[9] Watson, *As I Knew Them,* 202.

[10] Lodge, *The Senate,* 165–167.

[11] Louis Coolidge to Lodge, September 5, 1919, Lodge Papers.

and Johnson had been particularly successful in generating public sympathy for the ideals of the irreconcilables, if not complete public repudiation of the League of Nations.

The Republicans were able to mount a solid rebuttal to Wilson's speaking tour in September. Lodge believed that the Republican position was now unassailable. The events since March had convinced him that the president was vulnerable in his control of public opinion. He was braced by reports that Wilson's addresses were no longer met with public enthusiasm.[12]

When Wilson collapsed in Colorado, the Republicans felt they already had the upper hand. By the time the treaty passed out of the Senate Foreign Relations Committee onto the floor of the Senate on September 10, 1919, the Republican opposition already was solidified under the direction of Henry Cabot Lodge. During the spring and summer of 1919 Republican speeches against the League became more emotional, displaying the more rhetorical style of a campaign stump speech than a Senate oration. By August even Lodge was swept up in the tide of enthusiasm. He reported to Ellerton James:

> The cheering rose and fell three or four times, like a great excited mass meeting. They were all on their feet, not only applauding but yelling, especially the Marines, who were scattered through the crowd and who pounded their steel helmets, which added to the noise. John Sharp Williams [D,Mississippi] always semi-intoxicated got up and began to abuse me and was roundly hissed. It is a matter of no importance to me . . . what John Sharp Williams thinks of me, but the rebuke he got made a very pleasant wind-up.[13]

Lodge knew the public floor debate would be covered by the press, and that at least a significant portion of the press would favor the Republican stand. The Senate debates of the fall of 1919 were not simply aimed at an audience in the chamber, but also to the American public as a whole. Press coverage obviated the need for continued public speaking tours.

Senators would continue to speak outside the forum of the Senate, but would be less aggressive in searching out audiences. After Wilson's stroke in late September, the Republican party depended less on the insurgents' oratorical skills. During the spring and summer of 1919, New England had been stumped intensively by the irreconcilables. However, the fall marked a change in tone of Republican public speaking. In organizing programs for the Roosevelt Day celebrations, the state party organizations avoided irreconcilable speech makers and tended to favor reservationists.[14] The irreconcilables still shared the debate on the Senate floor

---

[12] Lodge to George Harvey, September 11, 1919, Lodge Papers.

[13] Lodge to Ellerton James, August 15, 1919, Lodge Papers.

[14] Borah, Knox, and Johnson were specifically barred from the proceedings in Massachusetts. See Robert Washburn to Lodge, October 8, 1919, Lodge Papers.

with the reservationists; however, reservationists Lodge and Watson controlled the party on the floor and began to exercise some authority on behalf of moderation.

THE SENATE REPUBLICANS AND THE FIRST RATIFICATION VOTE

The ultimate position on the Versailles Treaty taken by the Republican party was molded by Henry Cabot Lodge. He believed in the maintenance of a consensus among Republican senators, and engaged in constant negotiation with both the pro-League forces and the irreconcilables. Before July 1919 the leadership of the Republican party was concerned with insurgent factionalism. With the Penrose chairmanship receding into the past, and the successful use of the League of Nations as a unifying issue, Lodge drove for an even larger consensus. He was not willing to dismiss the political influence of the internationalists. While relatively weak in the Senate, politicians who favored Wilson's treaty were well entrenched in the Republican party as a whole. The opinions of Charles Evans Hughes, William Howard Taft, and even Nicholas Murray Butler had to be considered. While Lodge was dependent on the irreconcilable faction in creating the ideological basis for the Republican attack, he argued that those Republicans who favored Wilson's treaty should join the reservationist camp in an effort to contain the irreconcilable movement.

Lodge's drive to tie in the two wings of the party resulted in a Republican position that advocated a serious attempt to ratify a strictly modified Versailles Treaty. The negotiations between Lodge and Borah in March 1919 had resulted in a strategy whereby both irreconcilables and reservationists would vote for any amendments or reservations that would "Americanize" the treaty. The particular targets for these changes focused on issues of American independence of action. They included the defense of the Monroe Doctrine, the creation of mandated territories, voting procedures in the League of Nations, the commitment of U.S. troops in defense of League decisions, and the regulation of immigration. At this early stage of the Versailles Treaty debate, it was relatively easy for Lodge and Borah to work in concert. They had not yet been forced to deal with a concrete document; furthermore, they had a common cause in the defense of Senate prerogatives as Woodrow Wilson assailed the role of the Senate in foreign policy making.

Wilson feared the Senate's push for amendments and reservations to the treaty. He argued that American alteration of the treaty could spark similar action by other nations and the result would be an endless series of negotiations and counter proposals. When he first submitted the treaty, he claimed that any such changes made to the document would have to pass by a two-thirds vote. He based his stand on the constitutional provision for two-thirds vote to support ratification. In fact, such a conservative approach was highly pragmatic; it would severely limit the Senate's ability to alter the president's authority in policy making. Lodge responded by pointing out Senate Rule Thirty-seven, which stipulated a simple majority was required for amendments and reservations. The Senate rules clearly provided for that body's ability to take the initiative on creating the final language of the ratified version of the Versailles Treaty. It was now Wilson who was forced to choose between compromising his treaty, or killing any less-than-perfect version.[15] Lodge jealously guarded the authority of the Senate in foreign policy making and insisted that the Republicans had the right to use reservations in the ratification process.[16] The defense of the prerogatives of the Senate fit perfectly into the Republican philosophy of law making through the development of a consensus opinion.

Lodge used the process of attaching reservations to the treaty as a means of drawing Republican internationalists into his coalition. In July he conferred with the chairman of the Republican National Committee, Will Hays, to solicit modifications to the Versailles Treaty. Suggestions for reservations came from eminent Republican internationalists, including former president William Howard Taft. The general body of Republicans assumed that certain limitations would exist if the United States participated in the League. Lodge argued that the reservationists were separated from the Republican supporters of the League merely by their insistence that the limitations of American responsibility had to be openly stated, not assumed. When former president Taft presented possible reservation texts, he opened the door for a reunification between the reservationist and pro-League camps. The basic tenor of the reservations suggested by Taft conformed to the guidelines established by the reservationist Republicans. Taft advocated five limitations on the treaty: (1) the obligations of the United States under Article X of the League would be limited by an imposition of a maximum length of time for American involvement of five years; (2) American involvement in League interventions would furthermore be limited by the stipulation that all League-instructed intervention had to be specifically approved by Congress; (3) the provisions of the Monroe Doctrine could not be circumscribed by League action; (4) questions of immigration and international trade were domestic issues and not debatable by the League; and (5) the United States could withdraw from the League of Nations after giving a two-year notice.[17] The Taft reservations indicated the formation of a constructive partnership between pro-League and reservationist Republicans. Moreover, their stipulations concerning the sovereignty of the U.S. government demonstrated an effort to find a compromise position with the irreconcilables.

The separation between the various factions within the Republican party was not easily bridged. The reservationists were concerned with issues of national sovereignty, but assumed that American political and economic strength was sufficiently strong to prevent manipulation by the British or French. Potential problems could be avoided if the Senate attached stipulations to the treaty that clearly defined the relationship between the League Council and U.S. foreign

---

[15] Wimer, "Woodrow Wilson Tries Conciliation," 431.

[16] See Diary, August 22, 1919, Chandler Anderson Papers, Library of Congress.

[17] Will Hays to Lodge, July 17, 1919, Lodge Papers.

policy. The pro-League Republicans claimed that the reservationists' solutions were already extant in international law and unnecessary. Their position on the dangers of attaching reservations to the treaty vacillated. Although they would have preferred no alterations to the treaty text, they were willing to accept reservations. The reservations proposed by Taft provided pro-League and reservationist Republicans a common ground for discussion. However, they failed as an attempt to unify all Republicans. The irreconcilables continued to believe that the deficiencies of the treaty were so great that, under it, the United States could not protect its national prerogatives.

By the summer of 1919, Lodge had defined the parameters of Republican victory in the Versailles Treaty debates. He needed some level of consensus, so as to preclude fragmentation of the party. Wilson's version of the treaty would have to be defeated so as to weaken the Democratic party for the 1920 election and prevent Wilson's idealistic internationalism from supplanting the commercial nationalism that had been created by the Republicans after the Spanish-American War. So as to overcome possible accusations of obstructionism, the Republicans would also have to provide some alternative to the Versailles Treaty that Wilson had negotiated. Lodge needed to alter the treaty text to make it a bipartisan or Republican document.

Lodge's efforts to escape accusations of obstructionism were evidenced in his push to move the treaty through the Senate as quickly as possible. Lodge was presented with the difficult political problem of balancing the public's desire for a resolution of the European war and the irreconcilables' determination to protect American political independence. He did placate Borah and Johnson by allowing the period of committee hearings to serve also as a time when those senators could absent themselves for public speaking duties. However, Lodge also was attentive to speculation that the hearings were too prolonged. Rather than allowing public attention to focus on the length of the Senate Foreign Relations Committee hearings, Lodge wanted to shift interest to the subject of Republican modification of the text.

The Republican senators had two means of modifying the text Wilson had presented them. The more severe technique was through amendment, which would actually change the text of the treaty. This method was preferred by those who thought the document was fundamentally flawed. While the irreconcilables were ultimately committed to defeating the treaty in its entirety, they saw amendments as a means of making an unacceptable document an undesirable one. Reservations to the treaty provided a less severe approach to treaty modification. They simply explained the Senate's interpretation of the document that was presented to them. They would declare basic limitations to American action according to the treaty and areas in which the U.S. government would not recognize the jurisdiction of the League of Nations. Lodge favored the use of reservations over amendments, as being a more practical means of changing the treaty.

The issue had been raised that if the United States amended the treaty, other signatories would have to approve of the amended changes. This position was most strongly advocated by Senator Kellogg (R, Minnesota), who had emerged as the leader among the mild reservationists. Kellogg actively lobbied with Lodge to focus Republican attention away from amendments, arguing they would "cause more delay and could serve no useful purpose."[18] Mild reservationists and some Democratic senators would vote for reservations, but not amendments. Lodge defended the preferred use of reservations as a means of expediting the ratification process, and preventing charges of obstructionism.[19] He spent the summer and early fall of 1919 balancing the Republican party position, trying to pull the mild reservationists into the party while holding onto the irreconcilables who continued to sponsor amendments.[20]

When the Foreign Relations Committee referred the Versailles Treaty to the Senate it recommended forty-five amendments and four reservations. Under these circumstances the version of the treaty reported out by Lodge was sure to be attacked from two camps: Senate Democrats would hold with President Wilson and argue for ratification without change, and Republican mild reservationists would not accept amendments to the treaty. However, these two camps were not in total agreement; the mild reservationist Frank Kellogg was willing to promote a series of reservations sponsored by Republicans.

By referring the treaty to the Senate with amendments, Lodge was able to maintain a sense of leadership over the irreconcilable element of the party. However, he still needed to solidify his leadership over the mild reservationists. Pro-League Republicans had already made a concession to party solidarity by accepting the principle of treaty reservations. Lodge needed to reconcile the pro-amendment and reservationists camps in some way, but the nature of debate, as it evolved in the summer of 1919, indicated this would be a difficult task.

Republican opposition had focused on Article X and the provisions for enforcement of League sanctions. Two lines of attack had emerged. The first came from traditional populist fears of European manipulation in international politics, and as such was most strongly advocated by insurgent progressives. The second was more widely advocated and rose in defense of the prerogatives of Congress in setting policy.

Irreconcilable thought reflected the residual Anglophobia that had been prevalent in nineteenth-century American thought. As such, its adherents represented a hostility to Britain that more modern-thinking Americans viewed as outmoded. However, these fears were not deemed totally irrelevant, since they combined this Anglophobia with a strong, nationalist defense of Congress as a policy-making body. In this second area irreconcilables and reservationists could agree.

During the summer of 1919 Borah, Johnson, and other irreconcilables had focused their attacks on the allocation of votes in the League. They argued against the inclusion of various elements of the British Commonwealth as voting nations,

---

[18] Frank Kellogg to Lodge, July 7, 1919, Lodge Papers.

[19] Lodge, *The Senate*, 162–164.

[20] Herbert F. Margulies, *The Mild Reservationists and the League of Nations Controversy in the Senate* (Columbia: University of Missouri Press, 1989), 68–69.

claiming they would vote as a bloc on behalf of the interests of the major partner, Great Britain. The granting of voting rights to four of the British self-governing dominions might have been acceptable. However, despite its status as a colony, India also was given a vote. The Kingdoms of Hedjaz and Persia, which were under the influence of the British government, had received full status in the League. This pattern was seen to skew League decisions in the favor of Great Britain, and in turn, preserve the nineteenth-century balance of power. By attacking the apportionment of votes in the League, the irreconcilables took the debate from the pragmatic issues of the role of the United States in the League, to a more fundamental discussion over the role of sovereignty. In the irreconcilable vision, the sovereignty of the U.S. government was at risk; only the most extreme alteration of the League Covenant would protect the power of the American government.

Speeches by Borah, Johnson, and Knox were designed to alert the public to the potential dangers presented by the League. Even though they felt that public support for their position was mounting, the irreconcilables were not secure in the thought that the Versailles Treaty would be defeated. As a means of curbing potential threats to American sovereignty, the irreconcilables favored the Johnson Amendment, which would give the United States six votes in the League. The amendment required a radical change in the structure of the League Council, but was still supported fully by the Republican party leadership in the initial phase of floor debates. Henry Cabot Lodge commented, "How anyone can vote against it passes my comprehension. A man who votes to give Great Britain six votes to our one will have tied a weight around his neck which will go with him through all his public life."[21] Despite the efforts of Lodge, the amendment failed in a floor vote on October 27. The defeat of the Johnson Amendment was seen as a defeat of the irreconcilable interests in the Republican party, for they had chosen the Johnson Amendment as a fundamental debating point. The defeat of the amendment was not only viewed in the context of the Versailles Treaty. Insurgent Republicans who formed a critical segment of the irreconcilable movement saw the issue applying to American domestic politics as well. Hiram Johnson described the voting results as a defeat of progressive reform, and privately accused opponents of the amendment of "obeying the orders of Morgan and Company, and Kuhn, Loeb, and Company in voting against me."[22]

None of the amendments that were recommended by the Senate Foreign Relations Committee were attached to the treaty. Johnson's amendment stipulating that six votes be allotted to the United States was the first to be considered by the full Senate. It failed by a vote of thirty-eight to forty, with eighteen not voting. The support for the amendment came from both irreconcilables and reservationists; although eight Republicans crossed party lines, the opposition to the amendment was essentially from the Democrats. The failure of the Johnson Amendment was

---

[21] Lodge to John Weeks, September 22, 1919, Lodge Papers.
[22] Diary Letters, November 1, 1919, Johnson Papers.

not due to the number of defections to the Democrats, but rather it was a result of the substantial number of reservationist Republicans absent at the time of the vote. Another similar amendment presented by the conservative nationalist, George Moses, was defeated by a slightly higher margin. An amendment presented by Robert LaFollette stipulated that the United States could only go to war in response to a League decision if the question first passed a national referendum. Once again irreconcilables and reservationists joined to support the amendment, voting thirty-four in favor, forty-seven opposed, with fifteen senators not present for the vote. As had been the case with the Johnson Amendment, Republicans dominated the list of senators not voting.

The Senate considered six amendments that would assert Chinese sovereignty in Shantung and limit Japanese presence in that area. The Shantung amendment presented by Henry Cabot Lodge, which simply deleted all of the Shantung provisions, failed dramatically with twenty-six in favor, forty-one opposed, and twenty-nine not voting. This occurred despite the popular sentiment against Japanese territorial gains at the end of the war. The rest of the failed amendments would have limited American participation on the various commissions established by the League of Nations.[23] Superficial examination indicated that these amendments had unified Republican support. Each time an amendment came to a floor vote, it was supported by both irreconcilables and reservationist Republicans. However, as the process of amendment and debate continued between October 27 and November 19, mild reservationists slowly started to break ranks. More striking was the continuously high number of senators absent from floor votes. These absent senators were typically reservationist Republicans.

When the amendments to the Versailles Treaty failed, the nature of the debate over the treaty shifted. The voting structure of the League was assumed, as was active American participation on the various commissions established by the League. Furthermore, while Japanese control over Shantung was opposed, the Senate decided to negotiate these sovereignty issues in another context. Debate would not be defined by the radical nationalism of the irreconcilables, but would be couched in the moderate language of reservationism.

The pattern of reservations shifted the Republican focus away from the specific structure of the League of Nations toward the issues of future action within the context of an international system that included a League. The reservations were designed to promote a certain independence of American action. They conformed to Lodge's principal complaint about the enforcement mechanism of Article X—that the United States needed to limit the occasions of its involvement in international political disputes. He feared that American wealth and power would be misused in being called upon repeatedly to settle disputes. The newly found power of the United States would be wasted; he argued, "By meddling in all the differences which may arise among any portion or fragment of humankind we simply fritter

---

[23] See Lodge, *The Senate*, 178–180.

away our influence and injure ourselves to no good purpose."[24]

Control of the text of the reservations was contested by elements within the Republican party and at times by Democrats. The leading mild reservationist, Frank Kellogg, had been persuaded that the treaty would fail without reservations. Lodge focused on containing Kellogg's activity as a means of curtailing the power of the Democratic party in the Senate, and persuaded him of the practicality of more forceful reservations.[25] The tone of the reservations underscored the role of the United States Congress in the making of American policy. Particular attention was taken to ensure congressional control of expenditures, the commitment of troops in foreign conflicts, and the determination of immigration and international trade policy. By drawing in the pro-League Republicans and holding the irreconcilables to their earlier commitment to support all Republican-sponsored alterations to the treaty, Lodge was able to secure enough votes to attach his reservations to the treaty.[26]

The version of the Versailles Treaty that was put to a vote had been modified by the Republican reservationists. These limitations did not fully allay the fears of British domination that had marked the opposition of insurgent progressives like Borah and Johnson. The irreconcilables were not convinced that the mainstream of the Republican party was truly committed to the defeat of the treaty. Rather, they now suspected that Lodge would accept any version that was not Wilson's.

The ultimate decision on the Versailles Treaty and the League of Nations was made not by the Republican senators, but by the president. Contrary to the suspicions of Hiram Johnson, Wilson did indeed believe that the Republicans had "cut the heart out of the treaty" by attaching reservations to Article X. Through the Democratic floor leader, Gilbert Hitchcock, Wilson instructed Democrats to vote against the treaty. The irreconcilable faction was free to split from the Republican party under the original conditions of the March agreement between Borah and Lodge. On November 19, 1919, three separate votes were held on the Versailles Treaty. The Senate first considered the Lodge text with strong reservations. Irreconcilables and Democrats combined to defeat the treaty, with thirty-nine in favor and fifty-five opposed. Later in the day a second vote was held on the same text, but neither Democrats nor irreconcilables defected in large enough numbers to attain even a simple majority. A third attempt to consider the Versailles Treaty was made that day when Democrats reintroduced the original text presented by

---

[24] Quoted from *Congressional Record,* 66th Congress, 1st Session, August 12, 1919, pp. 3778–3788. Lodge made a phonograph recording of the speech on August 21, 1919, Lodge Papers.

[25] Lodge to J. T. Williams, August 20, and September 6, 1919, Lodge Papers.

[26] Thomas Knock argued that an examination of the reservations provides a means of understanding both the Republicans' foreign policy concerns and Republican complaints about Wilson's domestic agenda of progressive reform. Lodge was effectively consolidating Republican opinion regarding domestic issues such as labor regulation in preparation for the next election campaign. See Knock, *To End All Wars,* 265–267.

Woodrow Wilson. That version also failed, with thirty-eight in favor of ratification, fifty-three opposed, and four not voting. Ratification of the Versailles Treaty would not occur in the fall of 1919.

THE ATTEMPT TO REACH A BIPARTISAN COMPROMISE

While the entry of the United States into the League of Nations was blocked by the Senate in November, the issue was not yet resolved. Henry Cabot Lodge had successfully defeated the Wilson proposal, but he hoped to extend the Republican triumph by negotiating the American entry to the League under the terms of the Republican party. Such an achievement would undermine partisan charges of isolationism against the Republicans and thereby would improve the position of the party in the 1920 election.

William Borah understood that Lodge did not share his fundamental opposition to the League of Nations. He was also aware of Lodge's sensitivity to press accusations that the Republican party was isolationist. Unlike Lodge, Borah was not afraid of the accusations of isolationism. He was convinced that American entry into the League would result in British manipulation of American interests. Borah was confident that, if apprised of this political risk, the American people would agree with the irreconcilable position. He felt that the irreconcilable position was politically safe because it was not isolationist, but nationalist.

By the fall of 1919 it was apparent that Lodge had successfully consolidated his authority and that his public stand on the Johnson Amendment marked the final concession to the irreconcilables. Irreconcilables could no longer rely on Lodge to act as a political enemy of the League of Nations. Borah would have to turn to others to prevent American entry into the League. To this end he began to conspire with Democrat Senator Claude Swanson (D, Virginia). At Borah's encouragement, the conservative Democrat began actively lobbying in the White House, encouraging Wilson to hold a firm line against Republican resistance.[27] As long as Wilson refused to compromise, even after the first ratification defeat, Democrat members of the Senate were reluctant to compromise with Lodge.

However, Wilson had not fully recovered from his stroke. He continued to be bedridden and could no longer effectively control the Democratic caucus. After the November vote, Lodge had the upper hand. The position of the Republican party was further strengthened by Lodge's ability to portray Wilson as obdurate. One of the president's arguments against the Lodge reservations had been the reported European opposition to alterations in the treaty text. However, Wilson's position was undercut in the winter, as European leaders, including Viscount Edward Grey, announced that the Lodge reservations were completely satisfactory. Wilson did not accept this Allied concession to Republican demands with grace.[28]

---

[27] Roots, "The Treaty of Versailles," 82.

[28] Edward Corwin, *The President, Office and Powers* (New York: New York University Press, 1940), 215.

The Republicans had further evidence that Wilson was dangerously autocratic, and that the Democratic members of the Senate were slavishly loyal to him. Lodge had forged his weapon to use in the upcoming presidential election. Without the active presence of Wilson, and in the face of powerful campaign rhetoric, the Democratic solidarity in the Senate began to crumble. In December, Democrats began drifting toward compromise with Lodge.

After the November vote, Lodge pursued a course of quiet compromise, designed to pull Democrats over to the Republican reservationist side. By January 1920, Lodge was openly discussing a bipartisan accord.[29] The solution would require a rewriting of the November treaty reservations, using milder language. This would provide Democratic senators with a rationale for a decision to reverse their earlier vote. In the face of this activity by Lodge, the irreconcilables began to regroup.

The conflict came to a climax on January 23, 1920. Lodge had been regularly meeting with various senators to discuss compromise language for reservations. As Borah described the events, he received an anonymous telephone call that warned of an impending conclusion to the search for a compromise. Borah immediately contacted Republican irreconcilables and they gathered in Hiram Johnson's office to discuss their response to a Lodge compromise. It was decided that Lodge's friend, the conservative George Moses (R, New Hampshire), would go to the meeting in Lodge's office and insist that the majority leader immediately accompany Moses to Johnson's office. Lodge left his own meeting under protest and upon arrival at the irreconcilable meeting received a harangue from Borah, Knox, and Moses. After what Hiram Johnson described as "three corking hours," Borah ended the attack by threatening open rebellion on the floor of the Senate, saying, "I won't give you a chance to resign. I am going into the Senate Chamber Monday morning and say that the Republicans must have a new leader, and I will tell why one is needed." Although he was obviously enraged, Lodge kept his composure, returned to his office, and broke off all meetings with the Democrats and mild reservationists.[30]

This victory was directly attributable to the tenuous political position of the Republican party. Lodge needed a unified party in the Senate. Without such unification, the Republicans could suffer another political defeat like the one in

---

[29] Key to this was the role of Oscar Underwood (D, Alabama). Underwood and Gilbert Hitchcock were vying for control of the Democratic party in the Senate. This dispute was reflected in Underwood's attempt toward an accommodation with the Republicans that would undercut the power of the Democratic internationalists. Evans C. Johnson, *Oscar W. Underwood: A Political Biography* (Baton Rouge: Louisiana State University Press, 1980), 270–272 and 295–297.

[30] Johnson, *Borah*, 246–248. Other accounts of this meeting can be found in Garraty, *Henry Cabot Lodge,* 384–387 and Stone, *The Irreconcilables,* 156–159. While these accounts differ in detail, they agree in substance. Stone is careful to emphasize the pressure of Irish-American voters against Republican compromise and argues that this was a factor that encouraged the irreconcilables in their opposition to Lodge's authority.

1912. Lodge was much more willing to sacrifice a point of policy than the loyalty of a significant segment of Republican senators. While the Republican irreconcilables were of varied political outlooks, they did accede to the leadership of William Borah. Borah had already experienced a sense of betrayal over the failure of amendments to the treaty. He had argued that the reservations were the product of sinister pro-League forces and that the irreconcilables had been abandoned by Lodge's strategy.

This general level of dissatisfaction was intensified by the reports that Lodge was meeting with members of the Democratic party for the purpose of limiting the scope of reservations to the treaty. Borah accused Lodge of trifling with the vital interests of the nation, and announced that he could no longer cooperate with the party leadership in the Senate.[31]

More important than Borah's statement disassociating himself with the Republican party leadership was the possibility of his generating factionalism within the party. A simple withdrawal of members was dangerous enough. However, Borah was ready to call for new elections in the Senate for party leadership. Lodge was not willing to withstand an open fight for the Senate's leadership in an election year.[32]

Lodge's sudden decision to break negotiations with Democrat reservationists had to be explained to the public. In a letter to a J. T. Williams of *The Boston Transcript* he described the situation, not in the context of a potential Republican party split, but as further intransigence by the Democrats. Wilson had established a climate of acrimony, and the Democrats could not bring themselves to approve of reservations that would defend the Monroe Doctrine.[33]

The Senate considered ratification of the treaty a second time, on March 13, 1920. However, without further compromise between Lodge and the Democrats, the Senate was forced to consider a text essentially like the one of November. Once again, the treaty failed to gain the required two-thirds support.

Lodge had successfully defeated the Democrat foreign policy initiative. Wilson, his health broken, would not provide a formidable threat to a Republican presidential victory in 1920. No Democrat had emerged as a powerful contender for his party's nomination.

Lodge had also succeeded in papering over the major political fissures within the Republican party. While he had not forged a positive response to Wilson's peace, he had developed a consensus as to what the Republican party would not accept. For more than a year he had drawn the attention of Republican senators, and the Republican party in general, to the League of Nations. From June 1919 until March 1920, foreign policy had occupied the attention of Republicans, not the nationalization of the railroad system, not the revision of the tariff, not the regulation of campaign practices. To the best of his ability, Lodge had generated

---

[31] Borah to Lodge, January 24, 1920, Lodge Papers.

[32] Garraty, *Henry Cabot Lodge*, 384–387.

[33] Lodge to J. T. Williams, Jr., February 2, 1920, Lodge Papers.

a unified Republican party in the Senate. This unification would provide much of the foundation for the Republican party's efforts in winning the 1920 presidential election.

4

The New Republican Majority

Nineteen-twelve was a Sunday school convention compared to this.
—Hiram Johnson

The selection of the Versailles Treaty debate as the focus of Republican political activity provided the means for the reunification of the party. Issues of the European peace did not touch on the old questions of the relationship between government and business that had divided the party a decade earlier. The process of treaty ratification placed special emphasis on the Senate, where the Republican party was in control. Furthermore, the structure of the Republican party in the Senate encouraged the reunification effort. With only a slight majority, the importance of consensus was obvious to all Republican members. The placement of Henry Cabot Lodge as both majority leader and chairman of the Foreign Relations Committee provided an essential consolidation of authority. Lodge had an ideological agenda, but he understood the importance of the institutional agenda in reunifying the party and resuming control of government.

Lodge's efforts during the Sixty-sixth Congress had been successful. The factionalism that had marked the party in Congress since 1909 still existed, but a truce had been declared. The insurgents and Old Guard were ideologically at odds, but for one year they had mediated their differences and avoided open hostility. The party would now have to capitalize on this new-found peace. The achievements of the Republicans in the Senate would have to be extended to the party as a whole during the election of 1920.

THE PRESIDENTIAL ELECTION OF 1920 AND THE SEARCH FOR A CANDIDATE

Republican politicians were now confident of the strength of their party over the Democrats. The political situation in 1920 was quite different from that of 1912. The primary objective of Republican politicians was victory in November, not the absolute control of the party by one faction. Unrestricted intraparty warfare was a specter of equally frightening proportions to men of such varied ideological backgrounds as Henry Cabot Lodge and William Borah. Electoral success could only be guaranteed by compromise that would preclude a split in the party. Lodge's activity regarding the Versailles Treaty debate had formed a base for Republican consolidation, but the key to Republican unity would be the party's conduct during the 1920 presidential campaign. Lodge regarded the 1912 nomination process as "a great calamity" and feared the upcoming Chicago convention would be characterized by the same sort of divisiveness. Republican political gains in 1920 depended on the preservation of party unity.[1]

Lodge's efforts in the Versailles Treaty debates had rekindled the spirit of compromise in the party. However, this spirit alone was insufficient to return a Republican to the White House. The party needed a candidate who would personify the rediscovered strength of the Republican party.

In 1912 Republicans discovered the liabilities of refusing to compromise. It was not until 1916 that they discovered the depth of antagonism between the factions. The election of 1912 could no longer be dismissed as a referendum on the personality of Theodore Roosevelt. In 1916 Charles Evans Hughes seemed to be the perfect solution to the Roosevelt problem. He was one of the leading figures of progressive reform through his role in the formation of Public Service Commissions in New York. Appointed to the Supreme Court in 1910, he had been able to absent himself from all the political debate surrounding insurgency and the Roosevelt bolt. In 1916 he had been one of the very few Republicans who had offended no major segment of the party. However, Hughes had been reluctant to run for the presidency and had to be drafted at the convention. He never overcame his reluctance and maintained a lackluster campaign.

The consequences of this reluctance were greatest in the western states where the insurgency had been strong. Hughes was not a charismatic candidate and needed the support of local politicians who would work for his victory in November. However, his campaign staff often failed to coordinate with the political machines of the insurgents. This tendency had disastrous consequences in California, where the followers of Hiram Johnson were insulted by Hughes's apparent lack of deference.

Hughes faced problems in addition to the logistical difficulties of assuring full cooperation between the national campaign and state political organizations.

---

[1] Lodge to Lord Channing of Wellingborough, April 8, 1919, Lodge Papers.

Although he had a solid background as a progressive reformer, so did his opponent, Woodrow Wilson. In addition, the trend toward urbanization was proving to be an advantage for the Democratic party. The Democrats had been more astute in responding to the growing importance of ethnic politics. Charles Evans Hughes had not been able to overcome these problems in 1916 and he was defeated by the incumbent Woodrow Wilson.

The defeat of Hughes had been frustrating for Republican politicians. They understood that the party was not completely healed yet, that the reconciliation process needed to continue. Efforts at reconciliation were augmented by other attempts to strengthen the party base. During World War I the Republican party learned how to appeal to ethnic voting blocs more effectively. As inflation grew and economic uncertainty increased, the party was able to use its image as the defender of responsible business and fiscal stability. The Republican National Committee had continued its efforts to erase the rifts between party factions. By scheduling annual meetings of the Republican National Committee and requiring all campaign money be filtered through the national representative on the state Republican committees, factions could no longer manipulate—or be manipulated by—members of the Executive Committee of the Republican National Committee. In addition, the distribution of votes at the presidential nominating convention were re-allocated to reflect Republican voter strength and party loyalty.[2]

The party was in a stronger position in 1920 than it had been in 1916. Nonetheless, this increased party strength could only be fully utilized if the Republicans nominated a strong candidate. The performance of Hughes in 1916 indicated that the Republican candidate in 1920 had to be a man of energy who could lead the disparate factions of his party.

As leading Republicans began considering possible candidates for the next election, Theodore Roosevelt's name kept reemerging. While he had been president, Roosevelt exemplified the perfect Republican figurehead. He exploited nascent chauvinistic nationalism and made the United States the regional power in the Caribbean Basin. He was charismatic and cultivated a popular following by publicly castigating members of the Old Guard who opposed his reform measures. At the same time he was always willing to defer to conservative Republicans in Congress, occasionally vilifying them in public while negotiating with them in private. Until 1912 Roosevelt had been both attractive to the electorate and palatable to the party hierarchy. He had destroyed his links to the party machinery by bolting, but after his failed candidacy he hoped to ingratiate himself once again. His political activity against Wilson's wartime policies—the questioning of American military preparedness for both the Mexican dispute and the European war, attacks on Wilson's defense of American neutral rights, and opposition to Wilson's concepts of liberal internationalism—were designed to both weaken Wilson's position as president and strengthen his own position as a future

---

[2] Minutes of the Republican National Committee, January 7, 1918, p. 1, and February 18, 1918, p. 73.

Republican nominee. Roosevelt's attacks did weaken Woodrow Wilson. But by the end of the war, Roosevelt's health was failing; and he died before he could be nominated by the Republicans for a second time. However, the image of Roosevelt, the candidate, continued to mold the thinking of how the Republicans would return to the White House.

The death of Roosevelt in 1919 sparked a search for a new candidate who could re-create that progressive's magic. No truly strong political figure emerged, although several were clearly interested in the nomination. Roosevelt had never named a political successor. It is unlikely that he could have, given that his political leadership was so dependent on the force of his charisma. Nonetheless, many of the candidates saw themselves as his true heir and proceeded to portray themselves as wearing the Roosevelt mantle. The two most prominent figures in this contest were Leonard Wood and Hiram Johnson.

Leonard Wood claimed his position as Roosevelt's heir by virtue of their long-standing partnership in the development of a modern American foreign policy. The two had first worked together in the Spanish-American War where Wood had been Roosevelt's commanding officer. As military governor of Cuba, Wood was a leading figure in the creation of an American hegemony in the Caribbean Basin. During the European war, Wood was the most senior member of the army to join in Roosevelt's criticism of American military preparedness. The focus of Wood's campaign was on foreign policy. His two greatest assets were his ability to evoke the image of the Rough Rider and his acceptability to most of the former president's generous campaign contributors. On the other hand, Hiram Johnson linked his campaign to Roosevelt not through a long-standing personal relationship, but by virtue of his partnership with Roosevelt on the 1912 Progressive ticket. Johnson's advantages lay in his ability to appeal to the public's sense of outrage at political corruption and his ties to important progressive congressmen.

These two heirs apparent to the Roosevelt tradition were joined by a third major candidate, Frank Lowden. Lowden's political career began with his success as a corporation lawyer. Married to the daughter of the railway giant, George Pullman, Lowden was well connected in the business community. That support had brought him the governorship of Illinois. As a conservative, Lowden became the spokesman for the Old Guard. While he had a relatively small following, Lowden did have access to a substantial campaign fund.

Hiram Johnson had entered national politics as Roosevelt's running mate in 1912, having been selected for that position on the basis of his experience as the governor of California. As governor, Johnson had accrued significant progressive credentials. He had successfully advocated both the regulation of bidding for state contracts and the creation of an annual state budget. Both these reforms followed the general trend of the early twentieth century toward rationalization of business and government institutions. However, Johnson added to this general reform movement a quality of moral fervor. He viewed himself as one of the very few incorruptible politicians in America. According to this self-image, he alone defended the American people. Those who opposed him had been corrupted by "the interests."

Johnson's career in the Senate was not distinguished by the introduction of major pieces of progressive legislation. He came to the Senate in 1917 when progressive reform legislation was still dominated by the Democratic party. Furthermore, because he had been involved in the heresy of 1912, Johnson was not a favorite with the leadership of the Republican party. As an insurgent progressive he wanted to remain detached from party conservatives such as Boies Penrose and Francis Warren. Johnson was trapped in a political conundrum. As a member of a minority party, he could not author successful legislation without the assistance of members of his party whom he regarded as political enemies. His appointment to the Senate Foreign Relations Committee in 1919 had presented him with a new, uncomplicated political forum. Rather than retreating into the shadows of senators with foreign policy experience, Johnson chose to step into the forefront of the anti-League debate.

When Henry Cabot Lodge began his consultations with William Borah regarding the Republican response to Wilson's peace proposals, he was tying himself to a politician who could be seen as either an insurgent progressive or a foreign policy leader. However, when Hiram Johnson was added to the committee as an ally of Borah, their partnership emphasized the insurgent qualities of Borah's opposition to the League. The resulting formation of the irreconcilable movement possessed a pronounced insurgent tone. This was particularly evident in light of the public appeals made by Republican senators through the League for the Preservation of American Independence. The better orators of the Republican party had been trained on the old progressive campaign trails. As the Louis Coolidge organization sought out speakers for the anti-League position, they came to rely heavily on insurgent progressives like Borah and Johnson. The activities of those two senators guaranteed that opposition to the League of Nations would be made a major insurgent political issue.

Hiram Johnson's original intention in the anti-League speaking tour had been to garner support for the Republican position. However, his political interests had already passed beyond representing the people of California. His speeches in the Northeast had been applauded by large audiences. This positive reaction so far away from his power base on the West Coast enhanced Johnson's self-image as presidential timber. The Coolidge organization provided enormous logistical support. The advantages derived from such support made Johnson's appearances polished, and his speeches began to take on a tone of statesmanship. Through the summer of 1919 the favorable receptions his speeches received encouraged Johnson to consider an open bid for the Republican nomination in 1920. His confidence was bolstered by Gifford Pinchot's positive assessment of his candidacy. He began to consider a national primary campaign.[3]

---

[3] Johnson to Alex McCabe, July 16, 1919, Johnson Papers.

Hiram Johnson was a leading public speaker in the anti-League movement. He routinely absented himself from Senate sessions in the summer of 1919 to go on long public-speaking tours in the Northeast and Midwest. Louis Coolidge planned to use Johnson in an effort to raise public opposition to the League of Nations. He would be a member of the stable of orators that would precede and follow Wilson's public engagements. Wilson was to be exhausted and out-performed by a troop of well-rested, well-rehearsed Republicans. With Wilson's stroke, however, such an expensive enterprise seemed excessive. Johnson suddenly found that the logistical support of the League for the Preservation of American Independence was no longer available. He immediately assumed that the cutting off of funds was part of an effort to thwart his presidential aspirations.[4]

The insurgent opponents of the League of Nations were not willing to withdraw from the public debate. The philosophy of the insurgency assumed a high level of contact with the general public. In response to the loss of Coolidge's assistance, William Borah and Medill McCormick organized a Johnson speaking tour in the Midwest and Plains States. The speaking tour was designed to be anti-League and not electoral. However, Johnson could use the tour as the foundation of a nomination campaign. The summer and fall of 1919 provided Johnson with the means of gaining a high level of public recognition. He was able to promote himself as a defender of American foreign policy prerogatives as well as a defender of progressive ideals. The speaking tour was not used to its full potential; no consistent effort was made by Johnson or his supporters to build a nationwide political machine in the wake of his speaking engagements. In fact, Johnson equivocated on his candidacy until the primaries of 1920.[5]

During the summer and early fall of 1919, Henry Cabot Lodge had managed to paper over the insurgent/conservative disputes that had plagued the Republican party in the preceding ten years. However, with the first defeat of the Versailles Treaty in November 1919, members of the Republican party began to shift their attention away from issues of foreign relations. The most politically sensitive problem facing the Senate was that of the railroads. In an effort to ensure the efficient transportation of war materiel, the federal government had assumed control of the rail industry as an emergency wartime measure in 1918. This partial nationalization of the railroads had appealed to progressives, many of whom had called for such measures long before the war. Progressive politicians, joined by unionized railroad workers who had benefited from federal management, hoped to pass legislation that would prevent the return of the railroads to the control of their owners and guarantee permanent government management. In the Senate, the

---

[4] Diary Letters, September 8, 1919, Johnson Papers.

[5] Lower, *A Bloc of One*, 139–144. An earlier psychological study of Johnson points to a series of psychosomatic illnesses in the fall of 1919 and emphasizes Johnson's vacillation concerning the construction of his campaign; see John James Fitzpatrick, "Senator Hiram Johnson: A Life History, 1866–1945" (Ph.D. dissertation, University of California at Berkeley, 1975), 90.

discussion of the future of the railroad industry would begin in the Interstate Commerce Committee where Albert Cummins, Robert LaFollette, and George Norris would be critical participants in the debate. As Henry Cabot Lodge moved the issue of the Versailles Treaty off the Senate floor, the insurgents pushed to replace it with that of the reorganization of the railway system. With the return of a domestic issue that had been an integral part of progressive reform, the insurgents began a push for power in the Republican party.

In 1919 Hiram Johnson clearly wanted the Republican presidential nomination, but would not issue an official declaration of candidacy. Despite his reluctance to announce his intention to run, no other Republican rose to contest Johnson's position as the representative of the insurgency. When he did declare himself to be a candidate, Johnson was not merely a token representative of the old Progressive party of 1912. He quickly received the endorsement of key members of the Taft insurgency and his candidacy symbolized the emergence of a new agrarian progressive movement that had its roots in the insurgency of 1911. The key progressives who had stayed with the party in 1912 supported the California senator. William Borah, William Kenyon, Charles McNary, and George Norris all endorsed Johnson, not Leonard Wood.[6] After Johnson's declaration of candidacy in 1920 his supporters in the Senate began a press campaign. Johnson was already popular with the general public; the objective of this campaign was to translate that popularity into support by the Republican party leadership. In press statements his backers were careful to include references to the bolt of 1912 and speculate on the effects of a second bolt. George Norris provided a particularly ominous view of the 1920 nomination:

> The machines may control the Convention, because the selection of delegates . . . is in the hands and under the control of the machine; but the lesson of 1912 should be a historical guidepost for the Republican party. . . . The great bulk of the common people may have but little to say about the nomination, but Great God, how they can vote! . . . If the people's wish and voice are not heeded in the nomination of a Republican candidate for President, there is great danger that the Democrats will control the next Senate.[7]

The support of these senators was important in that they represented an earlier wave of Republican-dominated progressive reform. They had not bolted the party in 1912, and so remained Republicans in good standing. They had all served more than one term in the Senate, and so had begun to acquire significant levels of seniority.[8] William Borah's support was particularly crucial. Through his ability

---

[6] Fitzpatrick, "Senator Hiram Johnson," 121.

[7] Senator Norris's Press Statement, March 10, 1920, Johnson Papers.

[8] During the first half of the twentieth century, senators seldom served for more than one term. The chamber was largely populated by senators with fewer than four years of experience, and was dominated by those few who had served more than one term. See

to work with members of all factions of the party, he had become important in the national party organization. Lodge's decision to make Borah a near-equal partner in the League of Nations opposition had enhanced Borah's position as a leader in the party. Borah's prominence in national politics made him a likely chairman for the Republican National Convention in June. With these endorsements, Johnson's campaign took on significant dimensions in early 1920. He was not a fringe candidate or a dark horse, but rather the representative of an important minority faction within the Republican party.

Hiram Johnson finally ended his vacillation and announced his candidacy for the Republican nomination as the primary elections began. He entered his campaign without a national machine or even a large cohort of campaign workers. While he did possess important support among members of Congress, Johnson lacked organizations at the state levels that could translate popular support into convention votes. His California political machine was forced to bear the weight of his national campaign and would prove inadequate to the task.

Once he had decided to run for the Republican nomination, Hiram Johnson established a campaign dependent on a groundswell of public support. This conformed to established progressive ideals of representative government. Politicians were to represent the will of the people, not reflect the interests of business or the political establishment. As part of the reforms of the Progressive Era, several states had turned to the use of primaries to regulate the nomination process. However, the progressive drive for primary elections had been only moderately successful. While several states held primaries, the majority of delegates to the Republican National Convention were still under the direction of the state party caucuses or were uninstructed. Johnson's desire for widespread popular support led him to concentrate his efforts in the primary states, a strategy that could not mathematically guarantee him the nomination. Furthermore, such a strategy required strong local organizations in the primary states. Funding would be needed for the primary election campaign and support of the local newspapers would be necessary. Johnson lacked access to most state political machines and could not compete with the financial strength of his opponents, Leonard Wood and Frank Lowden.

Johnson's reliance on popular support and the primary states had an additional political liability. His oratorical style was fervid and his tendency to accuse political opponents of corruption alienated the moderate and conservative members of the Republican party. Henry Cabot Lodge, one of the most important members of the national party organization, viewed Johnson as a radical and a devotee of failed ideals such as government ownership of utilities.[9]

The vehemence of Johnson's campaign rhetoric damaged his credibility as the leader of the new reconciled Republican party, but it also made politicians chary

---

Barbara Hinckley, *Stability and Change in Congress* (New York: Harper and Row, 1977), 72–73.

      [9] Lodge to J. Otis Wardwell, April 16, 1920, Lodge Papers.

of supporting the targets of Johnson's attacks. The spring of 1920 was marked by the emergence of several favorite son candidates. They provided a convenient means for Republican leaders to escape the liabilities connected with endorsing any of the three major candidates—Johnson, Wood, and Lowden.

The campaign organizations of both Leonard Wood and Frank Lowden were well run and well financed. Both camps had developed a strategy of targeting those convention delegates who were uninstructed. This strategy placed a strong emphasis on maintaining good relations with state party leaders and those who controlled major Republican newspapers. Louis Emmerson, Frank Lowden's national campaign manager, argued that such a campaign strategy would result in a responsible nomination process, saying, "The national convention will be composed mostly of uninstructed delegates. We believe that it will be a truly deliberative convention and that the delegates will try to pick out the best man."[10] This strategy seemed on the surface to encourage deliberation; however, the financial strength of the Lowden and Wood campaigns resulted in high levels of spending. The combination of high levels of spending and uninstructed delegates led to accusations of buying delegate votes.

The ethical questions of campaign spending had been of great importance to the insurgent progressives. The Republicans had only recently risked a major party split over the seating of Truman Newberry. The focus of the attack on Newberry had been the extraordinarily high expenditures during his Senate campaign in 1918. The Republican party had held together in May 1919 to seat Newberry, but members of the insurgent faction had found merit in the Democrats' charges.

Insurgent fears of uncontrolled campaign spending reemerged in the spring of 1920 as reports of large gifts to the Wood and Lowden campaigns became public. Leonard Wood's national campaign manager, William Cooper Procter, became a figure of some notoriety. The millionaire Procter had no previous political experience but managed the candidate who claimed to represent modern progressive reform. He had personally provided much of the funding to the Wood campaign, and it was widely argued that Procter had bought the position as Wood's manager.[11] On February 26, 1920, the rumors of large campaign contributions led William Borah to move for the creation of a special Senate investigating committee. This first attempt to form such a committee failed.

Most of the delegates to the Republican National Convention were chosen between March and May of 1920. During this period the question of campaign spending rose as a major political issue. Frank Lowden had targeted delegates chosen by the state caucuses and spent virtually no time or effort in the primary campaigns. His strong ties to major corporate interests provided his campaign fund

---

[10] *Indianapolis News,* March 3, 1920, p. 1.

[11] Initial reports listed Procter's contributions at $500,000. However, Procter eventually sued the Wood organization for the repayment of campaign loans amounting to $745,433. Randolph C. Downes, *The Rise of Warren Gamaliel Harding, 1865–1920* (Columbus: Ohio State University Press, 1970), 408, and the *New York Times,* June 23, 1921, p. 29.

with ample resources for the pursuit of the nomination. He was also a free spender on the campaign trail. Controversies over his campaign tactics first emerged in Missouri. In that state, where delegates were not chosen via primary elections, Lowden had made cash gifts to delegates committed to him. Nat Goldstein and Robert Moore of St. Louis had each received $2,500 upon announcing their support of Lowden. Eventual investigations of Lowden's activities in Missouri uncovered payments of $88,000 to Missouri Republican leaders without any requirement for justification of expenditure.[12]

Similar reports began to emerge in the states of the deep South. Republican leaders in Georgia were accused of the acceptance of payoffs for convention votes. Lowden campaign payments to black delegates amounted to thousands of dollars. The extreme weakness of the Republican party in Georgia, combined with the near total disenfranchisement of black voters in that state, guaranteed that such campaign expenditures were designed not to elect a Republican, but to nominate the conservative Lowden.

Lowden and Johnson had targeted different groups of delegates. Despite little direct competition with Lowden over delegate votes, Johnson alluded to Lowden's free-spending practices in order to strengthen his own candidacy. While the two would certainly be competitors at the Republican National Convention, Johnson faced more immediate political threats from Leonard Wood and various favorite sons. Johnson took the theme of Lowden's improper spending practices and began applying it to all his opponents.

Johnson's nomination would be contested in every state, including California. California politics were traditionally subject to north/south splits. Johnson's center of political strength was in and around San Francisco. His career as a reform governor had antagonized a variety of elements in the California Republican party, most particularly the business interests of the Los Angeles area. This geographic division within California politics resulted in the candidacy of Herbert Hoover as a favorite son.

Hoover was a significant threat to Hiram Johnson. He had gained national recognition through his leadership of the American Relief Administration during World War I. Hoover's insistence on efficiency and generosity in the American relief effort had sparked admiration in both Europe and the United States. The success of these efforts made Hoover an important symbol of altruistic liberalism. During the war, Hoover had been a loyal deputy of Woodrow Wilson. Like the president, he was an ardent internationalist and supporter of the League of Nations. He had approved of Wilson's 1918 call for a Democratic Congress. He supported reforms of modernization, but was a friend of the business community. Hoover

---

[12] *Chicago Herald Examiner,* June 1, 1920, p. 1, and June 2, 1920, p. 1. The *Herald Examiner* (an unbridled supporter of the Hiram Johnson candidacy) added that E. L. Morse, a prominent figure in Missouri politics, reported that despite Johnson's widespread popularity among Missouri Republicans, thirty-three of the thirty-six Missouri delegates supported Lowden.

had the support of the major newspapers of the southern part of the state. In addition, his advocacy of internationalism had resulted in a strong following among internationalist members of California's Progressive party and women voters throughout California.[13] While Johnson won the primary election in California, the political battles for the support of his own state absorbed much of his campaign's precious energy and attention.

The most significant primary of Johnson's campaign was that of Indiana. Indiana politics were generally moderate to conservative, and would be more hospitable to the Lowden and Wood candidacies. Both Lowden and Wood had labeled Indiana as a key state and had established firm footings among the state's Republican leadership. A Johnson victory in Indiana would have a major impact at the National Convention.

Leonard Wood was a popular candidate in Indiana. He had key support within the party's state organization and the Indianapolis newspapers. He was also a highly visible candidate. His initial petition to be added to the primary ballot had more signatures than any other such petition in the history of the state's primary. During the campaign in May, he made more than seventy-five public appearances.[14] In comparison, Johnson had limited support among the leaders of the Republican party in Indiana and could not afford to purchase newspaper advertising at the rate established by Leonard Wood.

Nonetheless, Wood recognized that Johnson provided a substantial threat in Indiana. Wood sought to focus the contest on foreign policy issues, not domestic problems. The most dramatic distinctions between the Wood and Johnson platforms concerned the League of Nations. Wood supported the reservationist stance of the mainstream Republican party. Furthermore, he was not going to permit Johnson to become the self-proclaimed defender of "Americanism." He promoted an American foreign policy that would be activist and interventionist, but resoundingly defended congressional authorization of military actions. Wood proclaimed that reservations to Article X of the League Covenant were necessary to protect the sovereignty of the U.S. government.[15]

Wood was careful to use his military service and his associations with Theodore Roosevelt in projecting his image as a defender of American democracy. His supporters emphasized the radicalism of Hiram Johnson's reform ethic. On the eve of the election the *Indianapolis News* reported that "the fear that Johnson, by the combined vote of the malcontent and radical elements to which he has appealed, might win without representing the majority opinion of Republicans, has caused numerous Republicans who had been undecided or had leaned toward Lowden or Harding, to join the Wood forces." The reporting of the *News*, while politically

---

[13] Lower, *A Bloc of One*, 149–154.

[14] *Indianapolis News*, March 4, 1920, p. 1, and May 1, 1920, p. 1.

[15] *Indianapolis News*, May 1, 1920, p. 1.

colored, was accurate.[16] Leonard Wood won the hotly contested Indiana primary.

The result of the election was important, but it did not kill the Johnson candidacy. In fact, it provided him with a new issue. The amount of money spent in the Indiana primary exceeded all previous primary elections. Charges of buying votes flew about, with most Republicans agreeing that spending had become uncontrolled. While he did not win the primary, Johnson had a powerful weapon for the convention debates. In May and June the issue of spending by Wood and Lowden surpassed all others. It was an issue of particular divisiveness, as Johnson supporters charged others with corruption, and in turn, were charged with providing the Democrats with a new weapon against potential Republican candidates.

William Borah led the offensive against the spending practices of the Republican presidential candidates. Borah was appalled by the absence of controls on campaign finance, seeing it as an immediate threat to the election process of 1920 and as a general threat to American democracy. He argued that the introduction of massive amounts of money would skew the information available to voters and would eventually lead to bribery and corruption. After the Indiana primary, William Borah once again proposed that the Senate Committee on Privileges and Elections investigate spending practices in the 1920 campaign. This second attempt passed by a unanimous vote, and a special committee was formed under the chairmanship of Senator William Kenyon (R, Iowa).[17]

The work of the Kenyon committee remained on the front pages of newspapers throughout the Republican National Convention. The investigation quickly focused on the Wood and Lowden organizations. The principal line of argument against Wood concerned his relationship with his campaign manager, William Procter. Procter's massive contributions to the Wood campaign constituted a suspect link between big business and the candidate. The accusations of questionable behavior eventually led to the dismissal of William Procter on the eve of the convention and his replacement by Frank Hitchcock. The Wood campaign suffered a further blow, as Procter refused to accept his dismissal and continued to issue campaign instructions.[18]

The testimony concerning the Lowden campaign, however, was far more damaging. On June 2, two of the Missouri delegates to the Republican National Convention testified before the Kenyon Committee that each had taken $2,500

---

[16] *Indianapolis News*, May 3, 1920, p. 1. The political impact of such reporting should not be underestimated. The *Indianapolis News*, a supporter of Wood, furthered his candidacy by its coverage of the primary and other state primaries. The Maryland election, held on the same date, had an earlier poll closing. Wood's victory in Maryland was widely reported in the evening edition of the *News* hours before the close of the Indiana polls.

[17] Senator Kenyon was the second-ranking Republican on the Privileges and Elections Committee and had endorsed Johnson. See Wesley Bagby, "Progressivism's Debacle: The Election of 1920" (Ph.D. dissertation, Columbia University, 1960), 117.

[18] *Chicago Herald Examiner*, June 4, 1920, p. 1.

from the Lowden campaign.   Further investigation threw into question the legitimacy of all the Missouri delegates. On June 3 all the delegates from Missouri were expelled from the convention, with thirty-three of the thirty-six committed to Lowden. As Republicans gathered in Chicago to prepare for the opening day of the convention, they were exposed to the gleeful political hyperbole of the *Chicago Herald Examiner*. This supporter of Johnson's candidacy reported, "The testimony [in the Senate] indicated that the money-mad Missourians used mustard gas, sluggers, rump conventions, and forged election calls to cheat the people of any choice in the making of a president."[19] The Republican National Convention examined the credentials of the delegates while the Kenyon Committee heard testimony on the spending practices of the various Republican candidates. Lowden delegates were consistently contested, with charges of bribery leveled at members of several delegations.

The question of ethics remained a major issue throughout the nomination process. Supporters of Johnson argued that he was the one candidate who was not damaged by the Kenyon Committee.[20] As such, he would not be a victim of Democratic attacks in the November election. The issue of Johnson's untainted campaign was clearly a major concern to the convention delegates. However, the Wood and Lowden forces were successful in preventing the campaign spending issue from coming to open floor debate at the convention. The Johnson forces still could use this corruption strategy, only less directly. By threatening to force the issue onto the floor, Johnson was able to gain substantial concessions from his opponents. The most significant use of the issue occurred when Johnson needed to stop the Wood bandwagon that had begun in the third and fourth ballots.   William Borah threatened to take the platform and make a major address on campaign financing if he did not receive the requested adjournment.[21] When the convention reached the Wood/Johnson impasse on June 12, William Borah announced, "I have been a Republican all my life; I even stayed with Mr. Taft in 1912, and that's going some. I am willing to support now any clean man and I will not support any man who is not clean."[22] Senator Miles Poindexter insisted that the cleanliness issue was of critical importance to the Republicans of the western states and argued that the nomination of Wood or Lowden would result in the defection of the West to the Democratic party, loss of Congress, and the possible loss of the White House.

---

[19] *Chicago Herald Examiner*, June 3, 1920, p. 1.

[20] This factor has been used to explain the success of Warren Harding's nomination bid. Harding had received a gift from no individual that was larger than $13,000 and his campaign committee could legitimize its expenses. Downes, *The Rise of Warren Harding,* 409.

[21] Bagby, "Progressivism's Debacle," 117.

[22] *Chicago Herald Examiner*, June 12, 1920, p. 1.

THE REPUBLICAN NATIONAL CONVENTION AND THE LEAGUE OF NATIONS ISSUE

Foreign policy concerns were also a focus of attention at the Chicago convention. The question of admittance to the League of Nations—that one issue that had tied Republicans together during 1919—was still of critical importance. With the second failure of ratification in March 1920, the Republicans had to formulate some alternative response to the European peace. The first opportunity to present this Republican alternative would be in the Republican platform of 1920. Seven senators were appointed to the Republican National Committee's Committee on Policies and Platform; none of them were irreconcilables.[23]

The original draft of the League of Nations plank, written in early May, took the reservationist position. While this first draft did not bind the convention or any of the prospective nominees, it put Hiram Johnson in an extremely difficult position. Johnson was not only committed to irreconcilable opposition to the League of Nations, he was using that stand as a major argument for his nomination. Running on a position of absolute opposition to the League in the primaries, Johnson perceived this draft to be an act by the reservationists and internationalists to sabotage his campaign.

Henry Cabot Lodge was well aware of the schisms that were resurfacing in the Republican party. The fundamental debates of progressive reform had returned. Republican politicians had begun to divide over the issue of campaign spending. Conservatives were calling for a return to private control of the railroad industry, and an end to the nationalization that had been imposed as an emergency wartime measure. In response, insurgents insisted that the nationalization of the railroads had been beneficial and must continue as a permanent policy. Even the tariff began to reemerge as an issue, as conservatives began to promote the use of the tariff to increase revenue and protect the American economy. These issues had the potential of provoking a major party split like that of 1912. Lodge was not willing to permit the League of Nations controversy to push the progressive insurgent faction further from the rest of the party. He recognized that existing divisiveness made the League of Nations a critical issue. A reservationist plank would provoke a major battle or even a bolt if it were accepted by the Convention. Lodge understood the narrow channel he was navigating and lobbied for a foreign policy plank that would be so broad as to include "every argument from Borah's line down to McCumber's."[24]

Lodge's caution proved to be well founded. When the convention met in Chicago, Borah and McCormick announced that Johnson could not run on the

---

[23] The senators on the committee were Albert Cummins, Irvine Lenroot, Albert Capper, Harry New, James Watson, Reed Smoot, and Frank Kellogg. Will Hays to Lodge, January 28, 1920, Lodge Papers.

[24] Lodge to George Harvey, May 25, 1920, Lodge Papers. See also Will H. Hays, *The Memoirs of Will H. Hays* (New York: Doubleday & Company, Inc., 1955), 247.

initial version of the plank. Senator Brandegee, the conservative irreconcilable, threatened to refuse to run for reelection in the fall if the plank passed.[25]

While William Borah was willing to threaten a second split of the Republican party, his real objective was compromise between the reservationist and irreconcilable factions. In the days before the convention opened, Borah was careful to allow room for political maneuvering over the League of Nations issue. In an interview with the *Chicago Herald Examiner*, Borah stated, "I have had certain proposed drafts presented to me, but there were no formal conferences, and there has been no final agreement."[26] Several of the reservationists held firm and resisted the softening of the League plank. This resulted in an escalation of rhetoric by the Johnson supporters. They linked the reservationists with the traditional focus of agrarian progressivism. Hours before the convention was to determine the League plank, William Borah announced, "Just what influence is blocking this agreement? Senator Crane and the international bankers."[27]

Henry Cabot Lodge was able to bring enough pressure to bear against the reservationist plank to generate a compromise. This version was drafted by Elihu Root. The new language was sufficiently vague that both reservationists and irreconcilables could claim it represented their thought. Authorship by the internationalist Root helped to pacify those who had heartily supported American involvement in the League of Nations. Before the plank was to go to the floor of the convention for debate, it had to pass through the convention's Resolution Committee. The committee's chairman was James Watson, an ally of Lodge and an extraordinarily skillful parliamentary politician. Watson used this ability to prevent open divisiveness on the convention floor. The compromise plank was adopted unanimously, and the potential for schism was avoided.

The Root version of the plank committed the party to "an agreement among nations to preserve the peace of the world." It included the core of the argument against Article X of the League covenant, calling for U.S. action "without depriving the people of the United States in advance of the right to determine for themselves what is just and fair when the occasion arises, and without involving them as participants and not as peacemakers in a multitude of quarrels."[28]

The plank attacked Wilson's version of the peace as being "intolerable for an independent people" and "certain to produce injustice, hostility, and controversy." It dutifully commended the Republican senators' defense of "the time-honored policies of Washington, Jefferson, and Monroe" and failed to make even an oblique reference to the reservationist/irreconcilable split. In short, the plank maintained Republican solidarity through the method developed by Lodge in 1919. While the Republicans were incapable of generating a detailed foreign policy program, they

---

[25] Bagby, "Progressivism's Debacle," 129.

[26] *Chicago Herald Examiner*, June 7, 1920, p. 3.

[27] *Chicago Herald Examiner*, June 10, 1920, p. 1.

[28] Kirk H. Porter and Donald Bruce Johnson, eds., *National Party Platforms, 1840–1964* (Urbana: University of Illinois Press, 1966), 231.

could still maintain a full attack against the Wilson plan.

Both the reservationists and irreconcilables achieved significant gains. The irreconcilable faction had prevented the party from adopting a pro-League plank and kept Hiram Johnson's candidacy viable. Yet reservationists could interpret the compromise as a temporary expedient. Solidarity at the Republican National Convention would provide a Republican president and American entry to the League could be achieved at a later date. Lodge recognized the deficiencies of the League of Nations plank as a foreign policy statement but also recognized its necessity as a political tool.[29]

The controversy over the League of Nations platform set the tone for the convention. The delegates were faced with a complicated political situation. The principal divisions of the party were each symbolized by one of the three major candidates. In addition to Lowden, Wood, and Johnson, several states supported favorite son candidates. Not only would no candidate come into the convention with the majority required for nomination, no candidate would be in immediate striking range of the nomination until delegates began breaking away from support of the favorite sons.[30]

THE REPUBLICAN NATIONAL CONVENTION AND THE SELECTION OF A NOMINEE

The preliminary work of the Republican National Convention had achieved a limited success in terms of holding the party together. However, there were still opportunities for major divisions once the convention went into regular sessions. The determination of the permanent chairman of the convention would have an effect on the nomination process. William Borah was the most likely choice, but because he had endorsed Johnson and was openly hostile to Wood and Lowden, he felt it would be unethical to accept the position. The withdrawal of Borah resulted in the election of the temporary chairman, Henry Cabot Lodge.[31] The chairmanship of Lodge would help to prevent open splits at the convention. As he had used his position as chairman of the Senate Foreign Relations Committee to forge a Republican compromise on the League of Nations, he would use his position as chairman of the Republican National Convention to bring about a more generalized consensus within the party. This would work to the disadvantage of the Johnson forces. Lodge's predilection to compromise and moderation would not favor a candidate who virulently attacked Republican conservatives and who also had a history as a bolter.

---

[29] Lodge to Corinne Roosevelt Robinson, June 19, 1920, Lodge Papers.

[30] Leonard Wood had 287½ delegates, Frank Lowden had 211½ delegates, Hiram Johnson had 133 delegates, and the leading dark horse candidate, Warren Harding, had 65½ delegates. Nomination required 493 votes.

[31] Wesley Bagby, *The Road to Normalcy: The Presidential Campaign and Election of 1920* (Baltimore: Johns Hopkins Press, 1962), 123.

Hiram Johnson's strategy at the convention was twofold. He hoped his two main opponents, Lowden and Wood, would be discredited by accusations of corrupt campaign practices. At the same time, Johnson had to convince the delegates that he had support not only among the populist-oriented western voters, but with the general public. His anti-League speaking tours had given him a high level of recognition in the East. His powerful oratorical style had antagonized the more conservative Republican politicians, but had impressed the average voter.

Considering his lack of a genuine national organization, Johnson had done quite well in the primaries. He had been most successful in the West where agrarian progressive ideas were widely accepted. Johnson's campaign committee chairman, Angus McSwen, sought to demonstrate that Johnson's image was not that of a radical, but of a popular reformer. Despite the fact that Johnson's campaign was not as well financed as Lowden's or Wood's, he came into the national convention with a strong following. In a letter to Henry Cabot Lodge, McSwen argued that "in point of personality and vote-getting ability he [Johnson] occupies an unique place in American life today."[32] McSwen used the election returns in the various primary states to demonstrate Johnson's popularity and viability as a candidate. His argument was that Johnson was creating a western groundswell that would continue to grow and carry the nation. This strategy had serious flaws. Far too many state committeemen could not accept a Johnson candidacy. Despite the fact that Johnson was favored by the average Republican voter, he was perceived as a radical by much of the party leadership.

Johnson's primary campaigns had stressed his opposition to established conservatism in the party. The leadership feared that while voters enjoyed the rhetoric of Johnson's primary campaign, they would lose their enthusiasm for him when actually confronted with the possibility of putting him in the White House. The Johnson position at the nominating convention was hampered by the weak support for Johnson in some of his delegations. Some states, such as Oregon, committed all their delegates to the candidate who had won the primary. In the case of Oregon, Wood had run a strong second and had considerable support within the delegation. As the balloting continued, these delegates with weak commitments to the Johnson campaign began to defect to other candidates.[33]

Hiram Johnson failed to win the nomination for a variety of reasons. Conservative and moderate Republicans recognized that his popularity was greatest

---

[32] Angus McSwen [Johnson Campaign] to Lodge, May 20, 1920, Lodge Papers.

[33] Paul David, Ralph Goldman, and Richard Bain, *The Politics of National Party Conventions* (Washington, D.C.: The Brookings Institution, 1960), 236. Not all of Johnson's delegations were weakly committed to his candidacy. Johnson had demonstrated some astute political maneuvering with regard to some delegations. In several states, those running for delegate positions were listed on the ballot in alphabetical order. In those cases Johnson would permit only his supporters with names beginning with the first letters of the alphabet to run in the delegate elections. As a result, Johnson supporters appeared disproportionately at the top of the ballot and were disproportionately elected.

in the West, not in the highly populated areas of the East or Midwest. Johnson's support among Republican politicians tended to come from two groups: insurgent members of Congress who had resisted conservative leadership of the party, and former members of the Progressive party. Both of these groups were viewed with some suspicion by the leadership of the Republican party. The issue of the League of Nations had been blunted by the adoption of Root's compromise foreign policy plank. The issue of campaign spending would deny the nomination to Wood and Lowden, but had not turned the convention to support Johnson.

By June 12 it was clear to the convention that the 1920 figurehead of the Republican party would have to be a man who personified compromise and adjustment. Perhaps the image of Theodore Roosevelt was not the best yardstick for measuring a presidential nominee. The Republican party had created other great presidents. William McKinley symbolized reserve, compassion, deliberation, and generosity. Recently sanctified at the 1917 dedication of the McKinley Memorial, the martyred president occupied a prominent position in the memories of the delegates searching for a compromise candidate.

The initial direction of the convention was to shift support to Leonard Wood. However, the question of campaign spending prevented Johnson supporters from following this movement and accepting Wood as the nominee. After the adjournment of June 12, informal meetings were conducted by George Harvey in the hotel suite of the Republican National Committee chairman, Will Hays. As these meetings continued into the night, it became clear that a compromise could not be made on any of the three major candidates. This night marked the beginning of the rise of Warren Harding's candidacy.

Warren Harding was a known element in the Republican party. He was not dynamic, nor had he served long enough in national Republican politics to be a well-known leader among politicians. These characteristics, however, were positive points in his candidacy. He was essentially Ohio's favorite son candidate, though he did have support outside his state delegation. He was appropriately conservative, obliging to the party leadership, and untainted by charges of excessive campaign spending. His Senate career had been one of political moderation, normally following party line in a quiet manner, constantly diplomatic and cooperative with all his colleagues in Congress. In short, he was not offensive to any major faction of the party. His greatest political mistake had occurred when he referred to Theodore Roosevelt as "another Aaron Burr."[34] Harding's insult to the canonized politician was overlooked; his party loyalty was not. With some effort, he could conceivably become the heir to the party of McKinley.

The initial impetus for a serious Harding candidacy came from the more conservative elements of the party. Harding disapproved of controversy and could be relied on not to attack the wings of the party. Furthermore, his nomination would cancel the effect of the Democratic party's nomination of the Ohioan, James

---

[34] James T. Williams, Jr., to Lodge, May 11, 1920, Lodge Papers.

Cox. The informal discussions that occurred in Will Hays's "smoke-filled" hotel suite on the night of June 12 resulted in a general sense of the acceptability of the Harding nomination.[35] At that time, Harding gained the support of an essential figure at the convention, Henry Cabot Lodge.

As chairman of the convention, Lodge's support was crucial in determining the viability of Harding's campaign for the nomination. Lodge had entered the convention committed to the Massachusetts favorite son, Calvin Coolidge, but privately preferred the ideology of Leonard Wood. As controversies over campaign spending made Wood's nomination less viable, Lodge began to shift his support to the senator from Ohio. Harding conformed to Lodge's vision of a Republican candidate who would end the fragmentation of the party. The Ohio senator had proved his loyalty to the party while serving on the Foreign Relations Committee during the League of Nations debates. Lodge praised Harding's role as a conciliator.[36]

While Harding was not the first choice of most of the delegates, he was acceptable to a broad range of senior Republican politicians. George Harvey, a private citizen well connected in the party, reported that Henry Cabot Lodge, Reed Smoot, Murray Crane, James Watson, Frank Brandegee, and William Borah all would consent to the Harding nomination.[37]

THE INSURGENT REACTION TO THE HARDING CANDIDACY

Once the decision had been made to nominate Warren Harding, the only real threat of party division came from the Johnson camp. The political outlook of Harding was not offensive to either Lowden or Wood and they quickly came to support the Republican nominee. However, Johnson was known to dislike Harding, both personally and politically. Early in the nomination campaign the insurgent candidate described Harding as "spineless" and the candidate of crooked politicians.[38]

Johnson's claim to nationwide political support was questionable, but he did have a strong following in the West. The party was still weakened by factionalism and a bolt by Johnson could result in the defeat of the Republican party in November. Harding recognized that Johnson presented a threat to the Republican party and offered Johnson the vice presidential nomination. Johnson refused.

Before the convention was over, liberal journalists were beginning to condemn the Harding nomination as part of a conservative plot consummated in "smoke-filled rooms." The aura of conservative corruption was bolstered as the inquiry of the Kenyon Committee unearthed questionable campaign practices by Wood and

---

[35] Bagby, *The Road to Normalcy*, 87–91.

[36] Garraty, *Henry Cabot Lodge*, 394–398.

[37] Bagby, *The Road to Normalcy*, 90. See also, Alice Roosevelt Longworth, *Crowded Hours* (New York: Charles Scribner's Sons, 1933), 311.

[38] Diary Letters, February 22, 1920, Johnson Papers.

Lowden—the two candidates who had been most strongly supported by the Republican right. Campaign ethics had the potential of becoming even more controversial when William Procter sued the Wood campaign in July 1920. In this political climate, Johnson's refusal to endorse the Republican party's nominee was particularly menacing.

Hiram Johnson did not bolt the party, nor did he endorse Harding. He remained silent for almost a month. During this time he was under pressure from all quarters of the party to join in support of the Republican nominee. William Borah, one of Johnson's principal supporters, urged Johnson's loyalty to the party. Rather than arguing for the candidate, Borah concentrated on the platform. He claimed the insurgent victory with the League of Nations plank surpassed the Harding nomination. He urged Johnson to work for the Republican nominee for the purpose of sealing the insurgent gains at the convention.[39]

In July Hiram Johnson finally began to work on behalf of Harding's presidential campaign. While he was not enthusiastic about the candidate, he came to agree with Borah's analysis of the Republican party platform. Johnson had decided to maintain some allegiance to the Republicans; he was not ready to leave the party a second time. However, he still did not approve of Harding as a candidate. Not only was Harding essentially a conservative, he did not possess the virtues or convictions Johnson felt were essential to a politician. To Johnson, Harding was the antithesis of a progressive politician. Worse yet, he had a talent for shifting with political tides rather than carrying out a political program. Johnson was not convinced that Harding would keep the United States out of the League of Nations after the election.[40]

Harding was clearly relieved by the retention of Johnson in the Republican fold. Confronted with only one opponent in November, Harding's electoral chances were substantially improved. Harding thanked Johnson for his loyalty, and complimented the senator on his magnanimity.[41]

Harding's relief was shared by other party leaders. Henry Cabot Lodge also viewed Johnson's support as critical. A Johnson bolt could destroy the Republican chances to regain the White House. Furthermore, Johnson was one of the best stump speakers in the Republican party and his skills would be welcomed by the Harding campaign.[42]

The leadership of the Republican party understood the threat that Johnson presented, and continually worked to prevent his disaffection. Throughout the campaign Johnson was asked to make public addresses on behalf of Harding. In this way Harding benefited from Johnson's oratorical skills while simultaneously causing Johnson to publicly reaffirm his support of the Republican party and its candidate. As a concession to Johnson's position as the insurgent progressive

[39] Borah to Hiram Johnson, June 24, 1920, Borah Papers.

[40] Johnson to A. D. Lasker, July 8, 1920, Johnson Papers.

[41] Warren G. Harding to Johnson, July 27, 1920, Johnson Papers.

[42] Lodge to Warren G. Harding, July 8, 1920, Lodge Papers.

standard bearer, Harding called on Johnson for advice regarding policy questions throughout the summer and fall of 1920. Most conversations between Johnson and Harding were dedicated to the League of Nations issue. Unable to secure the nomination, Johnson hoped to at least preserve American nonparticipation in the League.

Murray Crane's near success in attaching a pro-League plank to the Republican platform had worried the irreconcilables of the party. Root's compromise version of the plank marked a temporary victory over reservationism, but no one in the irreconcilable camp considered the compromise a final solution to the problem.

During the campaign it was clear that Harding did not diverge from the basic reservationist position. Despite his seat on the Senate Foreign Relations Committee, Harding had never developed any exceptional expertise in foreign policy. However, his basic advocacy of modern commercial conservatism made him sympathetic to the commercial internationalism advocated by Henry Cabot Lodge. Harding's political inclinations, combined with the vaguely worded Republican foreign policy plank, could easily lead to a Republican-sponsored entry into the League of Nations. In the winter of 1919–1920, both the British and French indicated that the conditional entry of the Americans was acceptable. It would be difficult for the irreconcilables to defeat entrance into the League a third time if a Republican president submitted a treaty. The threat of a denunciation by Johnson before the November election had been sufficient to prevent Harding from openly advocating American entry into the League of Nations. The Republican party held together in 1920 and Warren Harding was elected in a landslide with over 60 percent of the popular vote. The question remained as to whether Johnson could still influence Harding's public statements.

The memory of the 1912 bolt was still strong. Harding continued to be reluctant to dismiss Johnson's power as an opponent. Even after his success in the November election, Harding called upon leading Republicans to consult with him in Marion. Johnson was asked both in his capacity as a progressive and as a foreign policy leader.[43] Harding was committed to a unified Republican party even after the election. He was not willing to have his administration marred by intraparty disputes between the mainstream and the progressive wing. Johnson's support had been necessary for the maintenance of Republican unity during the election; it would be useful in the next four years. Harding's invitation to Johnson was designed to reaffirm the truce between the opposing factions of the Republican party. Johnson's acceptance of the position as postelection counselor marked the continuation of a spirit of cooperation within the Republican party. Johnson no longer referred to Harding as a "spineless sort of individual." In a letter to his son,

---

[43] Hiram Johnson was the only progressive irreconcilable to be invited to Marion, Ohio. Despite his experience in foreign policy questions, and his position as leader of the irreconcilables in the Senate, William Borah was not asked to advise the president-elect. The selection of Johnson was undoubtedly linked to his ability not only to present political problems in the Senate, but also to spark opposition among the general public.

Johnson reported that the Republican nominee had been converted to the insurgent cause and would only initiate foreign policy programs that had the full agreement of the Republicans in the Senate.[44]

As a counselor to Harding, Johnson had as his objective the curbing of the internationalist influences on the president-elect. Just as the Republican platform had not advocated American entry into the League of Nations, the new head of the Republican party could not advocate American entry into the League of Nations. As a means of preventing Harding's later support of the League, Johnson and other irreconcilables hoped to prevent avowed internationalists from becoming the president's principal advisors.

The position of secretary of state would be of undoubted importance. The Republican secretary would have to possess the respect of the leadership of the party. He would also have to be a man of sufficient stature and intellect to promote American interests in the postwar world. Henry Cabot Lodge's position on the Senate Foreign Relations Committee guaranteed that he would have some influence in the selection of the new secretary of state.[45]

Lodge supported the appointment of Elihu Root, Theodore Roosevelt's secretary of state. The selection of Root would guarantee a smooth working relationship between the White House and the Senate. His foreign policy goals were similar to those of Lodge. He had been a member of the Senate from 1908 to 1914 and had served on the Foreign Relations Committee. As a result, he had an appreciation of the role of the Senate in foreign policy making. Root favored conditional entry into the League of Nations. Furthermore, he had proved his commitment to compromise at the Republican National Convention.

William Borah generated a movement for an alternative candidate—Senator Philander Knox. Knox had extensive experience in the area of foreign policy, having served as the secretary of state under William Howard Taft. He was irreconcilably opposed to American entry into the League. The appointment of Knox would also serve as an important bridge in intraparty politics. Knox was a conservative on most domestic issues. His appointment would provide a continuing political tie between conservative elements of the party and the insurgent progressives. During the Versailles Treaty debates Borah and Knox had become close political allies. Knox's appointment to the State Department would provide a potential lever against Henry Cabot Lodge and would effectively prevent American entry into the League of Nations. Knox's appointment had no support outside of the irreconcilable camp. During the League debates in 1919 Lodge and Knox were only united by their opposition to Wilson's version of the League of Nations. By early 1920 the two were openly hostile in their differences over the Republican party's position on the European peace. A working relationship between Lodge, as chairman of the Foreign Relations Committee, and Knox, as secretary of state, was impossible.

---

[44] Diary Letters, December 7, 1920, Johnson Papers.
[45] H. M. Daugherty to Lodge, October 26, 1920, Lodge Papers.

The position of secretary of state fell to Charles Evans Hughes. A former Republican presidential candidate, he was a formidable power within the party hierarchy. He had been serving as an informal counselor to Harding throughout the campaign and had developed a good working relationship with the president-elect. It was this close relationship that led Harding to select Hughes.[46] While Hughes did not have Root's long-standing experience in foreign policy making, he had a formidable intellect. In the brief time since the 1916 election, he had grasped control of the issues of international relations and had become a leading theoretician in the area of international law and arbitration. Hughes had been an advocate of the League of Nations, falling into the camp of mild reservationists. For this reason, irreconcilables had not supported suggestions of his appointment as secretary of state and would be cautious toward his foreign policy initiatives.

Other cabinet positions were also given to internationalists. During the campaign, Harding had come to rely on Herbert Hoover. Hoover had caught the public's imagination as coordinator of European relief projects. He had served to inspire broad segments of the population to internationalism. However, Hoover had deeply antagonized Hiram Johnson during the California primaries. As Harding was selecting his cabinet in December, Johnson openly questioned Hoover's loyalty to the Republican party and doubted his potential value to the American government. Despite this opposition, Harding selected Hoover as his secretary of commerce. He was careful to inform Johnson before the appointment was made public, explaining it as a necessary concession to powerful elements within the Republican party.

THE ELECTION OF 1920 AND THE CONSEQUENCES FOR PARTY SOLIDARITY

Borah and Johnson had a profound impact on the politics of 1920. Through the candidacy of Hiram Johnson, they had made opposition to U.S. entry into the League of Nations an insurgent issue. As such, they prevented the Republican party from officially advocating entrance under the Lodge Reservations. They were not able to control the executive branch, either by nominating one of their own at the Republican convention, or by selecting the president's principal foreign policy advisors. However, they had learned how to manipulate the party's more conservative leadership and modify party policy.

Borah and Johnson had forced concessions because of the party leadership's fear of a bolt like that of 1912. Both fully understood the impact of a threat to leave the party. However, the real objective of these two senators was to reform the Republican party, not to destroy it. In this way their motives conformed to the basic pattern of insurgency developed between 1909 and 1911. While they openly discussed leaving the party, they were not interested in establishing an alternative

---

[46] Robert Murray, *The Politics of Normalcy* (New York: Norton, 1973), 24–25.

political apparatus. They assumed that the enactment of progressive reform was more plausible under the sponsorship of the Republican party. While most insurgent members of the Senate concurred with this approach, there was one notable exception.

Robert LaFollette had maintained a continual conflict with the leadership of the Republican party during his tenure in the Senate. Dismayed by conservative influences in the Republican party, disillusioned by the collapse of Wilsonian reform during the war, LaFollette disagreed with the Borah/Johnson concept of pushing reform through an established party. He sought to unite the populist elements of both the Democrat and Republican parties into a new progressive coalition. LaFollette opposed the creation of a new party around a charismatic presidential candidate, just as he had been against the original Progressive party under Theodore Roosevelt. He was interested in generating a congressional movement that would eventually evolve into a national organization capable of sustaining a presidential candidate. To this purpose, he formed the Independent Congressional Campaign Committee.

LaFollette's committee was designed to generate a powerful progressive bloc within Congress. This bloc would benefit progressive politics on the congressional level. By freeing ideological progressives from the conservative leadership of both parties, LaFollette hoped to institute a new wave of progressive legislation in the 1920s. He envisioned a unified movement of congressmen who would concentrate their efforts on Capitol Hill. He invited those members of Congress he deemed to be leaders of progressive politics to come together as a formal bloc.[47]

The Independent Congressional Campaign Committee was obviously a response to the failure of the Republican National Committee to nominate a progressive candidate. However, by eschewing party loyalty and attempting to undermine the authority of senior party members who were conservative, LaFollette's organization had a limited following. LaFollette was convinced that William Borah's participation was important and made a special effort to enlist the senator in his cause. Borah, as a widely respected senior insurgent, would have been a valuable ally. In response to LaFollette's initial request, Borah said that he regretted that Idaho politics would consume all his energy in November 1920. Borah was not willing to risk party sanctions that would affect his seniority; whenever LaFollette asked his assistance, Borah demurred, apologizing that he did not have enough time. Nevertheless, LaFollette's organization remained part of congressional politics until the mid-1920s.

The election of 1920 marked the beginning of a new pattern in Republican politics. Progressivism was not dead, but rather was submerged in a party desperate to maintain control of Congress and take possession of the White House. The insurgent progressive movement had taken on a subtle and complex institutional role in partisan politics.

---

[47] Robert LaFollette, Sr., to Borah, August 13, 1920, Borah Papers.

5

The Making of a New Republican Foreign Policy

A party which is ineffective will soon be discarded. If a party is to endure as a serviceable instrument of government for the country, it must possess and display a healthy spirit of party loyalty. Such a manifestation in the Congress would do more than anything else to rehabilitate it in the esteem and confidence of the country.

—Calvin Coolidge

After the election of 1920, the Republicans needed to generate a positive response to the postwar international system created by the Versailles Treaty. It was clear that the divisions within the party that had existed during the League of Nations debates had not vanished during the process of party platform negotiation in 1920. These differences were the result of fundamental ideological disputes, the resolution of which would require intricate political negotiation.

The mainstream of the party favored a foreign policy approach based on the progressive diplomacy that had evolved during the Roosevelt and Taft administrations. This approach assumed that it was appropriate to expand American influence abroad and that such an expansion obliged the U.S. government to become a leader in international relations. During the presidency of Theodore Roosevelt, the United States had adopted an aggressive foreign policy. Roosevelt sought to expand the influence of the U.S. government, as exemplified by American intervention in the Dominican Republic's debt crisis, American mediation in the Russo-Japanese War, and the construction of the Great White Fleet. Roosevelt consistently advocated the moral superiority of American culture and positioned the U.S. government as the steward of modern civilization. This chauvinism was mitigated during the presidency of William H. Taft, as the emphasis on military might was replaced by the economic uplift of Dollar Diplomacy. Nonetheless, the fundamental element of nationalism would remain in place. The United States not only had the right, but also the obligation, to expand its influence in the world economy. The United States had to be active in the international system and that activity would be determined strictly on the basis of national self-interest.

The Republican administration envisioned the United States as a world leader. The war had brought about a shift in the relative power of the United States, Japan, France, and Great Britain, and that shift benefited the United States. Under Republican leadership, the American government would support neither Wilsonian nor Bolshevik internationalism. It would encourage the continuation of an international financial system where currencies would be fixed on a stable gold standard and governments would be responsible for their national economic obligations. The United States would take up its role as a leader in the international system and not behave as a lesser partner in dealings with Great Britain.

Although most Republican politicians believed that the United States could protect its national interest and come to dominate international relations, a significant minority disagreed. The existence of the irreconcilable movement in the Senate demonstrated that some members of the party had a different perception of the international role of the United States.[1] Despite their differences over domestic policy, the irreconcilables shared a negative opinion of the international system, which they believed to be dominated by Europeans. These senators were ardent nationalists who believed the League of Nations had been dangerous because it limited American independence. Under a League-based international system political decision making would be tainted by European interests. The insurgents argued that until the European nations became more like the United States, the American government could better serve its people by remaining aloof. Irreconcilables hoped to formulate an American foreign policy that would insulate the United States from international conflicts.

The irreconcilables could not be dismissed by the party leadership. Lodge had been able to hold them to the party during the Versailles Treaty debates by pointing out that reservationists and irreconcilables had a common cause in their opposition to Woodrow Wilson's League of Nations. The party would have to find a new issue that would serve to maintain unity.

HENRY CABOT LODGE AND THE CREATION OF A REPUBLICAN FOREIGN POLICY

Henry Cabot Lodge was the key figure in the formulation of Republican foreign policy. He was fully versed in the issues of international relations and also had a profound understanding of the politics of the Senate. The power he had attained

---

[1] Robert Johnson provided a detailed analysis of the philosophical underpinnings of this group. His study placed a greater emphasis on economic issues, but also provided a good explanation of how those economic values helped to construct a position toward security and armament issues. See Johnson, *The Peace Progressives.*

during the critical period between 1918 and 1920 was enhanced by the election of a Republican administration. Lodge's power had been derived from his control of crucial positions in the Senate's institutional structure. Because he had been both the Senate majority leader and chairman of the Foreign Relations Committee, Lodge had controlled all aspects of the Republican response to the Versailles Treaty. This institutional position had provided him with enormous power in dealing with Woodrow Wilson. Although the partisan situation changed after the election of 1920, Lodge's power was not significantly altered. He maintained the potential ability to thwart Harding's foreign policy initiatives. The administration had to be prepared to defer to Lodge.

During the summer of 1920 there had been some discussion of giving Lodge an executive appointment. His friend, Senator George Moses, argued that such an offer was a reward for Lodge's long service to the party. However, it would also mean that he would have to abandon the power provided by the positions of Senate majority leader and chairman of the Foreign Relations Committee. In his reply to Moses, Lodge politely resisted efforts to move him to the executive branch:

> [M]y place . . . would be where I now am and that it would be wiser on all accounts and better for the country; for to shift the leadership and Chairmanship of the Foreign Relations Committee, if we came into power, would just now be a very risky thing.[2]

Without control over the institutions of foreign policy making, Lodge would lose control over the substance of Republican diplomacy. If Lodge stepped down from the chairmanship of the Foreign Relations Committee, traditions of seniority would give the position to Porter McCumber. McCumber's attitudes regarding America's role in international relations were quite different from those of Lodge. McCumber believed that Wilsonian internationalism had been the appropriate response to the European war. More important, McCumber did not possess a forceful personality and would have difficulty maintaining control over senators like William Borah and Hiram Johnson. Lodge's failure to continue as chairman of the Foreign Relations Committee would have consequences for the substance of Republican foreign policy and for the stability of the party in the Senate.

Lodge preserved his entrenched position in the Senate hierarchy and was able to maintain good relations with the executive branch. Although Lodge would have preferred the appointment of Elihu Root as secretary of state, he was able to work with Charles Evans Hughes. Both men agreed on the basic directions that foreign policy should take under the Republican administration.

Hughes supported the outlines of diplomatic activity that had been established under President Taft's Dollar Diplomacy. He believed that the expansion of American business into the international economy was both practical and morally sound. American entrepreneurs benefited from the profits earned in new markets;

---

[2] Lodge to George Moses, July 6, 1920, Lodge Papers.

foreign economies gained from access to American expertise. Tied to this was the belief that peace and international stability encouraged profitable economic expansion. In this system of economic growth, arbitration was preferred over military intervention and diplomatic negotiation was favored over war. Force would only be used when other means failed. Hughes advocated an American foreign policy that would promote international cooperation and economic interdependence.

Hughes recognized that the irreconcilable Republicans did not share his vision. Although they might not oppose American economic expansion, they were chary of the political responsibilities that accompanied expansion. They denounced "foreign entanglements" that might entrap the United States. The irreconcilable commitment to an aloof foreign policy provided a substantial political problem. Hughes agreed with Lodge's assessment that foreign policy making in the Republican party required a consensus between internationalists, reservationists, and irreconcilables. Those senators who had been irreconcilably opposed to the League of Nations could not be alienated from the party. He believed that it was possible to construct such a Republican consensus. In fact, he argued that during the Versailles Treaty debates the enemy of compromise had been Wilson, not the irreconcilable faction.[3]

In December 1920 Hughes emerged as Warren Harding's principal foreign policy advisor. Daily meetings between the president and secretary began immediately after the inauguration. Harding never developed strong convictions regarding foreign policy. He was impressed by the intellect of Hughes and remained deferential to the will of Lodge. As a result of Harding's passiveness, the formulation of foreign policy was left under the joint control of Hughes and Lodge. Although the foreign policy perspectives of Hughes and Lodge differed in emphasis, they were of the same conservative-modernist ideology.[4] The resulting Republican foreign policy was marked by cooperation between the legislative and administrative wings of government, not dictation from one central focus.

Lodge was convinced that Republican foreign policy under Harding needed to shed the image of isolationism. He argued that the United States had to maintain a strong posture abroad and that involvement in international politics would strengthen American democracy.[5] The barrier facing Lodge was the presence of opposition within the Republican party. The irreconcilables had made their position clear at the Chicago convention. As long as the party leadership feared insurgency, the United States could not join the League of Nations. The threat of

---

[3] David J. Danielski and Joseph S. Tulchin, eds., *The Autobiographical Notes of Charles E. Hughes* (Cambridge: Harvard University Press, 1973), 214.

[4] For a concise survey of the foreign policy views of these men, see Dexter Perkins, *Charles Evans Hughes and American Democratic Statesmanship* (Boston: Little, Brown Co., 1956) and Widenor, *Henry Cabot Lodge.*

[5] The most succinct explanation of Lodge's foreign policy goals under the Harding administration appears in Henry Cabot Lodge, "Foreign Relations of the United States, 1921–1924," *Foreign Affairs* 2 (June 1924), 538.

a bolt at the Chicago convention had forced the party to adopt a vaguely worded foreign policy plank. Throughout the election campaign, the party attempted to circumvent conflict by avoiding any clear foreign policy statements. Although this approach to the election campaign had prevented a bolt by Johnson and his supporters, it had not totally alleviated the tension between the irreconcilables and the mainstream of the party. Harding's vagueness inspired suspicion and a continuing level of uneasiness in the irreconcilable camp.

Harding's campaign strategy was designed to reinforce the party's reunification efforts. Replicating the McKinley front porch campaign, the candidate confined his efforts to meetings in his hometown of Marion, Ohio. The tasks of stumping, debating, and jawboning fell to the party machine. The Republican party's national chairman, Will Hays, issued position papers to the supporters of Warren Harding. Republican politicians were then instructed to use these position papers as the basis of speeches and other public statements. In an effort to prevent intraparty friction, the position papers regarding the League of Nations issue were vague, vague enough to permit widely varying interpretations. A problem arose when Hiram Johnson realized that he was making anti-League speeches based on Harding's campaign statements while William Howard Taft was making pro-League speeches based on the identical documents.[6] Harding's position regarding the League continued to remain unclear after the election. With the failure to secure Philander Knox as the secretary of state designate, irreconcilables feared a Republican-sponsored attempt to enter the League of Nations. During the winter of 1920–1921, William Borah and Hiram Johnson continued to pressure Harding on the League issue.

Irreconcilables did not accept Harding's disavowal of the League until the president's first address to Congress. During that speech, Harding elaborated on the party's platform position. He affirmed that the League covenant would not be sanctioned by his administration and declared that the preservation of senatorial power was absolutely necessary.[7] Harding had ended the suspicion that he would promote American entry into the League of Nations. However, he had been careful to preserve his options regarding other international organizations. He was also careful to assert the executive branch's prerogatives in formulating foreign policy.

Johnson's reaction to the Harding speech was particularly important. He had led the criticism against Harding's refusal to take a definitive position during the election campaign and he still could become openly hostile to the administration. The Harding speech abated Johnson's concerns, and he remarked in his diary that "I was delighted with it."[8]

The party had been successful in preventing a major split over the League of Nations issue. Nonetheless, Harding's commitments were not a suitable foundation

---

[6] Internal memo, Box 3, Part III, Johnson Papers.

[7] Warren Harding, speech to a Joint Session of Congress, *Congressional Record*, 67th Congress, 1st Session, April 12, 1921.

[8] Diary Letters, April 13, 1921, Johnson Papers.

for foreign policy. International conditions dictated that the Harding administration either join the League of Nations or generate some sort of American response to the League. Vague passivity was not a viable diplomatic solution.

Henry Cabot Lodge and Charles Evans Hughes both favored American activity in some sort of international judicial system. In a system of international arbitration, the court would be limited to previously designated, justiciable issues. Unlike the League of Nations covenant, a carefully worded arbitration treaty would pose no threats to American sovereignty or independence of action. Lodge favored an international system grounded in an international court, and promoted the actions of Elihu Root in establishing a world court built out of the Hague Convention.[9]

American entry into a world court or participation in general arbitration treaties was an ultimate objective. However, the issues of international arbitration were still quite close to the issues of international government raised during the League of Nations debates. Many of those senators who had been irreconcilably opposed to the League of Nations would be skeptical of a world court system, particularly if it had any relationship to the League.

Furthermore, Lodge's record was weak concerning the issue of international arbitration. The last time Lodge had been actively involved in this issue was during debates over the Anglo-American General Arbitration Treaty of 1911. Lodge had led the opposition to the treaty, and was successful in blocking its ratification. Although Lodge's opposition to the treaty had been based on the way it had been negotiated, not on the fundamental issue of arbitration, his arguments could be used by opponents of a world court system in the 1920s. The formulation of a Republican foreign policy would have to commence with a less divisive issue.

INSURGENT POLITICS AND THE ISSUE OF NAVAL DISARMAMENT

Neither the Harding administration nor Lodge had found an issue that was at the same time dramatic and uncontroversial. Fear of controversy discouraged the Republican leadership from inaugurating any new direction in foreign policy. This hesitation provided William Borah with an opportunity for action, and he attempted to seize the foreign policy initiative. During the war, Borah had become concerned with the level of naval armament in the world. His uneasiness stemmed from basic insurgent progressive concerns. Just as the British navy had guaranteed the Empire and defended the interests of London bankers, a strong American navy could be misused to preserve the investments of New York businessmen. The United States could accidentally follow the British path of a naval empire. This uneasiness with the potentially undemocratic nature of a large navy was further intensified by a desire to exercise general spending cuts at the end of the war. Military spending had become a particular target after E. B. Rosa of the Bureau of Standards reported

---

[9] Lodge to Warren Harding, September 17, 1920, Lodge Papers.

that 92.82 percent of all federal spending was devoted to past and future wars.[10]

In December of 1920, Borah had introduced a resolution calling for Britain, Japan, and the United States to begin discussions for the purpose of reducing naval armaments by 50 percent. The resolution had the potential for becoming the focus of public attention. It was sent to the Senate Foreign Relations Committee for further consideration.

On February 28, 1921, Borah introduced the subject of a 50 percent naval reduction once again. Referring to the Anglo-German naval race that preceded the war, Borah argued that naval disarmament was a prerequisite to peace. During League-sponsored disarmament talks in Geneva, the head of the Japanese delegation, Viscount Ishii Kikujiro, defended his country's level of naval armament by arguing that it was no more than a response to the American naval building program of 1916. Borah used Ishii's statement as a major weapon against the supporters of a big navy in the Republican party. From the floor of the Senate he challenged the governments of the three great naval powers to ease the tax burden on their citizens and diminish their military strength.[11]

This was not designed to be a simple push on the governments of Japan and Great Britain. Not only was it a very public prodding of the Harding administration to move in a direction dictated by the insurgent progressives, but it was also a provocative attempt to undermine the authority of Henry Cabot Lodge in the making of Republican foreign policy. The issue was moved to the Foreign Relations Committee for further consideration.

Henry Cabot Lodge had been one of the strongest proponents of a powerful American navy. At the turn of the century the U.S. government adopted the strategic theories of Admiral Alfred Thayer Mahan and transformed the United States Navy from a fleet of ramshackle gunboats to a modern blue water navy. Lodge had been one of the principal figures in this transformation, prodding congressmen to appropriate funds for a navy that would rival that of the British Empire. The naval building program of 1916 provided an American fleet that was both large and technologically advanced. The virtues of this modernized navy had been commended by the mainstream of the Republican party. Much of the Republican press, including Harding's *Marion Daily Star*, hailed increased naval building, equating it with American commercial supremacy.[12] Lodge assumed that the defense of American interests abroad required a large and powerful navy. He had encouraged Harding's support of naval building programs during the presidential campaign of 1920, arguing that it would be folly for the United States

---

[10]Leonard Hoag, *Preface to Preparedness: The Washington Disarmament Conference and Public Opinion* (Washington, D.C.: American Council on Public Affairs, 1941), 73.

[11] *Congressional Record*, 66th Congress, 3rd Session, February 28, 1921, p. 4046.

[12] Harold Sprout and Margaret Sprout, *Toward a New Order of Seapower: American Naval Policy and the World Scene, 1918–1922* (Princeton: Princeton University Press, 1943), 84.

to cut back on naval construction while Great Britain and Japan were constructing new battleships.[13] Lodge had come to personify the Republican commitment to a navy second to none. By throwing into doubt the sincerity of the Republican commitment to naval arms limitation, Borah was testing Lodge's ability to control Senate debate.

As Borah continued to push his plan for a 50 percent reduction in naval armament, the level of popular support began to increase. A growing number of letters and telegrams were sent to Borah in support of naval disarmament. The senator understood that the strength of the insurgent progressives was based on their ability to generate waves of public pressure. He realized that the issue of naval disarmament would create a favorable political climate for the insurgents. The insurgents who had formed the core of the irreconcilable movement could be presented as respectable statesmen, and would lose their image as nay-sayers and alarmists. A concentration of public interest on naval disarmament would increase the relative bargaining position of the insurgents in their discussions of foreign policy making with the administration and the rest of the party in the Senate.

The initial reaction of the Republican party leadership to Borah's call for a multilateral disarmament conference was negative. Each time Borah initiated debate, the subject was passed on to the Foreign Relations Committee, where Henry Cabot Lodge would determine when it was ready to be returned to the floor. In May, Borah tried once again by proposing an amendment to a naval appropriations bill. As before, he called for the major naval powers to begin negotiations with the objective of reducing fleet sizes by 50 percent. By this time popular support for the issue was strong enough to prevent the resolution from being buried once again in committee. For the most part debate followed the guidelines established by Borah and centered on the issues of expenditure. He relied heavily on the shock value of a budget analysis that had been produced for the executive branch. Borah appealed to the public's established concern for "Americanism," claiming, "For research, for educational work, for the building of citizenship, for the building of character upon which republican institutions may rest, we appropriate 7% of the entire expenditures of 5 billion and odd dollars, and 93% for war."[14]

While Borah avoided a direct discussion of the issue of American imperialism, he alluded to it in the debate over naval manpower. He argued that the mandate system after World War I had extended the responsibilities of the British navy, which had become responsible for maintaining peace over one-third of the globe. With no huge empire to protect, and no mandated territories, the United States certainly did not have the same naval personnel needs as Great Britain.[15]

The issues of the debate were expanded by Senator George Norris, who argued

---

[13] Lodge to Harding, February 25, 1920, Lodge Papers.

[14] *Congressional Record*, 67th Congress, 1st Session, May 13, 1921, pp. 1408–1409.

[15] *Congressional Record*, 67th Congress, 1st Session, May 13, 1921, p. 1406.

that with the German navy destroyed the U.S. building program was no longer based on national defense. An American drive for the largest navy was not determined by security needs, and the economic ramifications were dangerous.[16]

It was well known in the Senate that neither Lodge nor the administration was enthusiastic about a multilateral naval disarmament program. Nonetheless, Borah was able to undercut maneuvers against his amendment. During the Senate floor debate, Borah was asked about alleged administration opposition to the movement for disarmament. Borah asserted that Harding supported disarmament and argued, "My opinion is that if the President of the United States had anything to say to Congress upon so vital a matter, he would say it in a manner which becomes the President of the United States, and he would not pass it through the subterranean channels to those whom he thought it might affect."[17]

Borah had cornered Harding. He had announced on the floor of the Senate that the president did not oppose a multilateral disarmament conference. If Harding disavowed the statement, he would risk the anger of the insurgents and the condemnation of a public that was clamoring for a reduction in naval armaments. By claiming his amendment had administration support, Borah prevented its disappearance. On May 25, 1921, the Senate voted unanimously in support of Borah's call for an international disarmament conference.

Despite appearances of the final vote, the amendment did not have the complete support of the party. Lodge and the administration simply shifted the field of discourse to another level. The debate quickly moved to the House, where an alternative version of the call for disarmament could be originated. The differing House and Senate versions would then pass into conference; Lodge would choose the Senate conferees and the Borah resolution would be killed quietly. However, the strategy was unsuccessful. An attempt was made to spark House support for a more limited version of disarmament, governed by the navy's desire to continue aggressive modernization and expansion of the fleet. However, representatives who supported continued naval modernization and preferred to delay disarmament talks could not muster the necessary votes to pass legislation that would force the Borah Amendment into conference.

The victory was important for the insurgents. Active debate was the best means of maintaining the political cohesion of the group. The passage of the amendment permitted William Borah, not the party leadership, to define the topic of debate. Insurgents had successfully controlled the irreconcilable movement, but the controversy over the League had quieted and it was no longer a means of marshaling political energy. William Borah had found a new cause for the insurgent movement; the survival of the disarmament movement would keep the insurgent element active in the foreign policy debates.

The passage of the Borah disarmament amendment presented the administration

---

[16] *Congressional Record*, 67th Congress, 1st Session, May 13, 1921, pp. 1413–1415.

[17] *Congressional Record*, 67th Congress, 1st Session, May 13, 1921, p. 1418.

with a problem. Although Henry Cabot Lodge had paid lip service to the idea of naval disarmament, his support was limited to a disarmament that still provided the United States with a technologically advanced navy that was capable of dominating two oceans. Secretary Hughes was a less emphatic defender of the American navy, but saw disarmament as a complex problem that could not be resolved immediately. The passage of the amendment demanded some action, but the administration's movements would be cautious. Other foreign policy issues demanded attention in mid-1921 and the administration sought to balance the various questions while maintaining a hold on the insurgents.

The insurgents were frustrated by their inability to force the administration to act. Hiram Johnson, who was always quick to suspect the motives of the party leadership, feared the Senate insurgents could not maintain the steady pressure necessary to control foreign policy. He was frustrated by the fact that Secretary Hughes, and most of the American diplomatic corps, supported the League of Nations. He questioned appointments to the major ambassadorial positions, alleging a conservative bias. The insurgents had prevented American entry into Wilson's League of Nations, but they had only limited success in formulating a new Republican foreign policy. Johnson depicted this failure as the culmination of character flaws in the members of his party, asserting,

> Even the men, like Brandegee and Knox, whose past records as the advocates of government exploitation we all forgot in our enthusiasm for the good fight of which they were a valiant part, are now supine, subservient, miserable, contemptible lackeys of power. The Foreign Relations Committee once so powerful, that stood immovable for the preservation of our independence against a popular opinion at its flood tide after the war now meekly takes its orders and while whining to itself, accepts a [Ambassador to Great Britain, George] Harvey or [Minister to China, Jacob Gould] Schurman.[18]

Johnson's appraisal of the problem was overstated, but he did correctly recognize that the insurgents had not yet attained control of the foreign policy-making process. Through its control of the policy-making apparatus, the administration maintained the upper hand in foreign policy making, but found its flexibility extremely limited. The Borah naval disarmament amendment had thrown into question the authority of the administration. The administration, while still in a strong position, no longer exclusively controlled the foreign policy initiative. This became even more apparent as the administration attempted to create a peace treaty with Germany.

---

[18] Diary Letters, June 12, 1921, Johnson Papers. George Harvey had become a leading conservative Republican. The former editor of *Harper's Monthly* had been a leading figure in the "smoke-filled room meeting" that had led to the nomination of Warren Harding. Schurman was less notorious, but had been the president of Cornell and received his position due to his long friendship with Charles Evans Hughes.

AMERICAN FOREIGN POLICY AND EUROPEAN POLITICS

In December of 1919 as part of an effort to separate the issues of the League of Nations from those of the end of the European war, Senator Philander Knox called for a simple peace treaty with Germany. In the spring of 1921, Knox resumed this tactic by pushing the Harding administration for a separate peace treaty with Germany that would end the existing state of war. The Knox Peace Resolution called on the administration to act independently of its allies, who had ratified the Versailles Treaty. The measure passed in the Senate, but languished in the House. Tensions rose as it was rumored that the delay was the result of pressure by Charles Evans Hughes and Herbert Hoover.[19]

Charles Evans Hughes wanted to establish a formal peace treaty with Germany, but he wanted that peace to be framed in the existing Versailles Treaty structure. The Knox Peace Resolution pressured him to act quickly. If the pro-League Republicans were willing to compromise, the German peace treaty could be used to smooth the rift that still remained between the reservationists and irreconcilables. The construction of a policy toward Germany would not be easy. Irreconcilables still suspected Hughes would somehow twist the separate peace and force American acceptance of the Versailles Treaty. Johnson wrote to Charles K. McClatchy that "one of the prominent Senators told me yesterday that the plan was to make a gesture towards a separate treaty with Germany, and then to say the attitude of the Germans rendered this impossible, and there was nothing else but to accept the Versailles Treaty."[20]

Hughes sought to assuage the skeptics while conducting a foreign policy that adhered to his objectives. The first months of the Harding administration were marked by limited cooperation with the Allies in Europe. The United States maintained troops on the Rhine and participated in reparations talks. American policy maintained a delicate balance between maintaining a working relationship with its European allies and pacifying the irreconcilables. In an effort to block an organized opposition in the Senate, Hughes fell back on an established practice in Republican foreign policy making—he sought the counsel of key senators during the negotiation process. While the Americans were negotiating the peace terms, they were creating secondary treaties designed to deal with specific questions. Before negotiations were complete, Hughes showed Borah the text of the treaty regarding the property that had been confiscated from Germans.[21] Such discussions were designed to ameliorate the tensions between Hughes and the insurgents.

The Treaty of Berlin created a separate peace with Germany in August of 1921. The language of the treaty was chosen carefully, using the Knox Peace Resolution as a model. The treaty did not oblige the United States to become a member of the

---

[19] Johnson to Raymond Robbins, June 18, 1921, Johnson Papers.

[20] Johnson to Charles K. McClatchy, July 23, 1921, Johnson Papers.

[21] Pusey, *Charles Evans Hughes*, 444. See also Danielski and Tulchin, eds., *The Autobiographical Notes of Charles E. Hughes*, 227–228.

League's Reparation Commission. Even so, the irreconcilables hoped to totally block any secret attempts to cooperate with the League of Nations by altering the treaty during the ratification process. After a "quite spirited and somewhat bitter exchange" in the Senate Foreign Relations Committee, Henry Cabot Lodge proposed a resolution stipulating that the United States could not enter the commission without specific congressional authorization.[22] Hiram Johnson then amended this Lodge resolution to prohibit U.S. entry into any Versailles Treaty–generated organization without specific congressional approval. The administration's peace treaty could pass only if its proponents accepted this condition. The irreconcilables had forced the administration to separate itself from the League of Nations. Lodge fully understood the importance of making a definitive break with the League. He conceded the triumph of the irreconcilables in the Senate debate, announcing, "[W]e give notice to Germany and to the world for the first time in a formal, diplomatic, and international document that we assume and will assume no obligation under those provisions of the treaty of Versailles."[23]

The Lodge/Johnson stipulations eliminated nearly all of the opposition to the Treaty of Berlin. The only significant opponent of the treaty was William Borah. He still feared that the United States had taken the first step on the path to the League of Nations. He spoke eloquently in the ratification debates, hoping to stir some opposition. Despite his efforts, Borah was not able to generate any substantial congressional opposition to the Treaty of Berlin.

The Harding administration and Henry Cabot Lodge had been successful in establishing an aura of conciliation in the party. The ratification of the peace treaty set the stage for the party's next efforts in establishing a Republican foreign policy. The Treaty of Berlin also provided an indication of weakness within the insurgent movement. Heretofore, leadership in foreign policy issues had been amicably divided between Borah and Johnson. The ratification of the Treaty of Berlin demonstrated that the strong personalities of these two men could come into conflict. Insurgent philosophy encouraged its adherents to believe that all opponents were scoundrels or dupes. The League of Nations battles had demonstrated the triumph of the virtuous, and neither Borah nor Johnson was willing to suspect he had fallen from the ranks of the just. The two remained political allies, but they would never be able to return to the co-equal status established before the election of 1920.[24]

By focusing on the issue of a separate peace with Germany, the leadership of the Republican party was able to divert the attention of the Senate from the issue of

---

[22] Diary Letters, September 23, 1921, Johnson Papers.

[23] *Congressional Record*, 67th Congress, 1st Session, September 26, 1921, p. 5791.

[24] Diary Letters, September 23, 1921, Johnson Papers. See also Robert Burke, "Hiram Johnson's Impressions of William E. Borah," *Idaho Yesterdays* 17 (Spring 1973): 2–11.

naval disarmament, but only for a brief period. In June and July it was clear that the public pressure for naval disarmament was insurmountable and that action could not be delayed indefinitely. Furthermore, the debates regarding naval appropriations indicated that Congress was not going to support the expenditures necessary for a naval building war.

THE POLITICS OF COMPROMISE AND THE CREATION OF A NEW ORDER IN THE PACIFIC

The problem of naval armament had destabilized the relations between the major powers. Changes in naval strategy after the Battle of Jutland, combined with developments in submarine and air warfare, had affected the course of the naval building war between Japan, Great Britain, and the United States. During the war, all three had expanded their navies tremendously. However, the expense of these building programs had set politicians on a search for some means of discontinuing the arms race. By 1920 naval strategists and elected politicians in all three countries were at odds, trying to develop an equilibrium between national security and fiscal responsibility.[25]

The problem of relative naval power was further compounded by the changing relationship between Great Britain and Japan. For the previous two decades the balance of power in the Pacific had been maintained by the Anglo-Japanese Alliance. By forming a security pact, both Japan and Great Britain had been able to deter any encroachments on their positions in East Asia. The agreement, first made in 1902 and renewed in 1911, was scheduled to expire in 1921.

Politics within the British Empire were forcing a reassessment of the Anglo-Japanese Alliance. The relationship between Japan and Great Britain had deteriorated by the end of World War I, largely due to the growing strength of the Japanese navy and political stress triggered by increasing levels of Japanese immigration in the Pacific Basin. The British dominions bordering the Pacific—Canada, Australia, and New Zealand—had begun to view Japan as threatening. They hoped to use the forum of the 1921 Imperial Conference to initiate a new relationship between the British Empire and Japan, where the competitive nature of the relationship would be recognized. London was interested in both guarding against Japanese encroachments on the British Empire and preventing political conflict with the dominions over immigration restrictions. After long and heated discussions in the summer of 1921, the British arrived at a policy that recognized the concerns of the Canadians, Australians, and New Zealanders. The government of David Lloyd George favored the idea of replacing the Anglo-Japanese Alliance with a tripartite agreement that would include the United States. The inclusion of the American government was designed to give the

---

[25] Sprout and Sprout, *Toward a New Order of Sea Power*, 38–46, and William Braisted, *The United States Navy in the Pacific, 1909–1922* (Austin: University of Texas Press, 1971), 477–504.

British greater leverage against the Japanese. In addition, it placated the Canadians whose fears of continuing Japanese immigration and expanded Japanese commercial activity in the Western Hemisphere were parallel to those of the Americans.[26] In an effort to pull the United States into such an agreement, the British government proposed to connect the issue of East Asian security to the naval disarmament question.[27]

During the summer of 1921 the British and Americans discussed the logistics of negotiations regarding security in the Pacific. The British favored a sequential approach, with a preliminary discussion of security issues to be held in London before a disarmament conference. The Republican administration immediately recognized the danger to domestic politics presented by the British proposal. The core of the insurgent-irreconcilable opposition to the League of Nations had been based on the assumption of the perfidious nature of British diplomacy. The intense debate that had surrounded the League and Article X had encouraged public suspicion of the English. Hughes feared that any preliminary discussion held in London would attract the suspicions of Borah and Johnson.[28] If sufficiently aroused, these senators could generate a public opposition to American involvement in Pacific security discussions. For the sake of party unity, Hughes had to avoid any foreign policy initiatives that would antagonize the insurgency. The Treaty of Berlin would provide an important foundation for creating a foreign policy consensus between reservationists and irreconcilables. Discussions of naval armament would be key to the continuation of this reconsolidation process. Hughes concluded that good relations with the insurgents were of a higher priority than good relations with the British government.

The politics of insurgency were still very much a part of Republican policy formulation. From 1918 until 1920 insurgent activity had been swept up in the discussion of the League of Nations. However, after the first defeat of the Versailles Treaty, insurgent Republicans began once again to concentrate on domestic problems. Debate on the Senate floor in 1920 and 1921 demonstrated a growing concern on the part of insurgents for resuming the progressive Republican reform that had been sidetracked after the election of 1912. The problems of railroad organization, campaign ethics, and the economic plight of the American

---

[26] William Roger Louis, *British Strategy in the Far East, 1919–1939* (Oxford: Clarendon Press, 1971), 85. The prime minister of Japan, Hara Kei, also sought to extend the Anglo-Japanese Alliance to the United States. Roger Dingman, *Power in the Pacific: The Origins of Naval Arms Limitation, 1914–1922* (Chicago: University of Chicago Press, 1976), 128.

[27] Thomas Buckley, *The United States and the Washington Naval Conference, 1921–1922* (Knoxville: University of Tennessee Press, 1970), 34.

[28] Hughes also recognized that if the preliminary security talks failed, successful naval disarmament would be much more difficult. The administration had to make a credible effort toward naval disarmament and could not risk the creation of additional diplomatic obstacles.

farmer had to be addressed immediately. By 1921 a number of the Taft insurgents had achieved seniority; Albert Cummins, William Borah, and George Norris were men of stature in the Senate. Insurgents served on all the major committees and held some key chairmanships. In many respects the insurgency was better equipped to pass reform legislation in 1921 than it had been in 1911.

In an effort to coordinate reform, several of the insurgents formed the bipartisan Agricultural Bloc in May 1921. The membership was dominated by senators from the old populist strongholds in the South and Plains States. While it had no official leader, the movement's de facto chairman was William Kenyon.[29] The first opportunity for the Agricultural Bloc to test its strength came with the Norris Farm Bill in the summer of 1921. The Norris Farm Bill was the first of a series of attempts to give the federal government the authority to support the export of surplus agricultural production. Under this bill, the War Finance Corporation would identify key agricultural areas that suffered from surplus production. The Corporation would then be able to extend low interest loans to those financial institutions that engaged in the export of those surplus products.

The Norris Farm Bill was opposed by the administration, and a defense was quickly put in place. The presiding officer of the Senate, Vice President Calvin Coolidge, had agreed to permit the Norris bill to come to the floor. However, Coolidge absented himself from the chamber and turned over the gavel to Charles Curtis with the instruction to recognize Frank Kellogg, the sponsor of the administration's version of the farm bill. This feat of parliamentary legerdemain effectively blocked any discussion of Norris's more radical proposals.[30]

On the heels of the farm bill question came the issue of tax reform. Secretary of the Treasury Andrew Mellon had advocated a lowering of the federal tax burden on upper incomes as a means of spurring economic growth. Chairman of the Senate Finance Committee Boies Penrose agreed and sought to lower the tax rate in the higher income brackets. This included an effort to lower the maximum surtax from 65 percent to 25 percent. Insurgent Republicans opposed any efforts

---

[29] The initial members of the Agricultural Bloc were William Kenyon (R, Iowa), Arthur Capper (R, Kansas), George Norris (R, Nebraska), F. R. Gooding (R, Idaho), E. F. Ladd (R, North Dakota), Robert LaFollette (R, Wisconsin), Ellison D. Smith (D, South Carolina), J. B. Kendrick (D, Wyoming), Duncan U. Fletcher (D, Florida), Joseph E. Ransdell (D, Louisiana), J. T. Heflin (D, Alabama), and Morris Sheppard (D, Texas). Those who joined later were Charles L. McNary (R, Oregon), Peter Norbeck (R, South Dakota), John W. Harreld (R, Oklahoma), A. A. Jones (R, New Mexico), William J. Harris (D, Georgia), H. F. Ashurst (R, Arizona), Pat Harrison (D, Mississippi), Wesley L. Jones (R, Washington), Robert N. Stanfield (R, Oregon), Frank B. Kellogg (R, Minnesota), Charles A. Rawson (R, Iowa), and Claude A. Swanson (D, Virginia). Neither William Borah nor Hiram Johnson joined the Agricultural Bloc, though Borah routinely attended its meetings. A thorough statement of the organization and goals of the Agricultural Bloc can be found in Arthur Capper, *The Agricultural Bloc* (New York: Harcort, Brace & Company, 1922).

[30] William Allen White, *A Puritan in Babylon* (New York: Macmillan Co., 1938), 237.

to generate a less progressive tax system and threatened to join with Democrats to block the Penrose proposals. Faced with ardent opposition on the floor of the Senate, Penrose agreed to allow a high surcharge in the Senate version of the tax bill, but then simply rechanneled his efforts to have the rate lowered in the conference committee.[31]

Despite the margin of the Harding victory in 1920, the activities in the Senate demonstrated that he did not lead a unified party. Insurgents were separated from the mainstream of the party by both foreign and domestic issues. The party's leadership had solved the problem of revolt in 1920, but these solutions only quieted the insurgency, they did not eliminate it. Actions by insurgents regarding such diverse questions as peace with Germany, disarmament, farm policy, and tax levels had forced the Republican party leadership into defensive maneuvering.

In an effort to create bargaining time for the administration, Henry Cabot Lodge attempted to throw the Senate into a three-week recess in late July. Hughes was faced with intensely complex foreign policy problems. Negotiations for the Treaty of Berlin were underway. Great Britain was pressuring the United States for a commitment to a tripartite security arrangement in the Pacific. Hughes needed to define the diplomatic position of the United States in a way that would draw the insurgents to the party. A Senate recess in July would curtail the public speeches of Borah and Johnson, and relieve some of the immediate pressure on Hughes. However, Lodge was unable to get a recess. The combined concern over the administration's tendency to cooperate with the British government, desire to reformulate the tax burden, and reluctance to provide price supports to agriculture were enough to block Lodge's attempt for a recess vote.[32]

The first priority of the Republican party leadership was to keep the party unified. Because they feared an insurgent split, Hughes and Lodge decided that Borah's disarmament resolution required immediate action. The problem lay in how to use naval disarmament to solve other foreign policy problems.

After the war, relations between the United States and Great Britain had deteriorated. The failure of the Senate to ratify the Versailles Treaty, British requests for forgiveness of war debt to the United States, and increased British commercial influence in the mandated territories in the Middle East had all led to tension between the two governments. Hughes was committed to repair the breakdown of Anglo-American relations if at all possible. Furthermore, the expansion of Japanese influence threatened the American commercial position in East Asia.

The growing conflict between the primary naval powers threatened Hughes's

---

[31] Ripley, *Majority Party Leadership*, 100, and David Burner, *The Politics of Provincialism: The Democratic Party in Transition, 1918–1932* (Cambridge: Harvard University Press, 1986), 162–163. For a thorough explanation of the Mellon tax plan, see Andrew Mellon, *Taxation: The People's Business* (New York: Macmillan Co., 1924).

[32] Ripley, *Majority Party Leadership*, 100, and John Mark Hansen, *Gaining Access: Congress and the Farm Lobby* (Chicago: University of Chicago Press, 1991), 32.

vision of an international system where conflict was resolved rationally. The progressive development of American commerce required stable international markets; it was in America's national self-interest to promote peaceful situations that were conducive to commercial expansion. In the interest of stability, Hughes was willing to accept collective security arrangements. He believed that it was possible to negotiate a security treaty that would be ratified by the Senate. During the debates over the Versailles Treaty, Republican reservationists were concerned with a defense of congressional power, not collective security agreements per se. The British suggestion of a tripartite pact in the Pacific would solve the problem of stability in East Asia, would alleviate diplomatic tensions between the three signatories, and could be framed in a manner acceptable to Henry Cabot Lodge.

Hughes favored British suggestions for a new security agreement in the Pacific, but recognized that such an agreement might well be attacked by the same senators who had been irreconcilably opposed to the League of Nations. The issue of security in the Pacific was less volatile than security in Europe, but still, the irreconcilables' fears needed to be accommodated. Ratification of a security arrangement between the United States, Great Britain, and Japan would be possible if Lodge and Borah could resume the unity of purpose they had achieved during the Versailles Treaty debates. A commitment to collective security in the Pacific needed to be directly linked to Borah's demands for a naval disarmament conference.

William Borah had focused the American electorate's attention on the issue of naval disarmament. The administration could not delay action indefinitely. At the same time the administration sought to strengthen diplomatic ties with Great Britain and ensure political stability in the Pacific. As a result of this confluence of pressures, Secretary of State Hughes decided to call for a conference of extensive scope. The Washington Conference for the Discussion of Disarmament and Pacific and Far Eastern Questions would accommodate the goals of both the administration and the insurgents. The issues of disarmament and Pacific security were not elements of a single, grand foreign policy strategy. They represented the unconditional requirements of the foreign policy programs of two disparate elements of the Republican party. The desire for consensus required that both be included and somehow crafted into a unified foreign policy.

The invitations to the Washington Conference promised negotiations of extensive scope. By linking disarmament to the more general topic of Far Eastern questions, the Conference would direct its efforts to a comprehensive approach to the balance of power in the Pacific. The decisions made between nations at Washington would constitute a complex web of interests and objectives. However, when Charles Evans Hughes decided on the scope of the conference, the creation of a comprehensive solution to East Asian problems was not his only objective. Hughes understood that the future of any diplomatic arrangement at Washington rested on the support of all wings of the Republican party. By extending the scope of the Washington Conference, Hughes had made common cause with the insurgents and strengthened the Republican party.

THE U.S. DELEGATION TO THE WASHINGTON CONFERENCE

The scope of the Washington Conference strengthened the administration's relationship with Republican insurgents. However, the maneuvering could not simply stop with the formulation of the conference agenda; Hughes recognized the importance of selecting the proper personnel for the American delegation. The construction of the delegation was designed to put the United States in a favorable position vis-à-vis the other foreign powers, but it was also important in determining the relationship between the administration and the Senate. The American delegation would be relatively large, with four principal delegates and their advisory staffs. Secretary of State Charles Evans Hughes was selected as chairman of the group without hesitation. Elihu Root's position as an elder statesman in the Republican party ensured his appointment. The remaining delegates would be selected on the basis of their importance to the legislative dimension of foreign policy making. Any treaty negotiated at Washington would have to receive the support of two-thirds of the Senate. Unlike the situation confronting Woodrow Wilson three years earlier, the source of potential trouble was not Henry Cabot Lodge, but William Borah.

Borah had a vested interest in any treaty generated by the Washington Conference. He wanted the Conference to produce a treaty that would make rapid, monumental reductions in naval armament. If not satisfied with the levels of disarmament, he would bring his skill as a political trench fighter to bear against the treaty. The administration had to devise a method of minimizing a potential insurgent threat. Disarming Borah required either appointing him as a delegate to the conference or appointing the one man who could conceivably control him in the Foreign Relations Committee and on the floor of the Senate. The politically palatable decision was to select Lodge over Borah.

The appointment of Lodge as the third American delegate served a variety of purposes. Throughout the twentieth century he had been a leading figure in the formulation of American foreign policy, and his presence on the delegation firmly placed the Washington Conference in the Republican policy continuum. Lodge would support the rise of the United States as a leader in East Asian diplomacy. This support would include a commitment to place the United States in the role of guarantor of stability in the Pacific. The selection of Lodge reconfirmed the working relationship between the administration and the leadership of the Senate, and exemplified the Republican reliance on cooperation between the executive and legislative branches of government. Lodge's appointment was, of course, meant as an honor, a tribute to his long service in the Republican party. The gesture was well received and Lodge made his gratitude clear. Lodge recognized that his service on the American delegation could serve as a capstone to his career, demonstrating his constructive role in the creation of foreign policy. He thanked Harding, admitting, "[A]s I draw toward the end I confess the work on this conference will be to me a close for my work in public life which I shall value beyond anything."[33]

The appointment of Lodge guaranteed his support for the treaties negotiated at the Washington Conference. Lodge's position on the delegation gave the administration a sound advantage in the ratification process. However, the requirement for a two-thirds vote still posed political difficulties for a controversial treaty.

Borah was a formidable problem. He had been the principal instigator in the movement for naval disarmament and had already captured a great deal of popular support. However, he was simply too unpredictable to be part of the American delegation to the Washington Conference. He was capable of being stubborn and dogmatic and could not even be counted on to cooperate with the members of his own delegation. Borah did not turn down an invitation to be a delegate as was suggested by some journalists; he was never asked, "or not so loud as I could hear." Still, Harding hoped to tie him to administration policy. In August Harding approached Borah for support. Borah sensed manipulation and refused an absolute commitment. He recognized that, as part of a minority element in the Republican party, his real strength lay in the potential of generating an open party dispute. Borah's power was dependent on his ability to conjure up memories of the Taft insurgency. As the administration prepared for the Washington Conference, the political maneuvering within the Republican party would become intricate. The administration would use its control over the membership of the delegation to manipulate Borah out of power; Borah, in turn, would use the leadership's fear of party dissolution to insinuate himself into power. The administration was faced with two groups in the Senate who might oppose treaties negotiated at the Washington Conference. The old irreconcilable group, under the leadership of William Borah, could apply its opposition to Article X of the League of Nations covenant to any collective security agreement reached at Washington. Simple partisan conflict could provoke Democratic opposition to administration treaties. The leadership of the Republican party had to prevent a political alliance between these two groups to guarantee the successful ratification of the Washington Conference treaties.

The Harding administration chose as its fourth delegate the Senate minority leader, Oscar Underwood. The senator from Alabama was well respected by Democrats in Congress and his participation in the negotiation process would attract substantial support from his party during the ratification process. Furthermore, Underwood was respected by Henry Cabot Lodge, who saw the minority leader as reliable and cooperative. The ability of the two men to work on critical foreign policy problems had been tested in the winter of 1919–1920. At that time Underwood had been a key figure in the attempt to reach a compromise between Republican reservationists and Democrats.[34] Underwood's position on the delegation would serve to create a bipartisan policy and to prevent any major

---

[33] Lodge to Warren G. Harding, July 21, 1921, Lodge Papers.

[34] Johnson, *Oscar W. Underwood*, 296–297.

alliance between the Republican insurgents and Democrats.

The Harding administration had considered the possibility that the Democrats might refuse to participate in the Washington Conference. Hughes and Harding had also developed an alternative method for confining Borah. Although the irreconcilable movement had been dominated by insurgents, it had political depth because of the presence in its ranks of conservative Republicans like Philander Knox and George Moses. Since the second defeat of the Versailles Treaty, Borah had strengthened his legitimacy as a foreign policy expert through close ties with former Secretary of State Knox. The concessions made by the administration during the negotiations for the Treaty of Berlin had pulled Knox closer to the administration. If no powerful Senate Democrat could be induced to serve on the American delegation, Borah's threat could be circumscribed by the appointment of Knox.[35] This more complicated political maneuver was not necessary, however. Underwood accepted the position as the fourth member of the American delegation.

The administration determined that the American delegation to the Washington Conference would be unified in purpose. The results of the Washington Conference would provide the framework for future Republican foreign policy. The four delegates selected all shared the same basic outlook regarding the foreign relations of the United States. Although they represented different segments of American politics, Charles Evans Hughes, Elihu Root, Henry Cabot Lodge, and Oscar Underwood were conspicuously similar in their philosophies. All had favored some version of American entrance into the League of Nations; none perceived it as an agency of nefarious European domination over international relations. None held the insurgent suspicions of British diplomacy, and in fact they advocated close cooperation between Great Britain and the United States.[36]

The choice of the three Republican delegates was clear-cut. Hughes, Root, and Lodge had served consistently as Harding's principal foreign policy advisors since the election. All three were astute politicians with an intellectual bent. Hughes and Root had well-established reputations among international lawyers. Root had served as secretary of state under Theodore Roosevelt. Lodge possessed a reputation as the senator most consistently associated with the growth of American power in international affairs. The stature of these men within the diplomatic community would give credence to the Harding administration's position.

The construction of the American delegation to the Washington Conference placed Charles Evans Hughes in a favorable position. He now was at the head of a diplomatic delegation that would work as a coherent group. The treaties negotiated at the Washington Conference might confront some opposition in the Senate, but the party leadership had done everything in its power to ease the process of ratification. Their hope was that the Washington Conference would be

---

[35] U.S. Department of State, *Foreign Relations of the United States, 1921*, vol. I, Hughes to Harvey, August 29, 1921, p. 65.

[36] Buckley, *The United States and the Washington Naval Conference*, 43–47.

the dramatic and uncontroversial foreign policy issue that would finally reunify the Republican party.

In the course of 1921 the insurgents demonstrated that they were still a force to be reckoned with. They were suspicious of administration motives and sought to generate political pressure that would force the president to at least modify policy to meet their goals. They were adept in congressional warfare and, in addition, understood that the administration feared a progressive bolt.

However, the formulation of the Washington Conference demonstrated that the leadership of the Republican party could exercise some control over insurgent politicians. The success of the Borah resolution for the reduction of naval armaments had been the only point where the administration completely lost control of the foreign policy initiative. It had been impossible to obviate the effect of the resolution, but Hughes managed to maintain control of the conference itself. The decision to sponsor the Washington Conference demonstrated that the ideological differences between Republicans would not paralyze the formulation of a postwar foreign policy.

6

The Washington Naval Conference

This is one of the most clever things that has ever been done in the world of politics.

—Hiram Johnson

The Washington Conference of 1921 was designed to be the pillar of Republican postwar foreign policy. Its agenda represented a near perfect equilibrium between all the factions of the Republican party. The more conservative leadership of the party saw it as a constructive means of negotiating a stronger position vis-à-vis the British and Japanese. Irreconcilables were comforted by the fact that the conference was totally detached from the activities of the League of Nations, and was directed at limiting the ability of the United States Navy to intervene in foreign conflicts. The scope was sufficiently broad to allow the American delegation latitude in generating the quid pro quo necessary for a stabilization in East Asia. However, the agenda did not permit the United States to be pulled into the diplomatic issues of Western and Central Europe. With the Republican party unified behind him, Secretary of State Charles Evans Hughes could focus his attention on negotiations with the two principal commercial rivals of the United States.

THE WASHINGTON CONFERENCE AND THE OBJECTIVE OF WORLD PEACE

In July and August, Charles Evans Hughes defined the scope of the Washington Conference through a series of exchanges with the governments of Great Britain and Japan. The basis of the talks would be Borah's call for a reduction in naval armament. However, Hughes did not want to set narrow limits on the negotiations.

Concerns in the British Empire and in Japan over the future of the Anglo-Japanese Alliance necessitated some discussion of balance of power in East Asia. The continued presence of Japanese troops in Siberia and the Japanese occupation of the Shantung Peninsula had generated a fear that American national interests in Asia were at risk. Hughes sought a new, fully integrated diplomatic balance in East Asia. Naval disarmament was a crucial building block to this new regional balance, but it was important only as one aspect of a much larger scheme. The five Principal Allied and Associated Powers of the First World War would all participate in the naval discussions. In addition, China would have to become an active participant in the conference.[1]

Hughes's decision to respond to British pressure by expanding the scope of the Washington Conference committed the Harding administration to an assertive position. The United States was now encouraging complex diplomatic settlements that were designed to alter the strategic balance in the Pacific.

The administration's decision to focus discussions on the Pacific demonstrated a desire to reinforce traditional American involvement in East Asian diplomacy. At the same time, the Conference could be used as a foundation for increased activity in other regions, including Europe. Although no clear plan was evident, Hughes recognized that any agreement reached at Washington would also have an impact on the balance of power in Europe. The secretary recognized the importance of European stability to continued American economic strength and was in the process of forming a new foundation for an Atlantic foreign policy. This Republican activity was quite separate from the Wilsonian internationalism that had dominated American diplomacy at Versailles. The Republican administration would be active internationally, but its activity would be based on pragmatic economic concerns. Hughes preferred to chart this new direction in American foreign policy in the context of Pacific affairs. Stability in the Pacific was perceived as more tenuous than in Europe. Furthermore, because the Asian situation was not marred by deep seated hatred among powerful rivals, a successful resolution was more likely. Hughes was leading the nation back to the traditions of national self-interest that had dominated the Republican foreign policy of the Progressive Era. In setting the stage for the Washington Conference both Hughes and President Harding were careful to make no overt reference to the League of Nations or the Versailles Treaty. Nonetheless, the symbolism of the opening days of the Conference demonstrated the Republicans' intent to make the Washington Conference the foundation for a comprehensive response to World War I.

The Washington Conference was originally scheduled to commence on November 11, 1921, the anniversary of the armistice. The Conference—and particularly its goal of naval disarmament—was portrayed by the administration as

---

[1] U.S. Department of *State, Foreign Relations of the United States*, 1921, vol. I, Hughes to Harvey, July 9, 1921, p. 24. The five Principal Allied and Associated Powers were Great Britain, France, Italy, the United States, and Japan. China was also a lesser Allied power after 1917.

the path to peace in the twentieth century. World War I had been false in its promise as "the war to end all wars"; however, the peace provided at Washington would be "the peace to end all wars." This commitment to the symbolism of a postwar peace was further solidified when the opening session was postponed one day. The U.S. government wanted to inter the American Unknown Soldier at Arlington National Cemetery on Armistice Day; to avoid scheduling conflicts, the Washington Conference would begin on November 12.

The interment of the Unknown Soldier was one of the great public events of the age. The United States was the last of the major Allies to commemorate the war dead in this fashion. As Americans read news accounts of the British, French, and Italian ceremonies earlier in the year, popular opinion demanded that those who made the ultimate sacrifice be remembered. When the U.S. government buried the Unknown Soldier it organized not a ceremony, but a spectacle.

The press helped to generate much of the excitement surrounding the interment. Armistice Day fell on a Friday, and the newspapers enjoyed almost a week of publicizing the event. The selection process of the Unknown Soldier was detailed; biographical sketches of the pallbearers appeared, with complete accounts of their military service; the invitation lists, including the 5,040 Gold Star Mothers, were published. Public fervor was so great that by the morning of November 11, logistical organization was nearly impossible. The bridge from Washington to Arlington was a mass of automobiles and people. President Harding's car was barely able to get through the confusion. Secretary of State Hughes arrived only by abandoning his car and running to the cemetery.

The breakdown of organization did not limit the administration's ability to portray the interment of the Unknown Soldier as a symbol of America's commitment to peace. The spirit of the day was one of celebration and all of Washington was swept up in it. The theme of armistice was everywhere, and linked to the Armistice Day celebration was the Washington Conference. The tie between the two events even extended to the mundane. In an advertisement for the Piggly Wiggly grocery stores, the management prayed, "May November 11th come to take its place alongside that of December 25th in world importance. It is within the power of the assembled delegates to the Conference for the Limitation of Armament to lay the cornerstone of a Temple of Peace in the hearts of all mankind."[2]

The interment of the Unknown Soldier and the opening day of the Washington Conference were melded into one grand event. The foreign delegates to the conference were honored guests at the Arlington services, as was required by diplomatic protocol. Their presence gave the press additional opportunities to link the Washington Conference to the postwar peace. The energy of the Armistice Day ceremonies naturally spilled over into the preparations for the opening session of the Washington Conference the next day.

The Washington Conference was to be held at the Pan American Building, one

---

[2] *Washington Evening Star*, November 11, 1921, p. 40. See also Buckley, *The United States and the Washington Naval Conference*, 68–69.

of the few venues with adequate facilities for a meeting of such scope. The only limitation of the building was that its auditorium was moderately sized. The Harding administration wanted extensive press coverage of the plenary meetings of the conference. The agenda for the first day was limited to welcoming statements, procedural announcements, and a speech by the chairman of the Conference. This sort of program was better suited to a large auditorium where the press corps could be present and a large audience could witness the event. Therefore, the first session of the conference was held at the Continental Memorial Hall so that 270 reporters could join members of the United States Congress and diplomatic corps to hear the opening address of the chairman of the Conference, Charles Evans Hughes.[3] The subsequent plenary sessions followed this pattern.

The Washington Conference began with a welcoming speech by President Harding. He asked for a reasoned effort to find international stability. He drew comparisons to the postwar conference at Versailles, arguing that the purpose of the delegates was not to impose the will of the victors, but to "apply the better attributes of mankind to minimize the faults in our international relationships."[4] Harding petitioned the delegates to conduct successful, rational negotiations. However, his speech's vague vision for an improved international order was a mere prelude to the opening address of Charles Evans Hughes.

The election of Charles Evans Hughes as chairman of the Washington Conference was fully anticipated.[5] The foreign delegations had shown no signs of unwillingness to accept the leadership of the American secretary of state. Hughes recognized the advantages of his position and sought to use the chairman's opening address to seize the initiative. Everyone in the audience at the Continental Memorial Hall anticipated some reference to naval disarmament. However, in the first few moments of his speech, Hughes went far beyond what any of the delegates had anticipated. He called for a complete reevaluation of the naval building programs that the major nations had engaged in since the outbreak of the European war. He proposed a dramatic ten-year building holiday, the destruction of older ships in the world fleets, and the establishment of ratios that would define the balance of power between the major navies of the world. The Hughes proposal was dramatic because it was specific. It called for the destruction of pre-Dreadnought ships built before 1906. However, fleet reduction would not be achieved by a simple destruction of slow, weakly armored battleships. At the same time the Hughes proposal called for the elimination of the fast, well-armored, heavily gunned post-Jutland ships. The super-*Hoods* of Great Britain, the *Saratoga*-class of the United States, the *Mutsu*-class of Japan were the linchpins of

---

[3] *New York Times*, November 11, 1921, p. 1.

[4] *Washington Evening Star*, November 12, 1921, p. 1.

[5] In October Hughes had suggested that Prince Tokugawa of the Japanese delegation be made temporary chairman. However, he was overruled by the other members of the American delegation. From this point on, Hughes's election as chairman was certain. "Washington Conference Diary," October 21, 1921, Lodge Papers.

the postwar battle fleets. They embodied national honor as well as national power. Hughes would relegate them to the scrap heap.

It was as radical a proposal as Borah's earlier suggestion of an across-the-board 50 percent reduction. It was far more dramatic, because it had some real hope of eventual implementation. By using such a dramatic appeal, targeted to the general public, Charles Evans Hughes effectively took control of the Washington Conference. Not only did he seize the diplomatic initiative and throw the foreign delegations into defensive positions, Hughes secured his control of the policy-making initiative within the American government and relegated the insurgent irreconcilables to a role of watchful waiting.[6]

Republicans in the Senate reacted favorably to the Hughes initiative. Most commended the proposal set by Hughes without reservation. The conservative irreconcilable, George Moses, was the only senator to attack openly the secretary's speech, saying, "[W]e had been too generous at the outset."[7] The reaction of the insurgents was particularly important. The summer sessions of the Senate had been marked by complicated maneuvering over federal support to agriculture. A new issue was about to reach the Senate floor that could have dangerous consequences for party unity: the issue of the legitimacy of the Truman Newberry election was going to be debated once again.

The return of the campaign ethics question, combined with the traditional insurgent/conservative debates over the government's relationship with farming, threatened the cohesiveness of the Republican party. Hughes's call for disarmament demonstrated that the conservative administration and the Senate insurgents had at least one important objective in common. Just as the Versailles Treaty debates had helped to unify the Republican party two years earlier, the issue of naval disarmament could also serve as a common cause that would bind Republicans together. Insurgents supported the secretary of state. Leading irreconcilable, Hiram Johnson, was impressed by the Hughes call for massive naval disarmament. In a press release he described the Hughes proposal as "the antithesis of secret intrigue and diplomacy."[8] Senator William Kenyon, who would be an important figure in the Newberry debates, was impressed by the call for radical naval building cuts.[9] However, the opinion of William Borah, the leader of the insurgent irreconcilables, was the most important.

Senator Borah was absent for both the Armistice Day ceremonies and the opening of the Washington Conference; he was on a speaking tour in New York. His statements to the press marked a cautious support of Hughes's opening proposal. Although he remarked that "too much praise cannot be given to Secretary Hughes," Borah also cautioned against too much enthusiasm, "Do not forget that the commendation that greeted the proposals of Mr. Wilson [the Fourteen Points]

---

[6] See Dingman, *Power in the Pacific*, 197–198.

[7] *Washington Evening Star*, November 13, 1921, p. 4.

[8] Press release to the *Washington Herald*, November 13, 1921, Johnson Papers.

[9] *Washington Evening Star*, November 12, 1921, p. 4.

surpassed the commendations that have greeted the proposal of Mr. Hughes."[10] Borah would not grant Hughes unqualified support. The secretary had promoted American entry into the League; he was willing to cooperate with League organizations; and he could be outmaneuvered by the Europeans just as Wilson had been. Borah was particularly concerned about the secrecy he was sure would blanket the Washington Conference. He had already expressed his fears in an Armistice Day speech in Schenectady, New York, asserting, "The 'unknown soldier' was not only unknown in this war, but he was unknown in all the proceedings, all the intrigues or understandings or policies, which first brought on the war and into which this nation was finally drawn. . . . Behind closed doors the unknown's life was treated as a miserable inanimate thing, a mere cog in the intricate and remorseless machine of modern diplomacy."[11]

Hughes had retaken the policy initiative from the insurgent irreconcilables, but he could not be sure his brand of disarmament would go uncontested by members of his own party.

THE FOUR POWER TREATY AND THE ISSUE OF SECRET NEGOTIATION

Following the drama of the Hughes call for massive naval disarmament, the Washington Conference slipped into the tedious detail of diplomatic negotiation. The problems on the agenda were complex. The conference was attended by the delegations of the Principal Allied Nations of the First World War (Great Britain, France, Italy, Japan, and the United States), three lesser European powers that had long-standing interests in Asia (Portugal, Belgium, and the Netherlands), and China. The interests of these nations were disparate and often in conflict. The intense public pressure on the delegations guaranteed that progress would be made toward naval disarmament; however, the achievement of this progress would require adjustments in other areas.

The balance of power in East Asia had shifted as a result of World War I. The Bolshevik Revolution had thrown former spheres of Russian control into chaos. The Versailles Treaty had mandated former German island possessions to the Allies, and more important, had recognized Japanese seizure of Shantung from the Germans. The financial crisis that followed the war made it difficult for Europeans to continue the economic development of colonial areas in the Pacific. Each of these factors contributed to increased turmoil in East Asia. As tensions between nations escalated, China suffered the most with widespread disintegration of government and economic collapse. The authority of governments in Asia needed to be established; once this was accomplished a new balance of power could be created in East Asia. The political control of the islands mandated by the Versailles

---

[10] *Washington Evening Star*, November 13, 1921, p. 1, and November 14, 1921, p. 13.

[11] *Washington Evening Star*, November 12, 1921, p. 13.

Treaty needed to be recognized by those nations that were not signatories. Conflicts between Japan and China over the future of the Shantung Peninsula needed to be resolved. The role of the Japanese army on the Asian mainland needed to be defined. These issues of sovereignty were complicated by the inability of the Chinese republican government to control economic relations within its borders. A balance of power in East Asia required a simultaneous resolution to the problems in all of these areas.

The complex issues of East Asian politics were to be discussed in conjunction with the naval disarmament proposal. Borah's resolution, which called for a multilateral disarmament conference, had been a simple document. Its advocacy of a 50 percent across-the-board cut in naval strength ignored the problems of naval strategy that had arisen as a result of World War I. Theories regarding conventional surface fleet strategy had been altered and the introduction of new weapons prompted naval strategists to reassess the futures of their fleets. The Battle of Jutland had provided the most profound test of established naval strategy. There, naval architects were reinforced in their advocacy of the expensive process of continual technological development of armor plating. More important, the Battle of Jutland demonstrated that alterations had to be made in conventional surface tactics. Heavily gunned and heavily armored battleships were still the focal point of fleet operations. However, Jutland had shown that they were only safe when accompanied by large numbers of higher-speed light cruisers and destroyers. Changes in conventional fleet tactics were accompanied by responses to the new weapons introduced during the war. Although the use of submarines against merchant shipping had been hotly opposed by all of the Principal Allies, their use against ships of war was seen as an acceptable alteration of naval tactics. In addition, the rise of air warfare and the viability of sea-launched air attacks promised to change the course of strategic thinking in the next decades. Actual disarmament negotiations would force a detailed assessment of the importance of all of these factors.

For the purpose of dealing with these issues in a coherent fashion, political and disarmament problems were addressed in separate committees. Scores of technical advisors produced position papers and met with their delegations. Most meetings of the delegates were held in the Pan American Building, the official meeting place of the Conference. However, more informal negotiations took place as well, usually at the homes of the American delegates. In the face of all of this activity, the insurgent irreconcilables remained quiet.

During the Versailles Treaty negotiations, Republican opponents had continually sniped at the president's actions. These attacks came from nearly every faction of the Republican party in the Senate and covered a broad range of topics. The American delegation to the Washington Conference did not suffer this sort of wide-ranging, relentless attack. The most dangerous group—the insurgent irreconcilables—had been temporarily placated with the promise of naval disarmament. Both William Borah and Hiram Johnson were willing to reserve their attacks until the conference produced tangible documents for discussion.

Only one issue emerged in the Senate debates of the late summer and fall of 1921 that would provide a forum for attacks on Hughes and the American delegation: the problem of secrecy in negotiation would not wait until Hughes presented the Washington Conference treaties to the Senate.

The irreconcilables had been convinced that the peace created by the Versailles Treaty was unsuitable because Wilson had been duped by the Europeans during secret conferences. They had extended the logic of progressivism's drive for open government to diplomatic negotiation. Borah feared that secret sessions at the Washington Conference would result in unacceptable treaties, and he led a drive to keep the negotiating sessions open. This push manifested itself long before the conference began its sessions. Less than a week after the Harding administration invited the participants to the Washington Conference, Congress considered a resolution to force open diplomacy. It called for press access to all sessions of the Conference as well as the maintenance of a detailed record of the session meetings. The first attempt at a congressional declaration for open sessions was tabled, but it reemerged on the eve of the Conference to announce a generalized congressional opposition to secret diplomacy.[12]

The Senate had clearly indicated its opposition to secret diplomacy.[13] The problem was now to define unacceptable practices. American politicians were unanimous in their flat opposition to secret treaties—diplomatic arrangements that were not announced to the public until they were to be put into effect. The problems over the definition of secret diplomacy surrounded the issue of negotiation. The administration supported the publicizing of the Washington Conference. The press corps was cultivated; it had been well represented at the opening session of the Conference and received a stream of detailed press releases throughout the period of negotiation. However, there was a limit to the degree of openness that Hughes was willing to advocate. Hughes appreciated the delicacy of diplomatic negotiations and recognized that no nation wanted its position under continual public scrutiny. Private sessions were an expedient for successful agreements and had to be preserved. The official American position defined continual press reports as an adequate defense against secret diplomacy.[14] This did not meet the ultimate goals of either Borah or Johnson. They still feared that the British would secretly coerce the American delegates into some dangerous

------

[12] *Congressional Record*, 67th Congress, 2nd Session, November 8, 1921, p. 7534. See also August 17, 1921, p. 5118.

[13] This attitude was reflective of public opinion; numerous petitions advocating open sessions had been sent to the Department of State and by December 9, 1921, the total number of signatures on them amounted to 20,645. "Resolutions Received by the American Delegation," December 9, 1921, Hughes Papers. See also Hoag, *Preface to Preparedness*, 95.

[14] "Delegation to the Washington Conference Report to the President," 8, Lodge Papers. See also Charles Evans Hughes, "Some Observations on the Conduct of Our Foreign Relations," *American Journal of International Law* 16 (July 1922): 365–374.

concession. However, they did believe that information was much more accessible at the Washington Conference than had been the case at the postwar talks in Paris.[15]

Although both Borah and Johnson made occasional public remarks about secrecy at the Conference, no coherent attack on the proceedings emerged during the first month of negotiations. As a result, the U.S. delegation to the Conference was relatively free to focus its attention on the concerns of international politics.

If Hughes was to achieve his objective of massive naval disarmament, he had to deal with the British and Japanese desire to replace the Anglo-Japanese Alliance. The British had been disappointed at Hughes's refusal to discuss a tripartite alliance prior to the Washington Conference.[16] In an effort to promote discussion, Shidehara Kijuro of the Japanese delegation drew up a tentative agreement and presented it to the British delegate, Arthur Balfour. Balfour amended the proposal slightly and submitted the draft for discussion. The text was quite similar to the Anglo-Japanese Alliance. It provided for a coordinated response in the event that a third-party country threatened the territorial rights of one of the signatory nations and required that any disputes between the signatory nations be resolved through joint action. It differed from the Anglo-Japanese Alliance in that it did not commit the signatories to a declaration of war in the event of an attack on one of the participant nations.[17]

Hughes was not willing to commit the United States to the agreement proposed by the Japanese and British. Sentiment among the insurgents opposed the formation of open alliances with colonial powers and the Shidehara proposal would certainly be condemned as a simple expansion of the Anglo-Japanese Alliance. The most bitter complaints of the territorial settlements made by the Versailles Treaty had centered on Japanese expansion in East Asia. Hughes wanted to avoid placing the administration in the position of defending Japanese colonialism. He hoped that if France were included in such an agreement he would be able to disperse any advantage the Japanese could gain from the treaty.[18] Hughes then charged Henry Cabot Lodge with the drafting of an alternative American proposal.

Lodge was the member of the delegation who most distrusted Japanese political motivations. He had once described the Anglo-Japanese Alliance as "the most dangerous element in our relations with the Far East."[19] If the United States was

---

[15] Diary letters, November 16, 1921, Johnson Papers.

[16] Thomas Buckley suggested that this was a significant factor in Lloyd George's decision not to lead the British delegation. Buckley, *The United States and the Washington Naval Conference*, 65.

[17] Baron Shidehara's "Tentative Draft of an Outline of a Tripartite Arrangement among Japan, the British Empire, and the United States of America, with Mr. Balfour's Amendments," November 27, 1921, Lodge Papers.

[18] Buckley, *The United States and the Washington Naval Conference*, 133–34.

[19] Lodge to Charnwood, November 18, 1921, Lodge Papers. See also Sadao Asada, "Japan and the United States, 1915–1925" (Ph.D. dissertation, Yale University, 1963), 147.

going to be an active participant in the arrangement that replaced the Anglo-Japanese Alliance, Lodge would be the best member of the delegation to draft an unassailable treaty. After extensive discussions between the American delegation and its technical advisors, Henry Cabot Lodge directed the State Department counselor, Chandler Anderson, to write the first draft of the Four Power Treaty.[20]

The draft that Anderson produced followed the general direction that had been established by Shidehara and Balfour. The agreement was designed to preserve the status quo in Asia. Any threat to the possessions and dominions of the signatories would trigger a coordinated response. No specific mention of intervention was made, but the signatories were pledged to "arrive at an understanding as to what measures should be taken to preserve the general peace and safeguard said rights and possessions."[21] The draft excluded any specific commitment to military or economic intervention, and so it avoided the issues of debate that had been generated by Article X of the League of Nations covenant.

After a final consultation among Anderson, Lodge, and Hughes, the draft was altered to specify the British Empire, the United States, Japan, and France as the signatories. It was also limited in scope. The issues of conflict to be regulated by the treaty were confined to disputes over the insular possessions of these nations in the Pacific. The Anglo-Japanese Alliance was to be replaced by a new multilateral commitment to the status quo in the insular Far East.

This process of negotiation had been conducted away from the scrutiny of the press. The exchanges that led to the drafting of the Four Power Treaty had been essentially private.[22] Hughes determined that the open discussion of the Four Power Treaty should occur quickly, so as to facilitate the continued negotiation of other issues. The next plenary session of the Conference was scheduled for December 10. This session would be open to the public and well attended by the press corps. The introduction of the Four Power Treaty at this session would

---

[20] Chandler Anderson had been active in American treaty drafting since the Roosevelt administration. He was one of the country's leading theoreticians on the binding nature of security commitments. His article, "The Extent and Limitations of the Treaty-Making Power under the Constitution," *American Journal of International Law* 1 (July 1907): 636–670, was a keystone in the legal defense of American adoption of security and arbitration treaties.

[21] Diary, November 21, 1921, Anderson Papers, and "Four Power Treaty Draft by Chandler P. Anderson," Department of State Records, National Archives.

[22] The first full account of the Washington Conference stressed the secret nature of the negotiations: "As all the negotiations in regard to the alliance were secretly carried on between Mr. Balfour, Mr. Hughes and members of the Japanese delegation, it is impossible accurately to trace the history of the treaty which was evolved." Raymond Leslie Buell, *The Washington Conference* (New York: D. Appleton & Co., 1922), 174. Although historians have uncovered much of the sequence of negotiation, Buell's assessment that the Four Power Treaty was a product of private negotiation is, for all intents and purposes, correct.

assure it instantaneous public recognition that would help to mitigate the private nature of the negotiations that created it.

The issues dealt with in the Four Power Treaty should have been discussed in the meetings of the Committee on Far Eastern Questions. However, from its inception that committee was directed to focus its attention on the problems of continental Asia—the sovereignty questions of China, Manchuria, and Siberia.[23] The security of island possessions had not appeared as a major issue of formal discussion. The exchanges between Shidehara, Balfour, and Hughes had been private, almost coincidental. Because the discussions that led to the treaty had not been included in the regular committee agenda, the Four Power Treaty was not automatically included in the agenda of the Fourth Plenary Session. The meeting was dedicated to a progress report of the Committee on Far Eastern Questions. The opening minutes reflected the basic agreements that had been anticipated. The participant nations had already announced their commitment to maintaining the territorial integrity of China. The committee reports were almost perfunctory in nature, describing the specific areas of discussion that might be covered by an eventual Far Eastern treaty. After these initial reports, Charles Evans Hughes announced that Henry Cabot Lodge needed to communicate to the conference some information of an immediate nature.

The public announcement of the Four Power Treaty was dramatic.[24] In his presentation of the document, Lodge argued that the security of the Pacific was essential to world peace. The solution presented by the Four Power Treaty was a simple one, "We make the experiment here in this Treaty of trying to assure peace in the immense region by trusting the preservation of its tranquillity to the good faith of the nations responsible for it."[25]

The Four Power Treaty was not an attempt at international government. However, it was an important departure in the diplomacy of the United States. Traditions in American security policy had followed two basic patterns. The United States had relied on independent, ad hoc actions to defend its security interests. When this most basic approach was unsuitable, then the U.S. government relied on limited arbitration.

The United States had developed a more active foreign policy in the first two decades of the twentieth century. As the United States expanded its participation in international organizations, made increasing use of military force in diplomacy, and entered into more complex arbitration treaties, debates over the relationship

---

[23] State Department Press Release, September 21, 1921, Hughes Papers. The original intent of the committee structure is confirmed by the minutes of the Washington Conference. See U.S. Department of State, *Conference on the Limitation of Armament*, Washington, D.C., November 12, 1921–February 6, 1922.

[24] Rumors of an impending security treaty were discussed in the *New York World* in the week before the plenary session meeting. Nonetheless, the press coverage after the meeting indicated that the presentation retained its drama.

[25] U.S. Department of State, *Conference on the Limitation of Armament*, 164.

between the executive and legislative branches became more vehement. As executives sought to make the United States a leader in international politics, critics in Congress feared an erosion of legislative control over appropriations and war powers. This tension between the two branches had first erupted as open disputes during the Taft administration with an attempt to commit the U.S. government to a policy of general arbitration. It had continued with the debates over American entry into the League of Nations. These earlier attempts to expand the role of the United States had failed because the Senate viewed them as being in conflict with constitutional preservation of legislative power. The Four Power Treaty constituted the Harding administration's attempt to solidify American diplomatic leadership in East Asia while still preserving the authority of Congress. The Harding administration's Four Power Treaty would have to survive the scrutiny of senators who were jealous of congressional power.

The presentation of the Four Power Treaty exemplified the political sophistication of the Republican party leadership. The conduct of the American delegation demonstrated a great understanding of the use of popular pressure in diplomatic negotiation. By presenting diplomatic goals suddenly in meetings well covered by the press, Hughes was able to control the diplomatic initiative and generate political momentum. The public presentation of the Four Power Treaty was not unlike that of the American goals for massive naval disarmament one month earlier. In the case of the Four Power Treaty, the political value of a sudden presentation was further reinforced by the enthusiastic support the other delegations gave the agreement. Support of the treaty in major newspapers would strengthen Hughes in a contest with the insurgent irreconcilables.

William Borah responded quickly to the announcement of the Four Power Treaty. During the Senate session on December 12, he raised a series of reservations regarding the Conference proceedings. He argued that the impact of the Four Power Treaty was totally dependent on the level of armaments in the world, "that unless there is real disarmament this must inevitably be a military alliance and nothing else—a determination to overawe and dominate the Pacific by force."[26] He feared that the Washington Conference would not achieve its primary objective, which was to lay down guidelines for substantive naval disarmament. Although some progress had been made, interim conference reports already indicated that the delegations would not come to any limitation agreement on the critical areas of naval air power and submarines. Borah argued that the danger of the Four Power Treaty was directly proportional to the level of naval armaments in the Pacific and that the Senate should approach the treaty with some skepticism until a final arms limitation was reached.

Despite his call for skepticism, Borah was confronted by Senate acquiescence of the Four Power Treaty. During the Versailles Treaty debates he had had marked success persuading insurgents that the collective security provisions of Article X

---

[26] *Congressional Record*, 67th Congress, 2nd Session, December 12, 1921, p. 231.

undermined efforts to strengthen the federal government while making it more responsive to popular will. The enforcement of League sanctions had been seen as a threat to the legislative branch's control over war and peace issues. The collective security provisions in Article II of the Four Power Treaty only required that the signatories "communicate with one another fully and frankly in order to arrive at an understanding as to the most efficient measures to be taken, jointly or separately, to meet the exigencies of the particular situation." Because the treaty did not specify any form of action, or even any means of arriving at collective action, threats to legislative power were less tangible in the Four Power Treaty.[27]

The insurgent Republicans did not automatically suspect a threat to democratic government. The re-creation of an irreconcilable movement would not be triggered by the announcement of the new collective security system in the Pacific. The insurgent irreconcilable Miles Poindexter (R, Washington) announced himself to be a vigorous defender of the treaty, and he took on much of the responsibility for countering Borah's speeches on December 12. George Norris (R, Nebraska), another important irreconcilable, also declared his support of the measure immediately after its public announcement. The weakness of Borah's opposition was emphasized when the ranking Democrat of the Senate Foreign Relations Committee, Gilbert Hitchcock (D, Nebraska), announced his support of the Four Power Treaty.[28]

Borah continued to pressure the administration. Although the treaty demanded no commitment of U.S. support in either military or economic intervention, Borah feared the existence of a secret protocol that would bind the American government. This suspicion of diplomatic intrigue, combined with an as yet unrealized disarmament program, prevented Borah from supporting the Four Power Treaty. Although he was not immediately successful in stirring up Senate opposition to the treaty, circumstances turned in Borah's favor with the formal signing of the agreement.

Rather than sign the Four Power Treaty immediately after the announcement on December 10, the delegates decided to hold a special ceremony at the State Department. In keeping with the established practice of encouraging extensive press coverage, the signing ceremony was scheduled to be public. However, when

---

[27] The lack of specificity in Article II was a clear response to legislative objections to Article X of the League of Nations Covenant. It is important to note that the language of the Four Power Treaty also circumvented objections to Taft's Anglo-American General Arbitration Treaty. That failed agreement had specified the establishment of an ad hoc Anglo-American arbitration panel that would determine appropriate solutions to diplomatic problems between the two nations. The Four Power Treaty was designed to avoid the creation of any supranational body that would jeopardize American sovereignty.

[28] *Washington Post*, December 13, 1921, p. 1; *Baltimore Sun*, December 13, 1921, p. 1; and *Washington Evening Star*, December 13, 1921, 1. On December 14 the Democratic Caucus announced that it would support the treaty; however, Carter Glass (D, Virginia) later issued a statement regretting the early announcement. *Baltimore Sun*, December 14, 1921, p. 2.

the press corps arrived at the Department of State on the morning of December 14, its members were informed that their invitations were canceled. The ceremony would continue as scheduled, but no reporters were permitted to witness the event. The press was confined to an anteroom and briefed by a Department of State representative. No explanation for the change was given.[29] By such action, the Harding administration undermined much of its earlier work in promoting the Washington Conference as an example of open diplomacy. Although William Borah had found little support among his fellow senators for his suggestions of secret understandings surrounding the Four Power Treaty, several newspapers, including the *Baltimore Sun* and the *New York World*, joined him in speculating about the existence of dangerous unspoken agreements. The Washington press corps had already chided Charles Evans Hughes for his support of the League of Nations. At the press corps 1921 "Gridiron Dinner," held the day after the announcement of the Four Power Treaty, Hughes had been presented with "the key to the backdoor of the League of Nations."[30]

The Four Power Treaty was not destined to meet the same opposition that had confronted the Versailles Treaty; however, the process of advice and consent still posed problems. Relations between the administration and insurgents were already strained by the delays in the debates over the seating of Truman Newberry. The debate over a federally managed agricultural marketing system had returned to the Senate with the introduction of the Capper-Volstead Bill. The continuing problem of agricultural surpluses encouraged congressmen from farming states to resume their efforts to give the federal government authority to purchase key commodities and sell them at a loss on the international market.[31] After consultation with Henry Cabot Lodge, President Harding announced that the submission of the Four Power Treaty to the Senate would be delayed until after the completion of the Washington Conference. The ratification process would not begin until Majority Leader Lodge and Minority Leader Underwood could devote their full attention to the process of advice and consent.

The signing of the Four Power Treaty marked two important victories for Charles Evans Hughes. The secretary of state had constructed a framework for peaceful resolution of political problems between the major powers of East Asia. The four powers would recognize the insular possessions of each other and were committed to the maintenance of the status quo in the Pacific. On this foundation, the United States could build a new, activist postwar foreign policy. The pressure for the Four Power Treaty had originated from the British and Japanese, who sought a

---

[29] One of the most critical accounts appeared in the *New York World*, December 14, 1921, p. 1.

[30] *Washington Evening Star*, December 11, 1921, p. 1.

[31] *Washington Post*, December 11, 1921, p. 17. An editorial cartoon in the *New York World*, entitled "Cruelty to Animals," depicted the Agricultural Bloc chasing the GOP elephant with a pitchfork. *New York World*, December 11, 1921, p. 2E.

replacement for the Anglo-Japanese Alliance.[32] American cooperation in this effort built good will with these two nations, and the inclusion of France in the agreement would aid later cooperative efforts with the French. The Four Power Treaty also served an important purpose in American domestic politics. The good will established by the Four Power Treaty was a prerequisite for the continuation of naval disarmament and resolution of problems in China. Hughes was aware that the American public expected the Washington Conference to result in naval disarmament and anticipated changes that would strengthen the republican government in China. He believed that the public would accept the Four Power Treaty as long as additional gains were made at the Washington Conference. The potential storm of insurgent opposition could be withstood if the Washington Conference ultimately satisfied the American public's desire for naval disarmament and a stabilization of China.

THE FIVE POWER TREATY AND THE PROGRESS OF NAVAL DISARMAMENT

Hughes's push for significant naval disarmament encountered difficulties on several levels. Problems of national budgeting had induced the governments of both Japan and Great Britain to favor disarmament, but neither nation wanted to accept a diminution of its ability to defend its sphere of influence. Japan was particularly adamant in the assertion that a large postwar navy was necessary for the protection of its enlarged role in Pacific politics after 1919. The French government presented a set of unanticipated problems. While France's military power rested in its land forces, it advocated the creation of a large submarine fleet and the aggressive use of submarines in naval warfare. Any curbing of French submarine construction hinged on giving France the prestige of inclusion in all major Conference agreements. Furthermore, the League of Nations Commission on Disarmament did not favor the disarmament talks in Washington. The Commission's director, Salvador de Madariaga, argued that the issues of land and naval disarmament could not be separated and that no disarmament efforts should be made independent of the League of Nations.[33]

Not only did Hughes have to deal with opposition from these external political forces, but he had to face resistance from strategic thinkers in the United States Navy. The desire to return to the American tradition of limited military strength, combined with the wish to limit federal spending, generated the American public's drive for naval disarmament. The strategic planners in the navy understood that

---

[32] This thesis is best explained in Buckley, *The United States and the Washington Naval Conference*.

[33] Madariaga eventually condemned the Five Power Treaty as the principal force that undermined the League's efforts at universal disarmament. See Salvador de Madariaga, *Disarmament* (New York: Coward-McCann, Inc., 1929), 228

this interest represented a political force that could not be ignored.[34] However, they also recognized that the naval building programs of World War I had left the Japanese in an improved position and that the Japanese navy was committed to further improvements in its status. The Japanese were perceived as the principal threat to the United States Navy and the naval officer corps wanted to make certain that its ability to defend American interests against the Japanese would be preserved.[35]

The Japanese building program that had become effective in 1914 promised a technologically advanced navy that was capable of meeting any military threat in the Pacific.[36] The Japanese navy hoped that the Washington Conference would guarantee that it would be permitted to maintain a fleet size 70 percent of that of Great Britain and the United States. It also hoped to retain the newly constructed battleship, *Mutsu*. Not only was the *Mutsu* the most advanced ship in the Japanese navy, it held a certain romantic fascination for the Japanese public. It was the first battleship designed by Japanese naval architects. The funding for its construction had come from public subscription, not tax revenues. These features had given the ship an image of belonging to the people of Japan, not the government; its destruction would not be easily tolerated.

The Japanese navy of 1921 was more modern than the British navy; in many respects it rivaled the technological capabilities of the United States Navy. The meteoric rise of Japanese naval power had generated an apprehension among American naval planners that would color their perspective as they prepared briefing papers for the Washington Conference.

By calling for a naval disarmament conference, Charles Evans Hughes had triggered an abrupt shift in American foreign policy. The Borah proposal, despite its popular appeal, was not a realistic means of dealing with the sophisticated problems of shifting naval strategy. The Hughes proposal was much more pragmatic because it relied heavily on position papers drawn up by the Department of Navy's General Board. Those papers explained American theories of naval warfare and the disarmament process would have to be compatible with this strategic thinking.[37]

The basis of American fleet structure was still the battleship. The linchpin of all successful naval engagements would be a large, heavily armored, heavily gunned vessel capable of obliterating all other classes of ships as well as fortified shore

---

[34] Dingman, *Power in the Pacific*, 155–58.

[35] Sprout and Sprout, *Toward a New Order of Sea Power*, 88–103, and Braisted, *The United States Navy in the Pacific, 1909–1922*, 477–490.

[36] The plan was referred to as the "Eight/Eight Plan." It allotted eight capital ships to the Japanese fleet. (A capital ship is a battleship or a heavy cruiser with a displacement of over 10,000 tons.) Ships were to be replaced at eight-year intervals, thus assuring ultimate technological capability.

[37] "Report of the General Board on Limitation of Armaments," July 27, 1921, Hughes Papers.

installations. The Battle of Jutland had demonstrated that each battleship had to work in conjunction with large numbers of cruisers and destroyers. The speed of these smaller vessels made them useful for probing and scouting, and they served to intensify the attack capabilities of the battleship. The threat of air attacks had not yet been proven, and their use was not likely to be so great as to undermine the power of the battleship-based fleet.[38] In essence, the General Board argued that any naval disarmament had to be defined in terms of battleship reduction. This was the approach adopted by Charles Evans Hughes. The American proposal retained the concept of battleship based fleets, and defined disarmament as a limitation of the central element of those fleets.

During the first month of the Washington Conference, the other major naval powers constructed appropriate responses to the Hughes proposal. The delegations discussed the issues in good faith. However, important stumbling blocks emerged. The Japanese feared for the security of their island mandates and wanted some assurance that political instability on the Asian continent would not adversely affect Japanese interests. The Japanese government saw the navy as the means of preserving security in Japan's sphere of influence and was not eager to accept anything less than a relative increase in power.

Although the problems of naval armament levels in the Pacific constituted the greatest threat to a disarmament treaty, difficulties had also arisen in Europe. The French had defended their right to supplement their land-based military forces in Europe with a large submarine fleet; the British believed that the rise of such a fleet forced an expansion of the Royal Navy in response. As he was promoting the negotiation of the Four Power Treaty, Hughes hoped that it would provide the inducement to overcome the difficulties in the disarmament talks.

Hughes was correct in his perception of the political balance at the conference. During November the negotiations over a limitation of battleship construction had stalemated on the issues of fleet ratios and numbers of battleships to be retained.[39] The Japanese had asserted that they would accept only a 10:10:7 ratio of fleet size between the British Empire, the United States, and Japan. The U.S. proposal argued for a 10:10:6 ratio, which assumed the destruction of the battleship *Mutsu*. The Japanese government feared the impending loss of the protection provided by the Anglo-Japanese Alliance and sought to replace the alliance with increased naval power. It was not until the second week of December, and Lodge's announcement of the Four Power Treaty, that serious progress was made in forging a naval compromise. Within a matter of days the Japanese delegation seriously began to

---

[38] Although several proponents of air warfare had touted the danger of air attack to battleships, most naval officers had not yet seen enough evidence to believe that air attacks constituted a real threat to conventional fleet strategy. Brig. General Billy Mitchell's sinking of the *Ostfriesland* had been the only test of naval strategy and it occurred while the General Board's report was being written.

[39] See Buell, *The Washington Conference*, 150–171, and Dingman, *Power in the Pacific*, 202–214.

consider acceptance of the 10:10:6 ratio. A compromise emerged when the Japanese agreed to accept the lower ratio on the condition that the *Mutsu* be retained in the fleet. The battleship ratio was preserved by permitting both the United States and the British Empire to retain a comparable vessel. Although the disarmament negotiations continued through January 1922, the Four Power Treaty constituted the political breakthrough that provided an ultimate disarmament settlement.

THE WASHINGTON CONFERENCE AND THE FUTURE OF CHINA

The Four Power Treaty also was a factor in the determination of a political settlement on the continent of Asia. By the end of World War I, the Japanese had significantly expanded their area of control on the continent. In 1915 they successfully defeated the German defenses in the Shantung Peninsula and assumed administrative control of the area. In that same year they issued the "Twenty-one Demands," which would place the Japanese in control of the economic infrastructure of Manchuria and parts of northern China.[40] In 1918 the Japanese increased their military presence on the continent by sending troops into southeastern Siberia as a response to the political instability generated by the Bolshevik Revolution. The government of China needed to curb the growth of Japanese power on the Asian continent. The Western powers also had motivation for curbing Japanese expansion into the economy of northern Asia. Not only were the Japanese expanding at the expense of the Chinese and Bolshevik governments, but their extended presence provided a threat to those nations that had long-standing cultural and commercial interests in Asia. If Japanese hegemony were solidified in northern Asia, the interests of Western nations would be jeopardized.

The Chinese government clearly perceived Japanese expansion into the valuable areas of Manchuria and the Shantung Peninsula to be the greatest threat to the development of a modern democracy. However, the increasing pressure of Japanese expansion was not the only problem the Chinese faced after the war. Since the turn of the century, the communications and transportation infrastructures of China had been dominated by foreign-owned corporations. An inadequate Chinese banking industry had forced economic development in China to rely on capital from foreign sources. The continued economic growth of China was dependent on the involvement of foreigners, and this economic dependency manifested itself in a diminution of sovereignty. Furthermore, the Chinese had lost control over their tariff system in 1905 as part of the indemnity solution to the

---

[40] The "Twenty-one Demands" were submitted to the Chinese government in January 1915. They were designed to provide a secret agreement between the Chinese and Japanese governments that would legitimize Japanese control over former Russian spheres of influence that had been transferred to Japan as a result of the Russo-Japanese War. They also placed Japanese in important administrative posts in China and would force the Chinese to rely on Japan for military supplies.

Boxer Rebellion. As a result, the government had neither the instrument that provided the principal means of control of commerce nor the ability to raise revenues appropriate to the functioning of a modern republic. The government of China suffered obvious limitations with these encroachments on its sovereignty.

Much of the energy of the Far Eastern Committee of the Washington Conference was consumed by the issues surrounding Chinese sovereignty. The growth of Chinese nationalism in the previous ten years inspired the Chinese delegation to push for significant improvements in their nation's relationship with the colonial powers. Inspired by the rhetoric of the Versailles commitment to national self-determination, the Chinese sought the same sort of independence that had been granted to the nations of Central Europe. These Chinese demands for a new equal status were met with some sympathy from the Western delegations.

The U.S. government had been a particular supporter of Chinese economic and political independence. Since 1899 the United States had favored the Open Door Policy for the purpose of defending the concept of free trade between foreign investors in the Chinese economy. As part of the basic support for progressive expansion of democracy, the American people had welcomed the creation of a republic in China. This generalized advocacy of economic and political progress had provided the basis for the American public's condemnation of Japanese expansion into Chinese territory. The Versailles Treaty had supported Japanese claims in the Shantung Peninsula and the Republican party's attacks on this support had been met by popular approval. Consistency in Republican policy making demanded that curbs be placed on foreign encroachments in China.

The announcement of the Four Power Treaty in December guaranteed the Japanese control over their insular possessions. The question remained as to whether or not Japan also would be able to maintain a sphere of influence on the continent of Asia. The progress in the Committee on Far Eastern Questions pointed to a commitment to the preservation of Chinese sovereignty. This commitment would necessitate the establishment of a political equilibrium between Japan and China, where Chinese interests would be protected from Japanese power. All segments of the Republican party shared this desire to defend the interests of China. Freedom of commercial competition and support of modern government were goals of both conservatives and insurgents. The preservation of Chinese political integrity in the face of Japanese expansion provided a means of linking insurgent Republicans to the Washington Conference. This method of political linking was particularly useful in that its use alienated no faction of the Republican party.

The American delegation took the lead in generating a compromise between Chinese and Japanese interests. The success of the American push for a compromise was a result of the use of Elihu Root as the principal mediator. He was the member of the American delegation most capable of mitigating the Japanese government's desire to promote its economic interests on the continent by use of force. Root had been the architect of Japanese-American diplomatic relations in the twentieth century; his experience in direct negotiation with the

Japanese dated back to the Roosevelt administration. During his service as secretary of state, Root had created a workable definition of the relationship between Japan and the United States through the Root-Takahira Agreement. The former secretary of state was highly regarded by the Japanese delegation to the Washington Conference. Its members believed him to be sensitive to Japanese goals in the Pacific, and they were willing to accept his suggestions as well reasoned and mutually beneficial.[41]

Root was responsible for drafting the resolutions of intent that would form the basis for the Nine Power Treaty. The Chinese government had entered the conference with the goal of removing all the limitations on its sovereignty. Japanese resistance would prevent a serious consideration of the Chinese objectives. The American delegation provided a compromise designed to guarantee the open door in China and increase the authority of the Chinese republican government. By November 21, Elihu Root had created a set of principles that was acceptable to all parties. Taken together they provided a fundamental guarantee of national self-determination in China. However, they did not specify the exact means by which the Chinese republican government would take control of its political economy. These four resolutions of intent were referred to as the "Root Resolutions." Their declaration to the Fourth Plenary Session of the Washington Conference had served as the background to the announcement of the Four Power Treaty.

The Root Resolutions asserted the basic American diplomatic principles first declared in the Open Door Notes of 1899–1900. They did not specify solutions to the problems facing China, but were general statements of intent governing the relationship between the Chinese government and foreign powers: (1) the government of China would be treated as the sovereign power within the borders of China; (2) foreign governments would encourage the stability of the Chinese government; (3) all nations would be granted equal opportunity in the economic development of China; and (4) the current political instability in China would not be used as justification for special rights for foreign citizens or governments. However, debates over Chinese sovereignty were not confined to these general areas of policy direction. The diplomatic delegations began to recognize significant pressure from a variety of groups. Student nationalist groups both in the United States and China demanded a detailed resolution to Chinese problems. The chambers of commerce in Chinese cities called for a reordering of the Chinese government's control over the economy. Even more important, however, were the suggestions by members of the Senate that Chinese territorial integrity was an important issue. This push for a more specific approach to the problem of Chinese sovereignty manifested itself in two areas: the autonomy of the Chinese tariff system and the control of the Shantung Railroad.

The Chinese tariff system was under the control of an international board. The

---

[41] Buckley, *The United States and the Washington Naval Conference*, 151–155.

rates established were deemed by the Chinese republican government to be too low to provide sufficient funds to operate a modern state. The Chinese sought tariff autonomy, but were willing to discuss an interim agreement that would preserve foreign control of the system but secure a raise in tariff schedules of more than 100 percent. During the conference Japanese resistance proved to be too intense to meet the Chinese objectives of an improvement in tariff revenues. However, discussions at Washington did provide the basis for a later conference in 1925 that eventually led to tariff autonomy in 1930.[42]

The question of control over the Shantung Peninsula triggered a set of particularly difficult diplomatic problems. The Versailles Treaty had recognized Japanese claims in Shantung, and all of the nations participating in the Washington Conference except China and the United States were signatories to that agreement. As a result, it was inappropriate for the conference to direct itself to the debate over sovereignty in Shantung. However, the issue was the key target area of Chinese diplomacy. It had also served as a principal stumbling block to the American ratification of the Versailles Treaty. A resolution to this problem was essential to China and the United States for continued improvement in their diplomatic relations with Japan and the Western European powers. The American delegation hoped to solve this diplomatic difficulty by encouraging bilateral discussions between China and Japan simultaneous with the conference. Bilateral negotiations continued through the winter of 1921–1922 and focused on the central issue of control over the Shantung Railway. The railway system was the economic center of the peninsula and both nations recognized that governmental authority over Shantung was inextricably linked to control of the railway.

Although the United States had no direct interests in the talks, members of the Senate maintained an interest in their progress. In January 1922, Senator Thomas Walsh (D, Montana) introduced a resolution in the Senate that called on the president to ascertain the status of negotiations over the Shantung Peninsula. The Japanese perceived this as a threat of Senate resistance to the Washington Conference treaties and began to make concessions to the Chinese position.[43] The two nations were eventually able to come to an agreement over the transfer of the Shantung Railroad that reestablished Chinese control in the peninsula. Nonetheless, the strength of the Japanese economy ensured a continued Japanese presence in the development of northern China.

In addition to the treaty commitments that resulted from the Washington Conference, a series of resolutions was passed that was designed to strengthen the position of the Chinese republican government. The principal objective of these resolutions was the removal of foreign influence over the Chinese political economy. Extraterritoriality was to be ended in recognition of the Chinese

---

[42] Buell, *The Washington Conference*, 250–254, and Buckley, *The United States and the Washington Naval Conference*, 168.

[43] Buell, *The Washington Conference*, 261, and *Congressional Record*, 67th Congress, 2nd Session, January 20, 1922, p. 1432–1435.

government's progress toward establishing a modern legal system. The presence of foreign troops on Chinese soil was to be limited. Foreign postal systems and commercial radio stations were to fall under the jurisdiction of the Chinese government. The Chinese railway system was to be reorganized under one central administration and all future railroad construction would commence according to the needs of the Chinese government. Although this limitation of foreign power in China was not comprehensively enforced, it did constitute a clear commitment to the support of an independent Chinese nation-state.

THE WASHINGTON CONFERENCE AND THE CLIMATE OF AMERICAN DOMESTIC POLITICS

The Washington Conference closed on February 6, 1922. Its results demonstrated a complicated balance between the interests of the participating nations. Not only was it necessary for the American delegates to weigh the national interests of the United States against those of the other participant nations, but a balance also had to be maintained within the U.S. government. Despite the political pattern of intense animosity between Democrats and Republicans during the League of Nations debates, partisan conflict was not a significant factor in the formulation of the Washington Conference treaties.[44] The problems faced by the Harding administration were those of intra-party politics. The insurgent wing was a destabilizing element in the party; efforts had to be made to prevent issues of foreign policy from further separating the insurgents from the party leadership.

The administration had achieved a major victory when a number of important insurgents had announced their support of the Four Power Treaty in December. Borah could not rely on the issue of Pacific security alone to trigger an insurgent rebellion against the conservative administration position. However, in the winter of 1921–1922, Pacific security was not the only issue that faced Republican policy makers. The Harding administration and insurgent Republicans had been locked in a six-month-long debate over the federal government's responsibility toward agriculture, with no amicable compromise in sight. The issue of the seating of Truman Newberry had reemerged in the Senate in the first few days of the conference, but debate had been postponed. Although tension between the administration and the insurgents clearly existed, an open rebellion was avoided until January 1922.

On January 11, 1922, Thaddeus Caraway (D, Arkansas) introduced a motion to remove Truman Newberry from his Senate seat. Caraway's actions were motivated more by partisan hostility than by a desire for electoral reform. Nonetheless, his action sparked a full-scale battle over the continuation of progressivism in the Senate. Although he favored party solidarity, President Pro Tempore Albert

---

[44] The two leading Democratic senators, Oscar Underwood and Gilbert Hitchcock, both supported the treaties. Even Woodrow Wilson did not present any sort of forceful opposition to the Harding administration's efforts.

Cummins was also dedicated to the values of the progressive movement. Cummins not only permitted the Caraway motion to come to the floor of the Senate, but blocked the efforts of conservative Republicans to prevent the seating of Truman Newberry from becoming the subject of Senate debate.[45]

When the issue of the seating of Truman Newberry first came to the floor in 1919, the Republican majority was only two votes. Insurgents understood that support of Newberry was a prerequisite in maintaining control of the upper chamber. Despite the fact that many insurgents abhorred the amount of money spent on behalf of Newberry, and despite their questions as to whether Newberry genuinely represented the people of Michigan, they had all voted to recognize his election. However, after the election of 1920 the Republican majority was more substantial. Insurgents could now desert party direction in favor of a philosophical commitment without risking Democratic encroachment. They condemned the introduction of massive campaign spending as a repudiation of progressive principles. In a letter to Thomas Elliot, William Borah asserted, "[I]f Newberry can be seated upon the principles laid down in his defense, then we had just as well advertise seats in the Senate for sale on the open market."[46]

The January vote on the seating of Truman Newberry demonstrated a marked absence of party loyalty by insurgent Republicans. Not all insurgents disobeyed party direction; both Miles Poindexter (R, Washington) and Albert Cummins (R, Iowa) argued that Newberry had acquitted himself and had not engaged in improper spending practices. However, all of the Republicans who voted against Newberry were identified with the insurgency.[47]

Despite the defections of these senators, the party lines were strong enough to keep Newberry in his seat. The final vote was forty-six to forty-one in favor of Newberry and was reflective of the substantial power of the Republican party in the Senate. At the same time, the vote on January 13 did not end debate on the issue. Insurgent Republicans continued to snipe at the Newberry seating and the leadership of the party. William Borah was unrelenting in his attacks on the influence of wealth in Senate elections; he predicted that the leadership's defense of the Michigan senator would have dire results. In a letter to Frederick Landis he prophesied, "The Republican Party is voluntarily taking on a very heavy load. The supposition is that such things will blow over. My guess is that this will not blow

---

[45] *Washington Evening Star*, January 11, 1922, p. 1.

[46] Borah to Thomas Elliot, December 2, 1921, Borah Papers.

[47] Those Republicans voting against Newberry were William Borah (R, Idaho), Arthur Capper (R, Iowa), Wesley Jones (R, Washington), William Kenyon (R, Iowa), Edwin Ladd (R, North Dakota), Peter Norbeck (R, South Dakota), George Norris (R, Nebraska), and George Sutherland (R, Utah). Hiram Johnson (R, California) is reported to have opposed Newberry, but he was not present for the vote. *Congressional Record*, 67th Congress, 2nd Session, January 12, 1922, p. 1116, and *Washington Evening Star*, January 13, 1922, p. 4.

over until it has blown someone up."[48]

When insurgent Republicans broke party ranks over the Newberry issue, they demonstrated that the old reform ethic of the Taft era was not entirely dead. The nature of the movement had changed dramatically since 1912. The efforts for conciliation and compromise that were made by Senate Majority Leader Lodge and President Harding had eroded away much of the cohesion of the Taft insurgency. Some insurgents, like Albert Cummins, had been pulled into the orbit of Senate leadership and were now far more hesitant to break party ranks. During the summer and fall of 1921 the insurgent Republicans were united only in their opposition to the conservative leadership in the area of agricultural reform. Borah had tried to unite the movement around the disarmament question, but the success of his efforts was still in doubt. However, with the vote on the Newberry question it became clear that an insurgent consensus could arise in an area outside of agricultural policy. The leadership of William Borah in the attack on Newberry could be perceived as evidence of his role in a more broad assault on the conservative leadership. The problem that faced Secretary of State Hughes and Majority Leader Lodge was the question of whether or not Borah could marshal a coherent insurgent opposition to the Washington Conference treaties.

Taken as a whole, the Washington Conference treaties represented a balancing of the interests within the Republican party. The central goal—massive naval disarmament—had been defined by the insurgent irreconcilables. However, the specific achievement of that goal had been under the control of the conservative leadership of the Republican party. The success of the Harding administration in defining the postwar Republican foreign policy would be measured by an absence of opposition to the Washington Conference treaties during the Senate ratification procedure.

---

[48] Borah to Frederick Landis, January 17, 1922, Borah Papers.

7

The Senate and the Washington Conference Treaties

I have always found it difficult to edit a bad egg.

—Joseph France

William Borah rose to a position of prominence during the Versailles Treaty debates. He cultivated his status as a respectable insurgent and successfully manipulated the leadership of the Republican party. He continued to refine the politics of insurgency, and as a result, successfully blocked support of the League of Nations in the Republican party platform of 1920 and dictated one of the primary objectives of the Washington Conference. To the chagrin of the conservative party leadership, Borah had emerged as a powerful figure in the Republican party. However, the political climate that had promoted the rise of William Borah had begun to change during the Washington Conference.

Secretary of State Charles Evans Hughes had been able to dominate U.S. policy making during the conference. His decision to include Senate Majority Leader Henry Cabot Lodge and Senate Minority Leader Oscar Underwood in the American delegation effectively blocked the formation of any significant opposition in the Senate. Hughes also understood the importance of controlling public opinion; he was able to prevent potential opponents from inspiring a public outcry against the conference negotiations. During the Washington Conference, the more conservative elements of the Republican party demonstrated that the insurgency could be controlled.

BUILDING AN INSURGENT THREAT TO THE WASHINGTON CONFERENCE

William Borah was not satisfied with the treaties that emerged from the Washington Conference. He feared that the Four Power Treaty constituted an infringement on American sovereignty. He believed that the naval arms limitations of the Five Power Treaty were insufficient. Borah hoped to solidify an opposition movement to the Washington Conference treaties. The circumstances of the Washington Conference treaties were not conducive to the formation of a large opposition group. Only Hiram Johnson had shared Borah's broad skepticism of the Washington Conference. However, other senators who had been part of the irreconcilable movement had raised questions regarding specific aspects of the emerging treaties. During the course of debate, they could coalesce into an opposition group.

Furthermore, it was possible that some Senate Democrats would break away from the party leadership. Underwood's authority as Senate minority leader was not unquestioned. After his narrow defeat of Gilbert Hitchcock for the position of party leader in 1919, Oscar Underwood had not been able to gain the confidence of all the members of his party. Party discipline among the Democrats had broken down and Underwood was not able to curb those who sought revenge for the defeat of the Versailles Treaty or those who were opposed to any treaty that tied the United States to Great Britain.[1] During the winter of 1921–1922 Borah hoped to unify former irreconcilables and Democrats into a coherent force.

Borah's efforts would hinge on the Four Power Treaty. Even before the conference was over, William Borah had begun to construct an attack on the Four Power Treaty that was markedly similar to his strategy for the defeat of the Versailles Treaty. By linking criticisms of Article X of the League of Nations covenant to the Four Power Treaty debates, Borah hoped to inspire opposition within the Senate. Among these themes of criticism was the argument that American diplomats had been duped into secret agreements designed to protect established colonial empires. The treaty's requirement that the four signatories "shall communicate fully and frankly in order to arrive at an understanding as to the most efficient measures to be taken" was interpreted as a limitation on U.S. sovereignty by William Borah and other members of the Senate. In a letter to Arthur Vandenberg (R, Michigan), Borah asserted:

> [T]his is dynamite,—[sic] a little more subtle in its structure than that of the Versailles Treaty, but no less destructive in its nature of the things in which you and I believe. I shall carry this matter to the people the same as I did the other matter. It was botched, or contrived and built up up [sic], in secret and as the result of bartering and trading the same as Article X. It is a fearful betrayal of the purposes for which the Conference was called. Let us not be blinded by partisanship.[2]

Borah emphasized the idea that the obligations of the United States under the treaty were unclear. He and other opponents assumed that the members of the American delegation were not entirely forthcoming when describing the new American

---

[1] For an overview of dissent within the Democratic party, see Burner, *The Politics of Provincialism*. See also Johnson, *Oscar W. Underwood*, 294–341.

[2] Borah to Arthur H. Vandenberg, December 19, 1921, Borah Papers.

responsibilities.

Opponents worked under a cloud of disfavor. Despite a lack of support from the general public, the opposition movement in the Senate remained committed to the defeat of the treaty. It focused its efforts on depicting the Four Power Treaty as an example of secret diplomacy. Borah was not willing to forgo his opposition to the treaty for the sake of party loyalty. He would use his knowledge of the institutional politics of the Senate to see the treaty defeated.

Borah's organization of the opposition movement suffered from severe limitations. During the Washington Treaty debates he was in direct opposition to the chairman of the Senate Foreign Relations Committee, Henry Cabot Lodge. He was not able to use the committee's influence to alter the treaties by reservation and amendment.

Much of Borah's success in the Versailles Treaty debates had been a result of his partnership with Henry Cabot Lodge. As the chairman of the Senate Foreign Relations Committee, Lodge determined the nature of committee hearings and dominated the process of drafting a committee report. During the Versailles Treaty debates Lodge had insisted on extensive hearings, designed, in part, to provide the irreconcilables with enough time to launch a public-speaking program. In his efforts to weaken Wilson's treaty, Lodge had also sanctioned the attachment of irreconcilable-sponsored amendments in the committee's report to the full Senate. This sort of assistance from Lodge would not be forthcoming in the spring of 1922.

The Four Power Treaty was an unanticipated product of the Washington Conference. Because it was not the result of negotiations held in plenary sessions, no formal record of the negotiations existed. As a result, debate arose over the obligations incurred during the informal sessions. Remarks by supporters of the treaty came under intense scrutiny and could trigger outbursts of opposition rhetoric.

The debate over the treaty's obligations suddenly became complex after President Harding's press conference on December 20, 1921. At the end of the session, the president responded to a question regarding the definition of insular possessions. He was asked to explain whether or not the Japanese home islands were included in the insular possessions that were protected by the treaty. Although he had not been briefed on the issue, Harding did not defer the question to the State Department. He stated that the insular possessions covered by the treaty did not include the Japanese home islands.[3] The president's statement was not a reflection of the government's position. In a subsequent meeting with Charles Evans Hughes, Harding explained his decision to comment on the scope of the treaty by saying, "I didn't want to appear a dub."[4]

The president's definition of the treaty obligations provoked a sudden torrent of criticism. Although the administration quickly announced that President Harding's

---

[3] See Buckley, *The United States and the Washington Naval Conference,* 139, and Buell, *The Washington Conference,* 180–181.

[4] Beerits Memorandum, "The Four Power Treaty," Hughes Papers, 139.

exclusion of the Japanese home islands had been incorrect, treaty opponents seized the statement as a primary point of the debate.

James A. Reed (D, Missouri) used the president's error as an opportunity to launch a full-scale attack on the Four Power Treaty. Reed had been one of the Democratic irreconcilables during the Versailles Treaty debates, and agreed with Borah that the Four Power Treaty constituted the same threat as Article X of the League of Nations Covenant. He argued that the treaty demonstrated yet another act of foreign perfidy against naive American diplomats, remarking:

> Is it not astounding and is it not appalling that these conferences are so secret that the President of the United States does not know whether an agreement we are asked to sign and which is to last for 10 years is to bind us to send our sons to defend the mainland of Japan—its main islands—or whether it is a treaty that merely binds us to keep the enemy off little islands that Japan may have scattered through the ocean?[5]

The president's confusion over the interpretation of the treaty suddenly changed the nature of the Senate opposition. Before the press conference, criticism of the Four Power Treaty was unfocused. The vocal opponents of the treaty were former irreconcilables. Before a credible threat to ratification could be mounted, other factions within the Senate would have to join the attack. The confusion over the obligations of the treaty suddenly created a more complex treaty debate. The Harding statement propelled Gilbert Hitchcock (D, Nebraska) into the opposition camp. During the Versailles Treaty debates Hitchcock had become a formidable figure in foreign policy making. In 1922 he was the ranking Democrat on the Senate Foreign Relations Committee. His power in Senate politics was further enhanced by his leadership of those opposed to the election of Oscar Underwood as Senate minority leader. As a result of the Harding statement, Gilbert Hitchcock reversed his earlier support of the Four Power Treaty and declared himself to be an opponent.[6]

Other Democrats soon joined Hitchcock in criticizing the Four Power Treaty. They enjoyed the opportunity to chide a Republican president for excessive detachment. They used the theme of executive ignorance continuously, carrying it into the floor debates over the treaty. When the Four Power Treaty was submitted to the Senate, Hitchcock led the Democratic offensive by reminding the members of the president's gaffe in December.[7]

The suggestion that the United States might be compelled to defend the Japanese home islands (with no reciprocal commitment) generated a widespread criticism of the treaties. William Borah joined in the criticism of his party's president. In a statement to the press he mused, "We have now had two different interpretations inside of six hours. Let some mathematician tell us how many interpretations we

---

[5] *Congressional Record*, 67th Congress, 2nd Session, December 21, 1921, p. 629.

[6] *Baltimore Sun*, December 22, 1921, p. 1.

[7] *Congressional Record*, 67th Congress, 2nd Session, March 2, 1922, p. 3233.

will get inside of ten years."[8]

The Harding comments on the obligations of the treaty stirred an entirely new issue. Many of the Senate supporters had assumed the Japanese home islands were not covered in the treaty obligations. When confronted with the definitive interpretation by the State Department, their support was suddenly thrown into question. The *New York World* reported, "The Senate buzzed like an angry hive all day. The most menacing thing about the buzzing was the statement of various Republicans that they agreed with the president in his interpretations and if the treaty meant anything else they would oppose its ratification."[9] In the face of mounting public opposition in the United States, the delegates at the Washington Conference recognized that they had to exclude the Japanese home islands from the provisions of the treaty. In February the signatories of the Four Power Treaty signed a supplementary treaty that defined Japanese insular possessions as "only Karafuto, Formosa and the Pescadores, and the islands under the mandate of Japan."[10]

The signing of the supplementary treaty ended the debate over the definition of Japanese insular possessions. However, it did not end speculation over other secret commitments that had been included in the Four Power Treaty.

In an effort to reveal the true intent of the treaty, opponents pushed to have the president provide the Senate with all of the documentation related to the Four Power Treaty. They wanted not just the American delegation's report, but complete minutes of the negotiations as well as drafts of the treaty that had been considered by the four delegations. Because of the general support for the concept of "open diplomacy," the Senate approved of a resolution calling for all such documentation on February 16, 1922.

President Harding was not willing to provide this kind of detail to the treaty's critics. He emphatically refused to submit the documentation called for in the Senate's resolution. He defended the prerogatives of delegates to maintain confidential negotiations and asserted that minutes of informal discussions were not a required aspect of diplomacy.[11]

In fact, Harding's position regarding confidentiality had strengthened during the

---

[8] The *New York World*, December 21, 1921, p. 1.

[9] The *New York World*, December 22, 1921, p. 1. Other press coverage identified the Harding gaffe as a critical point in the ratification process. The *Chicago Herald Examiner*, which had favored the irreconcilable movement, saw the statement as an accidental revelation of a duplicitous plot, December 21, 1921, p. 1. Newspapers that supported the treaty agreed with the importance of the event; see the *Washington Evening Star*, December 22, 1921, p. 1, and the *Baltimore Sun*, December 21, 1921, p. 1.

[10] Thomas Buckley demonstrated that much of the force for this change came from Foreign Minister Uchida Yasuya. Uchida argued that the inclusion of the home islands set Japan apart as an inferior member of the agreement. Buckley, *The United States and the Washington Naval Conference*, 139–141.

[11] Warren Harding to Senate, February 20, 1922, Washington Conference Records, National Archives.

preceding weekend. The first draft of the president's response had argued that documentation could not be provided to the Senate because no such documentation existed. However, Secretary of State Hughes suggested that any reference to an absence of records be removed from the reply to the Senate. The president's refusal should be based exclusively in the terms of diplomatic protocol. In fact, informal records of the negotiation did exist, but Hughes felt it unwise to release them to the Senate.[12] The administration tried to stem the criticism by simple assertions that no hidden commitments existed.

Despite administration assertions that no secret agreements had been formed during the Four Power Treaty negotiations, speculation continued. Faced with constant denials of secret agreements by the delegation, treaty opponents began looking to other sources for information. On February 17, 1922, a meeting of the Council on Foreign Relations featured an address by Paul Cravath. Cravath was a noted authority in international law and the vice president of the Council. He was an advocate of international organizations and had been a supporter of American entry into the League of Nations. His speech endorsed the Four Power Treaty as a breakthrough in American diplomacy. Cravath's endorsement of the Four Power Treaty was anticipated; what was not expected was his claim that the treaty constituted the formation of a special relationship between the United States and Great Britain. This special relationship would provide the first step to American entry into the League of Nations under a Republican president.

Cravath subsequently denied that he had suggested a secret alliance existed between the United States and Great Britain. Nonetheless, William Borah interpreted his address as an accidental announcement of a secret pact. He argued on the floor of the Senate that Cravath was in a position to know the true meaning of the Four Power Treaty "as well as any man in the United States outside of the members of the conference itself." The old populist fear of Wall Street manipulation was suddenly introduced into the debate when Lee S. Overman (D, North Carolina) reminded the Senate that Cravath was "Morgan's attorney."[13]

The reaction to this address at the Council on Foreign Relations sparked a series of denials. Lodge, Underwood, and Hughes all denied that they had spoken to Cravath and that they had committed the United States to any special alliance. Elihu Root was conspicuous in his silence regarding the Cravath address. When asked by the press, Root refused to confirm or deny any conversations with Cravath.[14] Supporters of the Four Power Treaty assumed a defensive position and

---

[12] "Memoranda of interviews relating to Four Power Treaty together with drafts are in my office safe. Laurence Greene has had charge. I doubt advisability of suggesting any question of Department's possession of drafts. It should also be remembered in discussing records of conference that minutes of sub-committees were not sent to Senate." Hughes to State Department, February 20, 1922, Washington Conference Records, National Archives.

[13] *Congressional Record*, 67th Congress, 2nd Session, March 20, 1922, p. 4119.

[14] Buell, *The Washington Conference*, 185. See also the *New York Times*, March 21, 1922, and *Congressional Record*, 67th Congress, 2nd Session, March 10, 1922, p. 3666.

framed most of the debate as a proof that no secret agreement existed between the four signatories. The issue of secret treaties would remain one of the primary issues of debate.

THE SENATE AND THE FOUR POWER TREATY

The first level of debate would occur in the Senate Foreign Relations Committee. Lodge wanted to move the treaties out of committee quickly. As chairman, he determined whether or not hearings were needed. Lodge decided that additional information was unnecessary and did not schedule formal hearings or call for any expert testimony. Unlike the circumstances of the Versailles Treaty debates, opponents of the treaty could not use committee sessions to focus public attention on potential problems. William Borah would have to organize the opposition movement without the institutional assistance of the Senate's committee system.

Under the leadership of Henry Cabot Lodge, the Senate Foreign Relations Committee attempted to curb the debate through the language of the resolution for ratification.[15] When the Four Power Treaty was presented to the full Senate for consideration, its resolution for ratification stipulated that "there is no commitment to armed force, no alliance, no obligation to join in any defense." This legislative disavowal of an alliance was then reinforced by statements from members of the delegation to the Conference. Secretary of State Hughes sent a letter to the Senate declaring that no secret alliance existed between the United States and Great Britain.[16] However, most of the responsibility for blunting the claims of a secret treaty fell to Henry Cabot Lodge.

In his efforts to undermine the opposition's claim of secret diplomacy, Lodge argued that the negotiations between the Four Powers had been perfectly innocent. No minutes were kept because the meetings were informal and it did not occur to the delegates to ask that a stenographer be present.[17] Lodge went on to caution members of the Senate. He argued that the war had been fought for nothing if the powers of the postwar world could not achieve a peaceful international order. Resistance to the Four Power Treaty was not inspired by healthy skepticism; it was a result of unwarranted and destructive fear. If the United States could not participate in the construction of a new world order, the victims of World War I

---

[15] Garraty, *Henry Cabot Lodge*, 406, and Buckley, *The United States and the Washington Naval Conference*, 178–179.

[16] *Congressional Record*, 67th Congress, 2nd Session, March 21, 1922, p. 4158. The text of the letter was sent from Charles Evans Hughes to Oscar Underwood on March 11, 1922, Washington Conference Records, National Archives.

[17] *Congressional Record*, 67th Congress, 2nd Session, March 8, 1922, p. 3547. This disagreement had begun months earlier. In August Lodge and Borah had debated the nature of the Republican opposition to the secrecy of the Versailles negotiations. Lodge argued Wilson's fault lay in his refusal to respond to Senate inquiries, not in his presence at secret committee sessions; Borah claimed the whole process had been flawed. *Congressional Record*, 67th Congress, 1st Session, August 23, 1921, pp. 5510–5511.

had perished in vain.[18]

Notwithstanding these appeals to statesmanship, the opponents of the Four Power Treaty would not compromise. Those former irreconcilables who opposed it were too committed to a rigorous defense of American sovereignty. Those Democrats who joined them were too driven by partisan hostility to cooperate with a Republican administration.

Democrats dominated the opposition movement in the early days of the floor debate for the Four Power Treaty. The attack was an overt retaliation for the Republican opposition to the Versailles Treaty. One of the most biting criticisms came from the populist Democrat Tom Watson (D, Georgia):

> "Let us not blight the hope of the world," says the Senator from Massachusetts. That reminds me of what President Wilson stated to Congress when he said if they rejected the League of Nations it would "break the heart of the world." The thoughts are the same. Here are two hearts that beat as one, at last.[19]

This sort of sarcasm had limited force. Not only were the Democrats the minority party, but they were divided. Many followed the direction of the party leader, Oscar Underwood, and supported the Four Power Treaty. The success of the opposition movement was dependent on the combined efforts of Democrats and insurgent Republicans. As a result, a strange alliance was formed between Wilson internationalists and irreconcilables.

In the early days of the Senate debate the Republican opponents of the treaty refrained from making speeches. The energy of the early attacks came from Democrats led by Gilbert Hitchcock. These opposition speeches did not represent a consistent ideological focus. Partisan sniping notwithstanding, attacks on the treaty failed to concentrate on a single issue or set of issues. Like the earlier attacks on the Versailles Treaty, the debate covered the spectrum of political criticism. The attacks of the Wilson Democrats were strangely reminiscent of the irreconcilable attacks on the Versailles Treaty. At the same time, Democrats argued that the Four Power Treaty was a weak reflection of Wilson's attempt to reform international politics.

This inconsistency was symptomatic of a focus on partisan rivalry that held all Republican foreign policy suspect. One of the most complex attacks came from Senator Joseph Robinson (D, Arkansas). His initial efforts raised the old irreconcilable issue of naive American diplomats being manipulated by perfidious British politicians. He suggested that the Four Power Treaty was an element in some grand British design to preserve the Empire, that Lord Balfour had won more at the diplomatic table in Washington than any British army had gained on the

---

[18] *Congressional Record*, 67th Congress, 2nd Session, March 8, 1922, p. 3552.
[19] *Congressional Record*, 67th Congress, 2nd Session, March 8, 1922, p. 3561.

battlefield.[20] However, Robinson's criticisms were not a result of simple-minded isolationism. He argued that the Four Power Treaty was incapable of dealing with the complex problems of international cooperation. The treaty's deficiency was that it involved too few nations. The Four Power Treaty protected only the interests of the four signatories, not the territorial interests of other governments involved in Asian politics.[21]

The Democratic assault on the Four Power Treaty included an emphasis on the issue of manipulation—the American delegates had been manipulated by the British diplomats into creating an international system where powerful nations would control the weak. This aspect of the attack permitted an alliance with the former irreconcilables who opposed the treaty. Finally, on March 13, 1922, the Republican opponents joined in the Senate floor debate.

The Republicans who opposed the treaty had been active during the winter. William Borah and Hiram Johnson had led the public criticism of the Four Power Treaty from the day of its announcement. They both made extensive use of the press and public-speaking engagements. However, they had not participated in the first days of the floor debate. Those Republicans who spoke on the treaty in the early days of the debate were proponents of the treaty, led by Henry Cabot Lodge and Walter Edge (R, New Jersey). This pattern changed when Hiram Johnson took the floor to condemn Lodge's efforts to call for a close of debate and immediate consideration of the treaty. Johnson's attack was reminiscent of the Republican defense during the League of Nations debates; he asserted, "When advocates of the League of Nations and the new alliance rail at the Senate because it moves cautiously and with prudence and care, their shafts in reality are directed not at the Senate, but at the Constitution."[22]

Opponents of the Four Power Treaty wanted time. A drawn-out debate on the floor of the Senate might exhaust some of the supporters of the treaty. In the past the specter of acrimony had been enough to force concessions out of the leadership of the Republican party. The treaty could only be defeated if debate were extended. In an effort to continue the debate, both Johnson and Borah became active participants.

Once they joined in the floor debates, the Republican opponents focused on constitutional issues. Hiram Johnson's attacks on the Four Power Treaty mirrored the earlier defense against encroachments of war powers by the League Council. In 1919 the irreconcilables had feared that even the moral obligations created by Wilson's version of the treaty were too great a threat to legislative power. This fear was rekindled in 1922 during the Four Power Treaty debates. Hiram Johnson explicitly connected the Versailles Treaty and the Four Power Treaty debates; both constituted threats to congressional war powers.[23] Despite these appeals to a

---

[20] *Congressional Record*, 67th Congress, 2nd Session, March 10, 1922, p. 3667.

[21] *Congressional Record*, 67th Congress, 2nd Session, March 13, 1922, p. 3785.

[22] *Congressional Record*, 67th Congress, 2nd Session, March 13, 1922, p. 3775.

[23] *Congressional Record*, 67th Congress, 2nd Session, March 13, 1922, p. 3778.

defense of the Constitution, Hiram Johnson was not able to sway the Republican supporters of the treaty. Most Republicans were convinced that the Four Power Treaty did not infringe on the powers of the legislative branch.

William Borah also joined the debate on March 13. Rather than stressing constitutional issues or reiterating his charges of secret diplomacy, Borah questioned the efficacy of the Four Power Treaty. He argued that the treaty would incite hostility in the weaker nations of Asia, that "every outside nation will regard it as a covert threat to its interests."[24] By engendering this sort of opposition, the treaty would ultimately destabilize East Asia. Furthermore, the treaty's provisions for full diplomatic consultation would not be able to defuse tension once it had been generated. He reminded the Senate of the diplomatic situation that existed in Europe on the eve of the Great War:

> In 1914 there was machinery for conferring between [*sic*] the members of the entente; there was no difficulty about conferring between [*sic*] the members of the triple alliance. They had a perfect machinery and used it to confer repeatedly and effectively during the latter days of July, 1914 and the first days of August of that year. . . . Now I ask the supporters of this treaty where is the method provided by it by which to communicate and to confer between those who are outside of this group and the group?[25]

Borah's analysis of the treaty's deficiencies had no real impact on the course of the debate. His efforts to persuade more of the former irreconcilables to join the ranks of the Four Power Treaty opponents failed. Most of those Republicans who had helped him block U.S. entry into the League of Nations either spoke in favor of the treaty or sat in silent support. Only Robert LaFollette joined the Borah and Johnson position. Opposition to the Four Power Treaty could not be constructed as an issue in a broad insurgent agenda; rather it was a noisy manifestation of the Republican fringe.

The Senate continued to debate the Four Power Treaty until March 24. The tone of the debate remained essentially the same. Democrats dominated the attacks on the treaty. The Republican criticism was limited to the ardent attacks of Borah, Johnson, and LaFollette. Henry Cabot Lodge felt no need to compromise with the opponents in his own party. The supporters of the treaty firmly reiterated the benefits of the pact and denied any hidden objectives.

Henry Cabot Lodge had achieved his goals during the debates over the Four Power Treaty. Most members of his party were convinced that the treaty was not a result of secret diplomacy. The extensive press coverage of the conference plenary sessions, combined with the high level of respect for the integrity of Charles Evans Hughes, reinforced the declarations that the Four Power Treaty was

---

[24] *Congressional Record*, 67th Congress, 2nd Session, March 13, 1922, p. 3788.
[25] *Congressional Record*, 67th Congress, 2nd Session, March 13, 1922, p. 3787.

a product of open diplomacy. The constitutional issues of legislative control over war powers had been contained. Because the treaty made no clear reference to the use of military force, most Republicans felt it did not provide a clear threat to congressional prerogatives in foreign policy making. This interpretation had been reinforced by Henry Cabot Lodge's support of a reservation that stipulated complete congressional control over American actions in East Asian politics. The vigor of the opposition movement had not affected the general level of support for the treaty.

On March 24, 1922, the Senate ended debate on the Four Power treaty and held the votes for ratification. As the Senate considered the treaty article by article, the opponents attempted to limit its force through amendments.[26] These amendments concentrated on the same issues that had been raised in the debates over Article X of the League of Nations Covenant. Attempts were made to provide the signatories with the right to withdraw from the agreement before its ten-year expiration date. Several amendments were designed to narrow the definition of aggressive acts that would prompt joint resolution of diplomatic problems. A number of amendments defended the congressional control of war powers. Nearly all of these amendments were sponsored by Democrats; Hiram Johnson was the only Republican to introduce an amendment from the floor.[27] None of these proposed amendments attained the necessary majority support of the Senate.

When the Senate finally voted on the resolution for ratification of the Four Power Treaty, it voted on the text reported out by the Senate Foreign Relations Committee. Two-thirds of the Senate voted in support of ratification. Henry Cabot Lodge and Oscar Underwood were successful in holding together their bipartisan coalition. The final vote on the Four Power Treaty was sixty-seven in favor, twenty-seven opposed, and two not voting.[28] The administration succeeded with

---

[26] According to Senate Rule XXXVII, treaties had to be considered in two stages. First, the treaty was considered article by article; amendments from the floor were considered at this point. Then, the treaty was considered as an entire document; this second phase was the appropriate stage to make amendments to the ratification resolution or to any amendments or reservations recommended by the Senate Foreign Relations Committee.

[27] In all, nine amendments were introduced from the floor. James Reed (D, Missouri) proposed four; Joseph Robinson (D, Arkansas) proposed two; Gilbert Hitchcock (D, Nebraska) proposed one; John Shields (D, Tennessee) proposed one; and Hiram Johnson (R, California) proposed one. All of these amendments failed. The only amendment that was successfully attached to the treaty was the one proposed by the Senate Foreign Relations Committee. Sixteen attempts were made to amend that amendment; all of these attempts failed as well.

[28] Those senators opposed to the treaty were William Borah (R, Idaho), Joseph France (R, Maryland), Hiram Johnson (R, California), Robert LaFollette (R, Wisconsin), Henry Ashhurst (D, Arizona), Thaddeus H. Caraway (D, Arkansas), Charles A. Culberson (D, Texas), Peter G. Gerry (D, Rhode Island), Carter Glass (D, Virginia), William J. Harris (D, Georgia), Pat Harrison (D, Mississippi), James T. Heflin (D, Alabama), Gilbert Hitchcock (D, Nebraska), William King (D, Utah), Lee Overman (D, North Carolina), Key

a margin of four votes. The ratification demonstrated that the opposition was essentially partisan. Only four Republicans voted against the ratification. William Borah had failed to convince the former irreconcilables that the Four Power Treaty constituted a direct threat to American interests.

Despite the existence of a fundamental tension within the Republican party, William Borah and Hiram Johnson had been unable to make the Four Power Treaty an issue in insurgent politics. The signing of the supplementary agreement, which excluded the Japanese home islands from the Four Power Treaty, had assuaged the fears of many Republicans, regular and insurgent alike. The weak commitments of the treaty, requiring only that the parties negotiate fully and frankly, had not inspired a general fear for U.S. sovereignty. Some former irreconcilables, notably Miles Poindexter (R, Washington), were vocal advocates of the Four Power Treaty.[29] Other irreconcilable opponents of the League of Nations were simply unmoved by the cautionary pronouncements of Borah and Johnson.[30] Borah had not been able to provoke a credible threat to Republican solidarity. As a result, the politics of insurgency could not be applied in the Four Power Treaty debates.

With the passage of the Four Power Treaty, Henry Cabot Lodge sought to move the Senate to consideration of the rest of the Washington Conference treaties. Although the supporters of the administration had secured the first ratification vote, the opponents of the treaty were not willing to accept defeat. Joseph Robinson (D, Arkansas), one of the most active participants in the floor debate, moved for a two-day adjournment. He argued that so much time had been taken up by the Four Power Treaty debates that senators' other official duties had been neglected. He also announced that the opponents of the Four Power Treaty planned to offer amendments to the next item for consideration: the supplementary treaty, which excluded the Japanese home islands from the Four Power Treaty. The movement for a two-day adjournment failed; Henry Cabot Lodge was joined by Oscar Underwood in a call for continuation of debate.

On March 25 opponents of the Four Power Treaty reopened their assault. Led by Gilbert Hitchcock, the Democratic opponents argued that the previous day's vote had violated Senate rules. He claimed that these violations nullified the ratification vote and threatened to appeal the matter to the Supreme Court.[31]   An

---

Pittman (D, Nevada), Joseph Reed (D, Missouri), Joseph Robinson (D, Arkansas), Morris Sheppard (D, Texas), John Shields (D, Tennessee), Furnifold Simmons (D, North Carolina), Ellison Smith (D, South Carolina), Augustus Stanley (D, Kentucky), Claude Swanson (D, Virginia), David Walsh (D, Massachusetts), Thomas Walsh (D, Montana), and Thomas Watson (D, Georgia).

[29] See Allen, *Poindexter of Washington*, 232–235.

[30] George Norris, who had a record of adamant resistance to involvement in European diplomacy, showed no concern over the Four Power Treaty. His autobiography fails to even mention the controversy over the treaty.

[31] Hitchcock argued that two breaches of the Senate rules had occurred. First, official declarations of interpretation that had been signed by Charles Evans Hughes simultaneous to the signing of the Four Power Treaty should have been included as part of

extraordinarily acrimonious debate ensued and occupied the Senate for two days. Despite the vehemence of the debate and a near breakdown of Senate protocol, Henry Cabot Lodge was able to bring the Four Power supplementary treaty to a vote. As promised, two attempts were made to amend the treaty; both failed. The resolution for ratification of the supplementary treaty passed with a vote of seventy-three for, none against, and twenty-three not voting. Many of those senators not voting had voted against ratification of the Four Power Treaty, but would not vote against the supplementary treaty.

With the vote on the supplementary treaty, the opposition movement collapsed. Of all the Washington Conference treaties, the Four Power Treaty had been the agreement most open to attack in the Senate. Because it addressed the sensitive issue of collective security, it was open to the same sort of opposition that had been aimed at Article X of the League of Nations Covenant. However, the opposition movement had not been persuasive enough. Republicans who had been fearful of the power of the League Council did not necessarily have misgivings regarding the Four Power Treaty's less specific calls for full and frank discussion. Opponents of the treaty had been unsuccessful in convincing a sufficient number of Republicans to break with their party's leadership. The Harding administration recognized the nature of its success. Charles Evans Hughes praised Lodge and credited the victory to the senator's astute sense of congressional politics.[32] The administration's victory with the Four Power Treaty guaranteed that the debate on the remaining Washington Conference treaties would be relatively uneventful.

THE COMPLETION OF THE DEBATE OVER THE WASHINGTON CONFERENCE TREATIES

The Five Power Treaty, which established limits on naval armament, had been the primary objective of the Conference. It recognized ratios of size between the signatories, giving the two-ocean navies of the United States and Great Britain parity and the navy of Japan a marginal inferiority. Technological innovation in battleship building was curbed through a naval-building holiday and through limitations on the caliber of weapons used on capital ships. Limitation on the number and size of battleships served to limit fleet strength to the status quo.

Secretary of State Hughes's decision to limit the naval arms talks to capital ship agreements was a departure from William Borah's original call for a scrapping of 50 percent of the ships in the world's major navies. Furthermore, the concentration on capital ship limitation neglected the rise of a new form of sea power—the aircraft

---

the text of the treaty considered by the Senate. Second, Senate rules require that after consideration of the articles of the treaty by the Committee of the Whole, the vote for the entire text of the treaty must lay over for one day. *Congressional Record*, 67th Congress, 2nd Session, March 25, 1922, p. 4548.

[32] Charles Evans Hughes to Henry Cabot Lodge, April 1, 1922, Washington Conference Records, National Archives.

carrier. During the negotiations in November and December, Charles Evans Hughes had continued to follow the recommendations of the General Board of the Navy, and focused his efforts on battleships and large cruisers. The navy was still reluctant to accept the preliminary findings of Billy Mitchell on the potential of air attacks in naval warfare. However, William Borah was impressed by Mitchell's efforts and became convinced that aircraft carriers constituted a serious threat to disarmament efforts.

Borah had publicly criticized the Five Power Treaty when the agreement was first made public. He continued his efforts into the floor debates on the treaty, arguing that the treaty neglected the destabilizing force of air warfare. He ultimately asserted that the treaty marked a triumph in disarmament, but his support was qualified, "I should regard this treaty as a disaster rather than a benefit if the treaty should be regarded either here in the Senate Chamber or elsewhere as comprising all that there is to do in the matter of disarmament even during the next 10 years, the life of the treaty."[33] Nonetheless, William Borah would vote in support of ratification.

The debates over the Five Power Treaty proceeded rapidly. The navy supported the treaty and few members of the Senate were willing to dispute the expert opinion of the General Board. The questions raised by senators centered on the issues of air warfare and fortification of the Pacific bases. All the senators but Joseph France (R, Maryland) were willing to defer to the Department of the Navy. Even Hiram Johnson, who was often an acerbic critic of career diplomats and military officers, was not willing to attack the provisions of the Five Power Treaty. He demurred, "I would not for an instant put any view of mine in contradistinction to the views of the experts and our military and naval strategists. . . . I shall therefore yield my personal views of article 19 [maintaining the status quo on the fortification of Pacific naval bases] and vote for the ratification of the treaty as reported."[34]

Despite any misgivings they had regarding the Five Power Treaty, both Borah and Johnson advocated its ratification. The partisan attacks, which had been led by Gilbert Hitchcock, also ceased during the consideration of the naval limitation agreement. The final vote for the treaty was seventy-four in favor, one opposed, and twenty-one not voting. Although the number of senators not voting was high, this could not be construed as a silent opposition to the treaty. Most of these men were absent on business of the Senate and had announced in the *Record* that they supported the treaty.

The rest of the Washington Conference treaties followed a ratification pattern similar to that of the Five Power Treaty. The treaty to limit the use of submarines and noxious gases passed with a vote of seventy-two in favor and none opposed after virtually no discussion. The resistance to the two treaties regarding China was minimal.

---

[33] *Congressional Record*, 67th Congress, 2nd Session, March 29, 1922, p. 4704.
[34] *Congressional Record*, 67th Congress, 2nd Session, March 29, 1922, p. 4706.

The Nine Power Treaty was designed to guarantee the territorial integrity of China. Such a guarantee had been part of U.S. foreign policy since the McKinley administration and was universally accepted by American politicians. Opposition to the Chinese Customs Treaty was based on its failure to transfer complete authority for customs collection to the Chinese government at once. However, William King (D, Utah) was the only member of the Senate to vote against the customs treaty. He based his vote on the argument that the United States had the moral obligation to guarantee complete Chinese sovereignty.

The insurgent support of the Nine Power treaty was typified by William Borah. The treaty was perceived as a simple symbolic act that would do no harm and could improve the status of the Chinese republican government. Although Borah's support was not enthusiastic, it was certain. He argued, "I do not think a man or a nation can make a moral resolution to reform himself or itself too often, although it may not be lived up to. I have always believed in taking a New Year's resolution, and I have found sometimes it has helped for a considerable period."[35] The treaties regarding China advocated nothing more than established American foreign policy objectives. No change in U.S. military power was generated; no new diplomatic responsibilities were created. As such, they could not spark an insurgent revolt.

On March 30 the debates of the Washington Conference treaties were completed. Six treaties had been considered during the previous month and in each case the resolution for ratification attained the necessary two-thirds majority of the Senate. The Republicans achieved the foreign policy victory that they had denied Woodrow Wilson two years earlier.

The success of the Washington Conference did not mark a simple partisan victory, however. It demonstrated that the leadership of the Republican party had developed a full understanding of the complexities of insurgent politics. Throughout the negotiation and ratification process, the Republican leadership had prevented the formation of any substantive opposition within their own party. As a result, the conference treaties could not be used as an instrument in intraparty politics. For the next two years, the party leadership would maintain control of the initiative in foreign policy making.

---

[35] *Congressional Record*, 67th Congress, 2nd Session, March 30, 1922, p. 4780.

8

The Election of 1924
and the Collapse of the Insurgency

Remember that you are Henry Cabot Lodge, the Senior Senator from
Massachusetts, the senior of all the Senators in the United States and the
leader of the majority in the Senate. Remember also that the National
Conventions are sucked oranges to you.

—George Moses

The Washington Conference was a triumph for Secretary of State Charles Evans
Hughes. The treaties that had been produced by the conference were heralded as
the cornerstone of postwar diplomacy. The Four Power Treaty, Five Power Treaty,
and Nine Power Treaty collectively created a new order in Pacific politics. The
Washington Conference would be the foundation for diplomatic relations between
the wartime Allies. However, Secretary Hughes's triumph went beyond the scope
of international politics. The Washington Conference had marked a decisive
victory over insurgency.

Between 1918 and 1921 Republican opponents of the League of Nations had
been successful in their use of insurgent tactics. The threat of a second bolt had
been enough to block any Republican party support of U.S. entry into the League.
Republican insurgents like William Borah and Hiram Johnson had been able to
defend their version of American nationalism. They saw the League of Nations as
a threat to sovereignty, and therefore cooperation with that organization had to be
avoided. However, the Washington Conference demonstrated that Borah and
Johnson would have trouble converting specific opposition to the League of
Nations to a more generalized opposition to collective security arrangements. It
was clear that a significant minority in the Senate opposed the membership of the
United States in the League of Nations as well as cooperation with that
organization. What was not clear was the acceptability of increased American
activity in other international organizations.

In fact, a paradox had emerged in American foreign policy. It had become obvious that substantial resistance to participation in international organizations existed in the United States. At the same time, politicians and their constituents accepted, and even encouraged, greater American activity in international relations. The expansion of American economic power, which had begun during the war, continued in the postwar years with little opposition from any segment of the Republican party. The political climate that had prevented U.S. entry into the League of Nations presented no barrier to increased banking and commercial activity abroad. Despite all the rhetoric concerning the evils of Wall Street, insurgents supported certain types of economic expansion in foreign markets, particularly in the area of agricultural exports.[1] They were willing to support legislation that would facilitate international marketing of key agricultural products.

As a result, Republican internationalists were able to secure support for federal intervention in the international economy. In 1919 the Edge Act was pushed by congressional Republicans. It removed Federal Reserve restrictions on international financial transactions by American banks and permitted American banks to establish operations in foreign countries.[2] This concern with international finance continued into the Harding administration. Across the spectrum of the Republican party, politicians sought to maintain high levels of trade with Europe through the manipulation of finance.[3] In 1922 it was William Borah who called for an international conference to restructure reparations payments; this call ultimately led to the creation of the Dawes Plan in 1923.[4] Insurgent support for economic expansion, particularly that which would benefit farmers, demonstrated that opportunities existed for the Republican party to call for accelerated American involvement in international relations. The party leadership could implement treaties by carefully skirting the problems that had been raised over Article X of the League of Nations. More important, objections by Borah and his supporters would not cover the entire scope of foreign policy. The administration could focus on the

---

[1] The most extensive treatment of this pattern appears in Johnson, *Peace Progressives.* See also Warren I. Cohen, *Empire without Tears: America's Foreign Relations, 1921–1933* (Philadelphia: Temple University Press, 1987), 22–27; A. B. Genung, *The Agricultural Depression Following World War I and Its Political Consequences* (Ithaca: Northeast Farm Foundation, 1954); and Edwin G. Nourse, *American Agriculture and the European Market* (New York: McGraw-Hill Book Company, Inc., 1924).

[2] See Mira Wilkins, *The Maturing of Multinational Enterprise: American Business Abroad from 1914 to 1970* (Cambridge: Harvard University Press, 1974), 50.

[3] Although they often differed with the administration on the specifics of international economic relations, insurgent Republicans either supported American commercial activity abroad or remained silent on the issue through 1923. Hiram Johnson provided an exception to this pattern, consistently condemning American involvement in international economic cooperation. After 1924 insurgents took on a more aggressive critique of American banking abroad. See Johnson, *Peace Progressives*, 151–167.

[4] Diary Letters, December 22, 1922, Johnson Papers.

areas of common ground between the party leadership and the insurgents. After the Senate debates over the Washington Conference treaties, Charles Evans Hughes concentrated his efforts on defining the boundaries of insurgent opposition and searching for a way to expand U.S. involvement in international organizations without dissent.

EXPANDING UNITED STATES COOPERATION WITH THE LEAGUE OF NATIONS

During the debates over the Four Power Treaty, pro-League senators predicted that the treaty's passage marked the first step toward U.S. membership in the League of Nations.   However, Secretary of State Hughes understood the divisiveness of the League issue. He did not construe his victory at the Washington Conference as the end of irreconcilable sentiment in the Senate. He understood that the U.S. government could continue to expand its involvement in international politics despite opposition to the League of Nations.

The Harding administration had maintained a limited working relationship with the League of Nations. This relationship was exemplified by the position of the U.S. government on German reparations. During the debates over the separate peace with Germany, insurgents had added an amendment to the treaty that prevented U.S. participation in reparations talks without specific congressional approval. Although this effectively blocked normal American diplomatic activity on the Reparations Commission, the United States continued to be a factor in the negotiations.   The United States stationed a permanent observer with the Reparations Commission. In addition, the Harding administration continued to maintain a force of American occupation troops in the Coblenz Occupation Zone. Despite pressure from irreconcilable members of the Senate, more than 12,000 troops remained in Germany and participated in the enforcement of reparations collection. The presence of these troops made the United States a de facto participant in the debates over the collection of reparations.[5]

Relations between the United States and the League of Nations followed the basic pattern of the American occupation force in Germany. Interaction tended to be idiosyncratic. Anti-League sentiment in the Senate prevented the formation of a consistent policy of formal relations. Nonetheless, the United States maintained a functioning diplomacy with the League. The Department of State continued to station observers with League agencies. These observers reported League activities to the U.S. government, as well as providing members of the League secretariat and representatives of member states with information concerning current American positions on policy questions. Relations with the League were then supplemented by diplomacy toward the leading member states. The United States could

---

[5] See Keith Nelson, *Victors Divided* (Berkeley: University of California Press, 1975). The United States finally withdrew from Coblenz in February 1923 in reaction to the French seizure of the Ruhr.

coordinate its diplomatic activities with the League and generate a de facto League policy.

The secretary of state believed the United States had a legitimate role in European political affairs. Such an involvement required a certain level of cooperation with the League of Nations. Hughes was particularly interested in expanding this activity in the area of international adjudication.

This interest in the international justice system was founded in the policies of earlier Republican administrations. The Republican party had advocated an expanded use of international courts since the end of the nineteenth century. The administrations of McKinley, Roosevelt, Taft, and Wilson had all encouraged an increased reliance on courts of arbitration. Under these presidents, the United States had come to rely on judicial arbitration to settle specific classes of disputes. Although this increased dependence on arbitration had been stalled in 1911 when the Senate failed to ratify the Anglo-American General Arbitration Treaty, the leaders of the Republican party continued to support the concept of international adjudication. During the administrations of Woodrow Wilson, Republican luminaries such as Elihu Root, William Howard Taft, and Charles Evans Hughes promoted the expansion of a world court system.

The Republican supporters of international adjudication were confronted with a new problem in the postwar period. The earlier Republican emphasis on arbitration and adjudication had assumed the use of the Permanent Court of International Justice at the Hague. However, this World Court was placed under the administration of the League of Nations after World War I.[6] The League's influence over the Permanent Court consisted of its control of the election of the eleven judges; each judge had to be elected by a majority in both the League Assembly and the League Council. U.S. participation in this reorganized World Court could be construed as an establishment of formal relations with the League, and so Secretary Hughes had been reluctant to advocate full American participation in the World Court during the first two years of the Harding administration. However, the success of the Washington Conference gave the secretary reason to believe that U.S. entry into the World Court might be accepted.[7]

THE CONTINUING PROBLEM OF THE REPUBLICAN INSURGENCY

During the fall of 1922 Hughes began to pressure Harding for entry into the World Court. The president resisted Hughes's counsel, arguing that controversies

---

[6] This transfer had occurred at the recommendation of an international commission headed by Elihu Root. The decision of this group of jurists was made before the power of the irreconcilables had fully demonstrated itself. The assumption of Root and the others had been that the League would be a genuinely international organization, with representation from all the major powers.

[7] U.S. Department of State, *Foreign Relations of the United States, 1923*, vol. 1, Harding to Senate, February 24, 1923, pp. 17–18.

over domestic issues already threatened the cohesion of the party. The effort to achieve U.S. membership in the World Court was further complicated by the congressional elections of 1922, when Republican conservatives suddenly saw their political power diminished.

The election demonstrated that progressive reform was not dead. The postwar economic slump had produced political dissatisfaction and conservative Republicans were under attack from both Democrats and progressive politicians from their own party. As a result of the election, the Republican majority in the Senate was reduced to nine.[8] This alone boded well for insurgents, whose votes now provided the Republican majority. In addition, the course of specific elections further energized agrarian progressives. The internationalist Frank Kellogg, who tended to support business interests when voting on domestic legislation, lost his seat to the Farm-Laborite, Henrik Shipstead. The North Dakota senator Porter McCumber, who had defended Wilson's League as well as several conservative domestic programs, was defeated in the Republican primary by Lynn Frazier. A further insurgent victory occurred when Robert Howell defeated the leading Democratic defender of Wilson's League of Nations, Gilbert Hitchcock. The election demonstrated that calls for federal restraint of monopolies and aid to distressed farmers still appealed to voters; it also indicated that support for American participation in international organizations was weak in the West.[9]

Even the victories of the more conservative Republican candidates implied advantages for the insurgents. Henry Cabot Lodge, who had represented Massachusetts in the Senate since 1893, faced serious opposition in the 1922 election. Victory would require more than a strong state organization, more than the endorsement of the Harding administration. To secure the election, Lodge needed the rhetorical skills of leading insurgent politicians. This fostered an unlikely alliance between Lodge and Hiram Johnson.[10] Other Republicans sought to use Johnson's gift for rhetoric. The insurgent senator suddenly found his talents in demand for the 1922 election. The implications for power within the Republican party were not lost on Johnson, who mused, "[W]e did not amount to much in the

---

[8] The previous Republican majority had been fifty-nine Republicans to thirty-seven Democrats. In the Sixty-eighth Congress that substantial majority was whittled down to fifty-one Republicans, forty-three Democrats, and two nonpartisans who had strong ties to the Republican insurgency.

[9] The new members of the Senate who would be sympathetic to the insurgent agenda were Smith W. Brookhart (R, Iowa), Lynn Frazier (R, North Dakota), Robert Howell (R, Nebraska), Henrik Shipstead (F-L, North Dakota), and Burton Wheeler (D, Montana). They would be joined by Magnus Johnson (F-L, Minnesota) after a special election in 1923.

[10] This relationship is revealed in a letter from Hiram Johnson to Henry Cabot Lodge. "I can't tell you how delighted I was to receive your note of August 31. It touched me very deeply. After all, the charm of the Senate is in its personal associations; and to have from one whose good opinion I value, and whose friendship I treasure, a note of such kindly expression, was a source of infinite pleasure and gratification." Johnson to Lodge, September 29, 1922, Johnson Papers.

intervals between political fights in the Republican Party, but when it came to going to the people, there was a different situation, then our stock went soaring."[11]

The results of the election were disquieting to the Harding administration. In an effort to preserve some of his administration's domestic goals, Harding called for a special session of Congress in December. In this way, his proposed legislation would confront a less hostile Congress. Harding's first priority was to clear the domestic agenda; Hughes was asked to postpone consideration of the World Court.[12]

THE PROPOSAL FOR U.S. ENTRY INTO THE WORLD COURT

Finally, in response to pressure from his secretary of state, on February 24, 1923, President Harding requested that the Senate consent to American adherence to the Protocol of Signature, which established the Permanent Court of International Justice. Under the court's protocol the United States already had the right to bring cases forward for adjudication. The American jurist, John Bassett Moore, was serving as a judge on the court. The primary effect of the Senate's consent would be the requirement that the United States provide financial assistance for the maintenance of the Court.[13]

The Harding proposal came to the Senate at the end of the Sixty-seventh Session of Congress. Adjournment was scheduled for March 3. If the Senate did not act immediately, final consideration of American entry into the World Court would have to be made by the Sixty-eighth Congress, which had been elected in 1922. Timely action by the Senate was problematic; acceptance of the Protocol of Signature would have to be approved first by the Senate Foreign Relations Committee. In an effort to ease passage through committee, the administration designed its position to placate the committee's chairman, Henry Cabot Lodge.

Hughes had been careful to qualify the conditions of U.S. entry into the Court. Members of the Permanent Court fell into two categories: those nations that were permitted to submit cases to voluntary arbitration and those nations that chose to submit all conflicts to compulsory arbitration.[14] Hughes recognized that efforts to bind the United States to compulsory arbitration would be futile. The issues regarding the protection of American sovereignty that had been raised in the debates over the League of Nations were not new in 1919. The Senate had considered numerous arbitration agreements; at no time had that body indicated acceptance of the concept of compulsory general arbitration.

During the 1911 debates over the Anglo-American General Arbitration Treaty,

---

[11] Johnson to Frank P. Doherty, May 13, 1922, Johnson Papers.

[12] Berrits Memorandum, 35a, Hughes Papers.

[13] U.S. Department of State, *Foreign Relations of the United States, 1923,* vol. 1, Hughes to Harding, February 17, 1923, pp. 10–17.

[14] Of the forty-six signatories of the Protocol of Signature in 1923, only fifteen had signed the clause for compulsory arbitration. Pusey, *Charles Evans Hughes*, vol. 2, 599.

when the Senate had last considered a commitment to general arbitration, Henry Cabot Lodge had led the fight to block ratification. Hughes understood the limitations of Lodge's commitment to American activity in international organizations. Henry Cabot Lodge was an ardent nationalist. He believed that the United States was a nation of sufficient stature to take a leading role in international relations. However, Lodge was reluctant to trade an authoritative position in international politics for a diminution of political independence.

The conditions on World Court entry set by the Harding administration were inadequate. Despite the earlier cooperation between Secretary Hughes and Senator Lodge, both at the Washington Conference and during Lodge's 1922 senatorial campaign, the administration's request would be stalled in the Senate.[15] Citing the committee's concerns over the protection of U.S. sovereignty, Henry Cabot Lodge requested additional information from the administration. Hughes responded to Lodge's concerns, but it was clear that there would be no Senate action before adjournment.[16]

The delayed action on the Protocol of Signature was a result of the hesitation of Henry Cabot Lodge. It worked to the advantage of the two Foreign Relations Committee insurgents, William Borah and Hiram Johnson. Both men were suspicious of the administration's motives. However, as long as Lodge maintained his resistance to the World Court, the insurgents would have to do little to block U.S. entry.[17] Nonetheless, they would have the opportunity to discuss the World Court as a political issue during the 1924 election campaign.

Hughes viewed the situation as only a temporary setback. This delay provided the administration with an opportunity to garner public support for the World Court, which could be used to inspire Senate action. The focus of Hughes's attention was the legal community. In April he spoke before the American Society of International Law and in June he participated in the Kent Centennial Celebration at Columbia University.[18] The Court was portrayed as the most viable mechanism for guaranteeing world peace. His arguments grew out of the classical progressive interpretation of international politics—that economic development and the

---

[15] Lodge faced a two-sided threat in the 1922 election. His nomination was contested by Joseph H. Walker, who polled a startling 68,000 votes in the primary. Massachusetts Democrats also saw Lodge as an important target. The Democratic national platform of 1920 had condemned him by name. The Democratic organization for his state placed most of its campaign energy into the senatorial race of 1922. Lodge recognized that he had been targeted and pointedly asked Hughes for assistance. Despite the fact that Hughes despised making campaign speeches, he made a major address in Symphony Hall in Boston on behalf of Lodge. Hughes to Lodge, September 28, 1922, Hughes Papers. See also Garraty, *Henry Cabot Lodge*, 408–414.

[16] U.S. Department of State, *Foreign Relations of the United States, 1923*, vol 1, Hughes to Harding, March 1, 1923, pp. 19–24.

[17] Insurgents would become more vocal in their criticism of the World Court after the death of Henry Cabot Lodge. Johnson, *Peace Progressives*, 171–172.

[18] Pusey, *Charles Evans Hughes*, vol. 2, 600–601.

expansion of democracy were predicated on rational discourse. Rational discourse could best be achieved in a climate of adjudication.

Despite the successful efforts of the secretary of state to promote public support of the Permanent Court of International Justice, the Senate would not consent to adherence of the Protocol of Signature. Although Hughes continued to urge Senate support of the World Court, domestic political problems in the summer of 1923 overwhelmed foreign policy concerns. Just as the League of Nations had been sacrificed to party solidarity in 1919–20, the Permanent Court of International Justice would be sacrificed to party solidarity in 1923–24.

THE INSURGENCY AND THE NOMINATION OF CALVIN COOLIDGE

Republican party politics would continue to be limited by the demands of the insurgency. That group was still a force to be reckoned with in 1923; however, the substantial Republican majorities in the Sixty-seventh Congress had undercut much of their political power during the previous two years. For two years western progressives had sniped at Harding's policies of lowering the profile of the federal government. Issues surrounding agricultural policy, tax rates, election reform, and collective security had all sparked debate within the Republican party. William Borah and Hiram Johnson were not alone in accusing the Republican leadership of abandoning progressive values. Robert LaFollette and George Norris continued to promote their visions of progressive reform with the same energy they had exercised in 1911. Other politicians from the old insurgent constituencies had been elected since the 1912 bolt; they joined the first generation of insurgents in the policy debates of the 1920s. However, although a body of insurgent politicians existed, they had great difficulty forming a coherent political movement. As had been demonstrated in the Four Power Treaty debates, those Republicans who could be described as insurgents did not agree on all issues.

Events in the summer of 1923 would lead to the reemergence of the insurgent threat. For months the Harding administration had been tainted with the speculation of scandal. The cronyism practiced by the president and his friends had never reached critical proportions in the first two years of his presidency. In part, this can be attributed to the protection Harding afforded his longtime political allies. The affable Harding was popular with the general public and inoffensive to the rest of the Republican party's leadership. His tendency to suppress rumors concerning misguided lieutenants served to defuse accusations of political corruption.[19] All this would change on August 2, 1923 when Warren Harding died of cerebral apoplexy.

Shortly after the president's death, the Senate opened an investigation into abuse

---

[19] Ellis W. Hawley, *The Great War and the Search for a Modern Order: A History of the American People and Their Institutions, 1917–1933*, 2nd ed. (New York: St. Martin's Press, 1992), 61, and Robert Murray, *The Harding Era* (Minneapolis: University of Minnesota Press, 1969), 426–437.

of power by members of the Harding cabinet. Questions regarding the disposition of federally controlled oil reserves in Teapot Dome, Wyoming, and Elk Hills, California, suddenly emerged to unify the Republican insurgency and spark the public's sense of outrage.

Presented with the Teapot Dome Scandal, the insurgents could capitalize on their strength in Congress. Although they were a disparate political group, the insurgents were not totally unorganized. On December 1, 1922, Robert LaFollette set the groundwork for a new congressional caucus dedicated to a progressive agenda. It was similar to his earlier attempts to forge an insurgent bloc in Congress; LaFollette was convinced that the election of 1922 was the beginning of a second era of progressive politics. This new group was to be chaired by George Norris; its ultimate goal was to end the influence of big business in American politics.[20]

By LaFollette's account this congressional caucus would be the instrument for antiadministration reform. It was a political refuge for those Republicans offended by the Harding administration's efforts to lower taxes and promote corporate growth. Although LaFollette assumed the group would be dominated by Republicans, he welcomed participation by Democrats and Farm-Laborites.[21] He hoped that the creation of a strong caucus would provide an institutional framework that would support the insurgent agenda.

LaFollette's objectives would be difficult to meet. Although there was significant support of the progressive agenda in Congress, politicians did not readily turn to him for leadership. His most caustic critic was Hiram Johnson, who accused him of appealing to "the lunatic fringe." In a letter to Charles McClatchy, the editor of the *Sacramento Bee*, Hiram Johnson described the December 1 meeting in LaFollette's office:

> Borah attended it for ten minutes, and in his usual clever fashion became both a part of the gathering, and not a part of it. [Peter] Norbeck would not attend. [Charles] McNary told me he would not be a part of the bloc, and the two Progressive Congressmen from California, [Henry] Barbour and [Philip] Swing, would have nothing to do with it. It is needless to say to you that I would not enter into a LaFollette organization, however much I might believe in some of the things he would suggest or do. Indeed, I would not become a member

---

[20] Belle Case and Fola LaFollette, *Robert M. LaFollette*, vol. 2 (New York: The Macmillan Company, 1953), 1066.

[21] LaFollette named William Borah (R, Idaho), Smith W. Brookhart (R, Iowa), Arthur Capper (R, Kansas), Joseph France (R, Maryland), Lynn Frazier (R, North Dakota), Edwin Ladd (R, North Dakota), Charles McNary (R, Oregon), George Norris (R, Nebraska), Robert Owen (D, Oklahoma), Morris Sheppard (D, Texas), Henrik Shipstead (F-L, Minnesota), and Burton Wheeler (D, Montana) as members of this progressive congressional caucus.

> of any organization here which might, in any degree, control my
> freedom of action in the future.[22]

Johnson's criticisms highlight the fundamental liability of this progressive caucus—Robert LaFollette. During his service in the Senate, LaFollette had alienated virtually every member of the body. Conservatives had to contend with the brunt of his attacks, but LaFollette frequently expanded the scope of his charges and accused other progressives of a lack of commitment to reform. His accusations against Theodore Roosevelt in 1912 had helped to divide the progressive movement that had formed under the Taft administration. More important, they had generated long-lasting resentment within the insurgency. His opposition to compromise was seen as an impediment to reform by more pragmatic progressives. His claims to seniority in the progressive reform movement were questioned by many who had been his partners in the Taft insurgency.

Nonetheless, the insurgency had some institutional structure. By the fall of 1923 it also had an issue—the Teapot Dome Scandal. Teapot Dome renewed the emotional debate over political corruption that was the heart of progressive reform. Robert LaFollette had been trying to raise the issue of leaseholds on the naval oil reserves since the congressional elections in 1922. On October 22, 1923, the Senate Committee on Public Lands began a special investigation under the direction of Thomas Walsh (D, Montana).[23]

The Teapot Dome investigations did much to discredit the Harding administration. The public careers of Secretary of the Interior Albert Fall, Attorney General Harry Daugherty, and Secretary of the Navy Edwin Denby were destroyed. Despite these blows to key members of the party's leadership, the credibility of the Republicans remained intact.

The party was salvaged because Calvin Coolidge was not implicated in the scandal. Coolidge had been an active member of the Harding cabinet. He was the first vice president to be made a regular member of cabinet meetings and was present during cabinet policy discussions. As the presiding officer of the Senate, he had been the chief liaison for the administration in Congress. Because he was an active member of the administration, Coolidge was a target of the investigation. He was not implicated because the corruption scandal at Teapot Dome was not about policy making; it was about cronyism. Although Coolidge had been an active member of the administration, he had been outside of Harding's private

---

[22] Johnson to Charles K. McClatchy, December 8, 1922, Johnson Papers. See also Diary Letters, December 9, 1922, Johnson Papers.

[23] Burl Noggle attributed much of this delay to the extraordinarily busy schedule of Thomas Watson. Watson served on more committees than any other member of Congress, and so had little time to devote to the preliminary investigation. However, in the summer of 1923, Watson believed enough questions had been raised to conduct a formal hearing. See Noggle *Teapot Dome: Oil and Politics in the 1920s* (Baton Rouge: Louisiana State University Press, 1962), 32–63.

circle. He had never encouraged the appointment of his own political colleagues to positions in the federal government.[24] By 1924 the Republicans' greatest liability, the Harding coterie, was gone. The most important objective of the new president, Calvin Coolidge, would be to suppress open hostility between the insurgent progressives and the more conservative elements of the party.

Although their political styles differed greatly, Warren Harding and Calvin Coolidge were both dedicated to preserving the cohesion of the Republican party. Harding, possessing no real commitment to any political ideology, had always been ready to advocate policies of consensus. He was willing to construct complicated quid pro quo arrangements; and when he could not, he preferred to withdraw legislation rather than risk heated debate. He relied on his affability to secure Republican solidarity. When that failed, he turned to the parliamentary skills of the Republican leaders of Congress.[25]

In a different way, Calvin Coolidge would also rely on the power of his personality to lead the Republican party. Although he was certainly no intellectual, Coolidge was ideologically committed to conservatism. His support of conservative legislation was less easily swayed in the face of hostile legislators. His strength in holding the party together would be his placid demeanor. He was not garrulous as Harding had been, but he did evoke an instant confidence throughout the spectrum of the Republican party. He took on the role of Republican paterfamilias, a stern but loving master of his household. Politicians as different as Charles Evans Hughes, William Borah, and Henrik Shipstead regarded Coolidge with fondness.[26] With a few exceptions, most of the party's senior members saw Coolidge as a stabilizing force, capable of smoothing over rifts between conservatives and insurgents.

Calvin Coolidge operated with important political advantages. He was the incumbent. His actions to quell the Boston police strike, which had launched his career as a national politician, had given him the image of a no-nonsense leader. Because he remained detached from the Teapot Dome Scandal, he continued to enjoy national popularity. He was a credible candidate for the Republican nomination in 1924. Members of the party hoped to overcome the difficulties of the Teapot Dome Scandal and retain control of the White House after 1924. Most of the party's leaders recognized that this stability would be facilitated by a Coolidge nomination. This sentiment extended to a number of important insurgents. William Borah argued that the Republicans would benefit from

---

[24] In 1924 Robert Woods published a biography of Calvin Coolidge that was essentially a campaign document. He emphasized Coolidge's refusal to engage in cronyism or to use his position to pay off political debts in Massachusetts. See *The Preparation of Calvin Coolidge* (Boston: Houghton & Mifflin Company, 1924), 187–188.

[25] See Murray, *The Harding Era*.

[26] See Pusey, *Hughes*, vol. 2, 565; Mary Borah, *Elephants and Donkeys: The Memoirs of Mary Borah* (Moscow: The University Press of Idaho, 1976), 113; and Martin Ross, *Shipstead of Minnesota* (Chicago: Packard & Company, 1940), 60–61.

continuity of leadership. He believed that Coolidge should be given an opportunity to demonstrate his ability to preside over the party. It was in the interest of all the members of the party to see Coolidge succeed.[27]

Despite this political acceptability, Calvin Coolidge's position as the leader of the Republican party was not undisputed. His fundamental conservatism repeatedly sparked opposition among insurgent politicians. William Borah, Hiram Johnson, and Robert LaFollette all eventually emerged as figureheads of movements to wrest power from Coolidge.

The earliest push for a progressive candidate actually preceded Warren Harding's death and the question of the Coolidge succession. The same political problems that had led to the insurgent victories in the 1922 congressional elections spurred discussions of the presidency. In the spring newspapers began to suggest the feasibility of a bolt by William Borah. By the summer the *New York Nation*, the *Washington News*, and even the *New York Times* advocated Borah's leadership in a third-party movement against Harding. Borah did not dismiss this attempt to draft a third-party candidacy, and carefully maintained a collection of clippings in his political scrapbook.[28] However, this interest remained only superficial. After Harding's death, Borah felt he did not have sufficient reason to challenge Coolidge's position as party figurehead and failed to create any kind of national campaign organization.

The real assault on conservatism within the Republican party began during the primary elections in 1924. Hiram Johnson was not interested in a third-party challenge to Coolidge, but sought to take the Republican nomination away from him. Johnson's chances to unseat Coolidge were slim. Once again, he had failed to establish a strong national organization to coordinate his nomination bid. He preferred to rely on state and local Roosevelt Clubs to promote his candidacy. The campaign's organizational weakness was made worse by financial problems. Hiram Johnson lacked the money to make proper use of his political network. He even suffered defeat in his home state of California. Calvin Coolidge won that primary contest in six of the eleven congressional districts in the state. Winner-take-all rules eliminated the presence of a vocal cadre of Johnson supporters at the convention.[29] Hiram Johnson's strength in the 1920 contest had been the number of delegates he controlled via primary elections; he had no such firm base in the 1924 convention.

The Coolidge forces entered the convention process assured of victory. Press speculation centered on the selection of the president's running mate, not on the nomination of the candidate. Opposition on the convention floor was marginal. Neither Hiram Johnson nor Robert LaFollette was capable of generating an upset from the progressive wing of the party. Calvin Coolidge easily took the

---

[27] Borah to John W. Miller, February 8, 1924, Borah Papers.

[28] Borah Scrapbook, February 1922–August 1922, Borah Papers.

[29] Louise Overacker, *The Presidential Primary* (New York: Macmillan Company, 1926), 54.

Republican nomination with 1,065 of 1,109 votes.[30]

The Coolidge nomination secured the power of conservatives in the party. Because the margin of victory over Johnson and LaFollette was so great, the incentive to placate the insurgency was lost. The position of vice president did not need to be used to assuage the progressive wing of the party. Press speculation the week before the convention indicated that William Borah would be Coolidge's running mate. However, any commitment to appease the insurgency had evaporated after Borah turned down the vice presidential overtures. Next the conservative Frank Lowden was courted by the White House, but he also refused to join the ticket. The position ultimately fell to Charles Dawes. Dawes's credentials as a national politician stemmed from his work with government finance, since he had served as the first director of the budget in the Harding cabinet and as an architect of postwar German financial reconstruction. These institutional credentials were supplemented by his activity in the Minutemen of the Constitution, a grass-roots organization of midwestern businessmen dedicated to exorcizing "socialist influences" in the Republican party.

Insurgents found little comfort in the Republican party's platform of 1924, despite its repeated references to progressivism. In the opening days of the convention, insurgent Republicans had attempted to secure the adoption of a "Wisconsin platform" modeled on LaFollette's agenda for reform. This effort failed quickly. The platform that emerged from the convention was a conservative document. It applauded the growth of American capital and industry and condemned earlier efforts to strengthen the federal government's regulation of business. Insurgent Republicans found themselves in an uncomfortable situation. Those standing for reelection would have to accommodate themselves to a defense of limited public expenditures, lower taxes, a protective tariff, and minimal government involvement in business affairs.

The Republican platform underlined a fundamental division over the objectives of progressive reform within the Republican party. Although virtually all members of the Republican party considered themselves to be progressive, by 1924 the political term was so vague as to be meaningless. Coolidge's platform sought the progressivism of efficiency, not the progressivism of regulation. For the insurgents, regulation was the core of progressive reform.

Hostility from the insurgent wing of the party continued after Coolidge's substantial victory in June. Frustrated in their challenge to the party's conservatives, many insurgents were left in a political limbo. This problem was exemplified by the candidate Hiram Johnson. He would not bolt, nor would he take his defeat with magnanimity. He accused Coolidge of being a pawn of big business and feared the press had abandoned its defense of the common man.[31]

Coolidge's triumph at the convention was a result of the strength of his political

---

[30] The convention votes were 1,065 for Coolidge, 34 for Robert LaFollette, and 10 for Hiram Johnson.

[31] Diary letters, June 9, 1924, Johnson Papers.

machine. His campaign manager, William Butler, had created a steamroller that overwhelmed everything in its path. The Coolidge machine was prepared to face all opposition with unwavering resolve. This commitment was taken to extraordinary levels during the convention's keynote address, delivered by Representative Theodore Burton (R, Ohio). Burton condemned the Republicans of Congress for being insufficiently supportive of the president. He called on the convention delegates to join Coolidge in an effort to purge the party of disloyalty on Capitol Hill.[32]

Under the direction of William Butler, the Coolidge machine effectively silenced opposition from the Johnson and LaFollette ranks. In addition, Butler had done much to curb potential opposition from more conservative members of the party. He had constructed a tight defense of his candidate. Powerful Republicans whose loyalty to the president was questionable found themselves relegated to the background of the convention. These sanctions were even extended to Henry Cabot Lodge.

Henry Cabot Lodge had been a leading figure of the Republican party since the 1890s. His stature within the party leadership would suffer a significant blow at the Cleveland convention. Although both Lodge and Coolidge came from Massachusetts, they represented very different elements in their state's Republican party. Lodge had supported Coolidge's favorite-son nomination in 1920 and promoted his renomination in 1924. However, William Butler knew this support was insufficiently enthusiastic.[33] Furthermore, Lodge recently had failed to support the president on two important measures. He had voted to override Coolidge's veto of the Veteran's Bonus Bill and had helped to stall Senate consideration of the Protocol of Signature for the World Court. As a result of the failure to support the president, Lodge was not placed on any committee at the National Convention, nor was he permitted to address the convention. The stifling of Henry Cabot Lodge bespoke the formidable organization behind Calvin Coolidge. Lodge's health was poor and this was likely to be his last presidential nominating convention. Nonetheless, he was consigned to an insignificant role.

Lodge accepted the rebuke with magnanimity. He expressed no resentment, even to his associates. Lodge wanted to see a Republican victory in 1924, and believed that Coolidge was the best candidate. However, Lodge also recognized that the Republican party faced considerable obstacles. The political juggernaut that had served Coolidge well in Cleveland might fail him in a national election. Butler's actions at the convention had jeopardized the allegiance of the more senior members of the party. Support from insurgent politicians ranged from lukewarm to nonexistent. A third-party bolt could take away a significant faction of the

---

[32] *New York Times*, June 11, 1924, p. 1.

[33] John Garraty, *Henry Cabot Lodge*, 416–418. Some of the Coolidge biographers place more weight on the attitudes of the president, arguing that he had a much more active role at the convention. See Donald R. McCoy, *Calvin Coolidge: The Quiet President* (Lawrence: University Press of Kansas, 1967), 243.

Republican constituency. Coolidge would need more than a well-oiled political machine to counter the threat of a third-party bolt.

THE LAFOLLETTE BOLT AND THE FATE OF THE WORLD COURT

Robert LaFollette was the primary problem for Coolidge. Not only had LaFollette run against Coolidge for the Republican nomination, but he had also made it clear that he would stay in the presidential contest with or without the support of the Republican party. Immediately after the Cleveland convention, Robert LaFollette announced he would run as an independent progressive candidate. With Burton K. Wheeler as his vice presidential running mate, LaFollette hoped to forge a political movement dedicated to providing government regulation and reform. Although few national Republican politicians joined in the bolt, LaFollette was able to construct a national political machine. Calvin Coolidge would have to deal with both Democratic and Independent Progressive opposition.

The key to the LaFollette threat was the Teapot Dome Scandal. His political objective was to tie the president to the scandal; even without a direct link between Coolidge and the oil leases, Coolidge could be considered culpable in the affair. The Department of Justice had been slow in organizing the prosecution of Albert Fall. This question of inattention to public corruption became a cornerstone of LaFollette's campaign.

The focus of this progressive attack was viewed with concern by the leadership of the Republican party. Guy Emerson of the Republican National Committee worked to rally the party behind Coolidge. He believed that the independent candidacy of LaFollette could throw the election into the House of Representatives, where the antagonism of insurgent Republicans threatened conservative interests.[34]

This fear of the election being thrown into the House of Representatives was shared by several political commentators. N. O. Messenger of the *Washington Evening Star* spoke of the "grave possibilities" and "direful effects" on the American economy if the election were not resolved by the Electoral College.[35] Even though most of the insurgents had not joined the LaFollette bolt, their support of Coolidge was not resounding. They were sympathetic to the LaFollette platform. Enough of them might break ranks with the Republican party leadership to block the presidency of Calvin Coolidge.

The key disputes in the Republican party during 1924 were over domestic issues. However, foreign policy concerns were also included in the debate. The platform's foreign policy plank began with a full commitment to U.S. membership in the World Court. In the days preceding the Republican National Convention Calvin Coolidge met with Elihu Root, one of the most vocal Republican supporters of the international organization. The president made it clear that he backed his party's plank and would sponsor continued efforts to gain Senate acceptance of the

---

[34] Guy Emerson to Hughes, October 20, 1924, Hughes Papers.
[35] *Washington Evening Star*, October 22, 1924, p. 6.

Protocol of Signature.[36] In theory, Coolidge would be able to use his widespread support in the Republican party as a lever against the World Court opponents in the Senate. However, Calvin Coolidge would not be able to translate his power at the convention into Senate support of the Protocol of Signature for the World Court.

The leadership of Republican opposition to the World Court did not come from insurgent ranks, but rather from more conservative elements of the Republican party. George Wharton Pepper (R, Pennsylvania), who had been placed on the Senate Foreign Relations Committee in 1923, led the movement to require that the administration fully define the responsibilities of the United States in the World Court. This included an attempt to limit the power of the British Empire in an effort that was strikingly similar to the Johnson Amendment of the League of Nations debates. Pepper introduced a resolution that would deny the right of British dominions to vote in the League Assembly and Council when those bodies considered the election of judges to the World Court. Like the irreconcilables five years earlier, Pepper argued that governments that were not fully sovereign could not exercise the rights of sovereign nations.

Pepper's activities provided Borah and Johnson with a substantial political opportunity. The Coolidge administration focused much of its attention on Lodge and Pepper because they led the opposition to World Court entry. In fact, the opposition by insurgents on the Senate Foreign Relations Committee was more extreme than that of either Lodge or Pepper. Borah and Johnson allowed others to lead the opposition to the World Court Protocol, but their position was clear. In a letter to Albert Beveridge, Borah announced his unhesitating opposition, "So far as the Protocol is concerned, it seems to me to be one of the worst things that has been proposed so far."[37]

William Borah and Hiram Johnson felt free to construct their own resistance without risking the brunt of White House pressure. Their efforts were of a dilatory nature. They argued that other issues, such as the Isle of Pines Treaty, demanded precedence over the World Court Protocol. By pushing other legislative matters ahead of the World Court, they hoped to exhaust administration efforts.[38]

The U.S. entry into the World Court became increasingly problematic. Secretary of State Hughes and other World Court supporters were sensitive to the political complexities surrounding the issue. These concerns for the future of the World Court were revealed in correspondence between Hughes and the ambassador to the Court of St. James, Frank Kellogg. After Kellogg's defeat in the 1922 congressional elections, his service to the party was rewarded with a key ambassadorial post. A supporter of American participation in international organizations, Kellogg was concerned with the progress of the World Court Protocol in the Senate. He recognized that the British government favored increased U.S. dependence on arbitration and hoped to encourage this British

---

[36] *New York Times*, June 1, 1924, p. 1.

[37] Borah to Albert Beveridge, November 28, 1924, Borah Papers.

[38] *New York Times*, June 1, 1924, pp. 1-2.

support. However, he also feared antagonizing members of the Senate who were suspicious of international government. In a letter to Hughes, he reported that he "took particular pains to say I should not discuss the World Court, as it was pending before the Senate."[39]

Kellogg's attitude was particularly well founded. His efforts to achieve U.S. entry into the League of Nations in 1919 and 1920 had been thwarted by the efforts of Republican insurgents. Furthermore, his defeat in the election of 1922 had been a result of efforts by the Non-Partisan League. The core of support for the Non-Partisan League continued to be voters who favored a strong government dedicated to curbing big business. The Non-Partisan League was supportive of insurgent Republican politicians and would continue to aid them. He cautioned Secretary Hughes, "I am intensely anxious about this situation as I think it would be an awful calamity to the country to have the election thrown into the House of Representatives with combinations of LaFolleteism [*sic*] and Bryanism to work with."[40]

As the election approached, the administration became increasingly apprehensive. Fears of the election being sent to the House of Representatives were not allayed by the strength of the Coolidge machine. The LaFollette campaign continued to hammer away at the Teapot Dome Scandal and the issue of money and influence.

As had been the case in the Roosevelt bolt of 1912, most of the congressional insurgents stayed with the party in 1924. They continued grudging support for their party and refused to condemn the Coolidge candidacy. However, like the progressive bolters, they did bring into question the issues of money and political influence.

Once again, in the fall of 1924, the issue of campaign finances was raised by Congress. The special investigating committee was headed by William Borah, who had a well-established record as an advocate of limitations on campaign spending. The committee concerned itself with allegations of large-scale contributions to congressional campaigns. The first, and most important, of these allegations came from Thomas Walsh (D, Montana), who had headed the investigation of the Teapot Dome Scandal. Walsh contended that eastern businessmen had pooled $100,000 for his defeat.[41] Fearing widespread public condemnation of the election process, senators running for reelection made their campaign finances public. William Borah began the process by announcing he had budgeted $2,000 for his campaign, and had spent $597 by the third week in October. Conservative Republicans joined the ranks of those who supported full disclosure. Walter Edge (R, New Jersey) announced a campaign budget of $5,200. Francis Warren (R, Wyoming) declared he would not spend any money at all to be reelected.[42] In this climate of congressional frugality, the Coolidge campaign continued to raise money to defeat

---

[39] Frank Kellogg to Hughes, February 8, 1924, Hughes Papers.
[40] Frank Kellogg to Hughes, September 23, 1924, Hughes Papers.
[41] *Washington Evening Star*, October 23, 1924, p. 1.
[42] *Washington Evening Star*, October 24, 1924, p. 4.

the dual threat of the progressive candidate Robert LaFollette and the Democratic candidate John Davis.

In the last weeks of the presidential campaign one issue overshadowed all others —the power of money. As LaFollette preached against the influence of big business on American politics, foreign policy receded as a public concern. The Coolidge administration feared weakening the already fragile party structure and stopped pressing the Senate for consent of the Signature of Protocol for the World Court. The election was the immediate concern; U.S. entry into the World Court could be delayed.

The Coolidge administration depended on the continued solidarity of the Republican party. Collateral issues would not be emphasized for fear of antagonizing those whose loyalty to Coolidge might not be complete. The commitment of insurgent Republicans was already being strained by the issues raised in the LaFollette campaign. Furthermore, the tensions surrounding the election demanded that the secretary of state avoid open conflict with the chairman of the Senate Foreign Relations Committee. Calvin Coolidge would win a resounding victory in 1924, but part of the cost of that victory would be the Signature of Protocol for the World Court.

In 1924 the Republican party's ability to chart a direction for U.S. foreign policy was stalled. Despite the clear desire of Calvin Coolidge and Charles Evans Hughes, and despite a momentum that encouraged increased involvement in international organizations, the United States did not become a full member of the World Court. This foreign policy development failed to take place because Republican foreign policy was predicated on consensus and no consensus could be achieved. Because opponents of U.S. entry into the World Court held key positions on the Senate Foreign Relations Committee, they could effectively block any Senate action. The Coolidge administration feared the breakdown in party solidarity during a critical election, so it would not try to force Senate action. Once again Republican foreign policy had been held hostage.

Epilogue

I may be a little irregular on the start, but I am quite regular on the finish. When the fight against the League of Nations began, there were just six of us in the United States Senate against it, and when it closed we had seven million majority. So while irregular at the start, I finish regularly.

—William E. Borah

The election of 1924 marked the end of an era in the politics of the Republican party. Ever since the bolt by Theodore Roosevelt in 1912, the Republican leadership had been dedicated to conciliation and unity. Senior members of the party were careful to share power among the various factions; this meant that all factions, including progressives from farming states, would have a voice in party decisions. The years between 1912 and 1924 were notable as a period of uneasy truce among the various factions of the Republican party. This pattern continued through the election campaign of 1924, but the results of that campaign demonstrated that conciliation was not a prerequisite for electoral success. Like William Howard Taft, Calvin Coolidge suffered a bolt at the Republican convention and faced reelection against two opponents at the national level. Unlike the situation in 1912, the conservative Republican candidate for president in 1924 won reelection. Furthermore, this victory was substantial, with Coolidge receiving 54 percent of the popular vote and an overwhelming majority in the electoral college.

During the election, the leadership of the Republican party had been concerned with the problem of the LaFollette campaign. Coolidge supporters regularly referred to the potential problems of an election thrown to the House of Representatives. They responded to LaFollette's candidacy by emphasizing the image of the Wisconsin senator as a radical. The progressive candidate was portrayed as a man who would shake the very foundations of private enterprise in America. As part of the effort to emphasize this portrayal of LaFollette's threat to the economy, the administration was willing to put aside other issues in the campaign. As the election date approached, the administration's push for U.S. entry into the World Court lost its urgency. The Coolidge administration preferred to concentrate on the issue of LaFollette's radicalism and wanted to avoid controversy over foreign policy issues that could prompt further breakdown of party discipline.

The reelection strategy worked for Calvin Coolidge. Defections to LaFollette's camp were limited; debates among the factions remaining in the Republican party did not descend into acrimony. By steering away from policy debates that were potentially divisive, the Coolidge administration avoided a general breakdown of party discipline. The less frequent mention of the president's support for U.S. entry into the World Court was not indicative of a change in policy, but rather a desire to maximize the strength of the Coolidge candidacy.

With the substantial Coolidge victory, the Republican leadership could turn to the issue of party discipline. Coolidge's campaign manager, William Butler, had already demonstrated the willingness to punish errant senators. Henry Cabot Lodge had been relegated to a minor role at the Republican National Convention for opposing administration positions. This did not bode well for those senators who had bolted with LaFollette. Because there were so few of them, their punishment would have virtually no consequence for the strength of the Republican party in Congress. Logic dictated that the bolters would be penalized for their actions.

The party leadership declared its position on party loyalty and discipline through Vice President Charles Dawes's opening address to the Senate on March 5, 1925. Dawes used his first opportunity to castigate members of the upper chamber who opposed Calvin Coolidge. He decried Senate rules, complaining that a militant minority could defy the will of the president. After ridiculing the swearing-in ceremony, Dawes walked out of the chamber, leaving the Senate without a presiding officer.[1]

This general announcement of antipathy toward rebellious senators was made specific when the Senate finally began its session. When the Senate was reorganized for the opening of the Sixty-ninth Congress, Robert LaFollette (R, Wisconsin), Edwin Ladd (R, North Dakota), Smith Brookhart (R, Iowa), and Lynn Frazier (R, North Dakota) were excluded from Republican conferences. More important, they were not named to fill any Republican vacancies on Senate committees. This policy of ostracism was similar to that which had been exercised against Miles Poindexter in the wake of the 1912 election. Unlike the earlier case, the bolters of 1924 continued to be treated with some sympathy by those insurgents who had stayed with the party. The insurgent faction objected to the punishment

---

[1] *New York Times*, March 6, 1925, p. 1.

and the Republicans began to divide over the issue of party loyalty. The display of conservative power continued when the issue of committee assignments came to a vote on the Senate floor. The four bolters found they had allies among the insurgents who had stayed with the party, and a protest was made.

In the past, opposition from a large minority faction had been enough to spark an atmosphere of compromise. In 1925 the Republican leadership felt confident in its ability to impose punishment. This change in attitude was possible because the Democrats chose not to take advantage of the divisions within the Republican party. Presented with a division in the Republican ranks, the minority leader suddenly asked permission for the members of his party to refrain from voting on committee assignments. The conflict became a purely Republican affair and resulted in the defeat of the insurgent challenge. The insurgents had lost their ability to coerce their own party leadership with a threat of an alliance with the Democrats. Two of the most senior insurgents, William Borah and George Norris, continued to object to the treatment of the bolters. Nonetheless, the ostracism of the bolters continued until the election of 1926.[2]

Not only were errant Republicans punished, the administration faithful were rewarded after the election of 1924. Henry Cabot Lodge, whose health had been deteriorating over the previous year, died in November of 1924. The vacancy created by his death was then filled by William Butler, the architect of the Coolidge campaign. Not only did Butler receive the appointment as interim senator, but he was also given a seat on the Senate Foreign Relations Committee, the most prestigious committee in the Senate.[3]

The sequence of events between the election of Coolidge and the organization of the Sixty-ninth Congress boded well for the future of the Protocol of Signature of the World Court. It seemed that opponents of the court had lost much of their ability to use the institutions of government to block the president. Nonetheless, the United States would not join the World Court during the Coolidge administration.

Henry Cabot Lodge had been the single most influential Republican in the foreign policy debates between 1918 and 1924. As chairman of the Senate Foreign Relations Committee and as majority leader of the Senate, he had been able to dictate when treaties came to the Senate floor for consideration. He had been able to determine the parameters of the debate and could orchestrate changes in the

---

[2] There were limits to the punishment for the four bolters. They continued to hold their previous committee assignments, although they lost their seniority on those committees. In addition, a proposal was made to limit the ability of these senators to make personal staff appointments on Capitol Hill, an important source of patronage. This measure was defeated with the argument that the four had been sufficiently punished. Haynes, *The Senate of the United States*, 291.

[3] Frederick H. Gillett (R, Massachusetts) wanted the seat. As the former Speaker of the House, he was a man of considerable influence. However, the Foreign Relations assignment was given to Butler. Haynes, *The Senate*, 293.

treaty text. He had used these abilities to block Woodrow Wilson's version of the Versailles Treaty. He had also used them to steer the Four Power Treaty past Senate objections. Lodge had indicated that he would use his skills to oppose, not support, the Signature of Protocol of the World Court. He had raised a series of questions when the issue was introduced in the special congressional session of 1923. Although his criticisms were not vehement, he had very clear reservations about American participation in that international organization. Lodge's death meant that the force of his personality and his knowledge of the institutions of foreign policy making would no longer be a threat to Coolidge's support of the World Court.

Furthermore, the politics of insurgency had been devastated in the election of 1924. The LaFollette bolt had demonstrated the fundamental weaknesses of insurgent politics. The senior insurgents did not readily recognize the leadership of one man, and were reluctant to participate in a bolt led by someone else. The insurgent movement did have a vaguely defined political philosophy; the ideology that cemented these politicians together had been derived from the populism of the turn of the century. However, what made the movement stand out was not its ideology, but its confrontational style. The insurgency was born out of frustration; its members were willing to risk destruction of the Republican party to achieve their political goals. As long as party leaders like Henry Cabot Lodge feared for the solidarity of the Republican party, the insurgents could demand concessions from the moderates and conservatives. As long as the Democrats were willing to use (and be used by) the insurgents for their own political ends, the insurgents could influence Republican policy. Without organization under a single charismatic leader, without the key conciliator Lodge, and without the cooperation of the Democrats, the insurgents were open to attack from party conservatives.

Nonetheless, insurgency remained a force in Republican politics and continued to influence foreign policy making. The way that it operated in the political system changed, however. When the insurgency erupted during the Taft administration, it was a result of cumulative frustrations. Senate rules magnified the power of senior members and made the committees the centers of law making. Because they were junior, and were excluded from some of the most important committees in the Senate, the Taft insurgents could not afford to be subtle. By 1924 this situation had changed. This change was not in the way the Senate operated; the insurgents had not reformed the Senate rules between 1911 and 1924. However, the insurgents could be more effective under those rules during the Republican Ascendancy. Many of those who had revolted against Nelson Aldrich as first term senators were still in the Senate and had accrued considerable seniority. Since 1913 committee assignments reflected the diversity of the Republican party and the major committees were no longer bastions of conservatism. When Henry Cabot Lodge died in 1924, the chairmanship of the Senate Foreign Relations Committee passed to the most senior Republican on the committee, William E. Borah.

During the debates over the Versailles Treaty, Borah had learned to use Henry Cabot Lodge's fear of party disintegration. The insurgent techniques of confrontation and threatened alliance with the Democrats in Congress worked as effectively in debates over foreign policy as they did in the domestic policy area. As a result, the insurgent concerns of manipulation by Europeans and the rise of militarism became important elements in the foreign policy debate.

Insurgent methods had worked to force changes in foreign policy; however, they proved to be an inefficient means of legislating change. They required the ability to marshal public opinion and to use that public opinion to force political compromise. Too much was left to factors outside the control of insurgent politicians. Once William Borah became chairman of the Senate Foreign Relations Committee, he had at his disposal much more reliable methods of controlling legislation. As chairman, Borah came to rely on the technique of referring treaties to subcommittees for detailed consideration. Questionable treaties languished on the tables of subcommittees, a fact that encouraged the Coolidge (and later the Hoover) administration to consult with the insurgents before submitting treaties for ratification votes.[4]

Borah's power over the Senate Foreign Relations Committee was reflected in other ways as well. As chairman, Borah had influence over the assignment of new members of the committee. The Republicans would continue to guarantee that committee assignments would reflect the political diversity of the party. Conservatives and moderates would find places on the committee, but the rise of the insurgent presence was striking. During Borah's tenure as committee chairman, Arthur Capper (R, Kansas), Arthur Vandenberg (R, Michigan), and Robert LaFollette, Jr. (R, Wisconsin) were added to the committee. By 1931 five of the eleven Republicans on the Foreign Relations Committee were western progressives. Not only did these men share a commitment to domestic reform that focused on the plight of the farmer and the problem of corruption, they were sympathetic to Borah's vision of an insurgent foreign policy. Although they did not always agree on particulars, they sought to avoid U.S. membership in international organizations as well as large scale military spending.

In addition, other politicians who were sympathetic to insurgent ideas joined the committee under Borah's chairmanship. James Reed (D, Missouri) had been one of the two Democrats to join the irreconcilable opposition to the League of Nations. During the League debates he developed a working relationship with William Borah that continued through the consideration of the Four Power Treaty. Reed became a member of the committee in 1925, joining a Democratic faction that was often in agreement with Borah's vision of a new American foreign policy. These men—Key Pittman (D, Nevada), J. T. Robinson (D, Arkansas), and Thomas Walsh (D, Montana)—were willing to cooperate with Borah for ideological reasons, not

---

[4] When Arthur Vandenberg (R, Michigan) became chairman of the Senate Foreign Relations Committee in 1947, he was shocked at the number of treaties under consideration in subcommittees. Nearly all dated back to the chairmanship of Borah. In many cases all the members of the subcommittee were dead. Needless to say, the administrations that had proposed the treaties had long since given up hope of ratification.

simply to pursue a partisan program against Republican administrations. This non-Republican contingent was joined by Henrik Shipstead (F-L, Minnesota). The appointment of Shipstead demonstrated the influence of William Borah. It was remarkable because Shipstead consistently allied himself with insurgent Republicans; more important, he was the only member of the committee in the twentieth century who was not from one of the two major parties.

Borah's dominant position on the Senate Foreign Relations Committee assured continued insurgent influence over foreign policy making. Despite the support of Calvin Coolidge and Secretary of State Frank Kellogg, the Senate did not support the ratification of the Protocol of Signature of the World Court. U.S. entry into the World Court did not occur until after William Borah's death. His influence prevented the United States from entering the League of Nations or any international organization that was affiliated with the League.

This influence was reflected in other areas of foreign policy as well. Borah and other progressive Republicans pushed for an expansion of the naval arms control achieved by the Five Power Treaty. In response to this pressure, Calvin Coolidge sent a delegation to the Geneva Naval Conference with instructions to negotiate limits on the smaller cruisers, which had not been covered by the Washington Conference agreements. The insurgent influence on foreign policy took a slightly different turn when William Borah adopted the cause of the outlawry of war. In an effort to end aggression without the use of collective security or international organizations, Borah urged the president to brand aggressors as outlaw nations. This approach to international security took form in the Kellogg-Briand Pact. Throughout the 1920s American foreign policy making continued to be the compromised product of conflicting forces within the Republican party.

The insurgency did not die out after the election of 1924; it metamorphosed. As the elder insurgents gained seniority, they entrenched themselves as committee chairmen. William Borah's chairmanship of the Foreign Relations Committee was not an isolated case. By 1925 seven committees were chaired by insurgents, including the Agriculture and Forestry Committee, the Commerce Committee, and the Immigration Committee.[5] The senior members of the insurgency could use the

---

[5] The insurgents who held committee chairmanships in the Sixty-ninth Congress were George Norris (Agriculture and Forestry), Wesley Jones (Commerce), Arthur Capper (District of Columbia), William Borah (Foreign Relations), Hiram Johnson (Immigration), Charles McNary (Irrigation and Reclamation), and Peter Norbeck (Pensions). This trend toward committee chairmanships falling to insurgent politicians continued and intensified after the stock market crash in 1929. Growing voter dissatisfaction with conservative Republicans shifted power in the party toward the insurgent wing. When the Seventy-second Congress was organized in 1931 fourteen Senate committees were chaired by insurgents. They were Charles McNary (Agriculture and Forestry), Wesley Jones (Appropriations), Peter Norbeck (Banking and Currency), Robert Howell (Claims as well as Special Select Committee to Investigate the Alaska Railroad), Hiram Johnson (Commerce), Arthur Capper (District of Columbia), William Borah (Foreign Relations), Lynn Frazier (Indian Affairs), George Norris (Judiciary), Robert LaFollette, Jr.

committee system to frustrate conservative legislative programs.

The insurgency had developed the capacity to manipulate the committee system in the Senate. Although they seldom had enough power or cohesion to turn their political ideals into law, they were capable of blocking offensive legislation. As before, even after the party leadership lost its commitment to conciliation and compromise, the insurgent politicians were able to generate quid pro quo. The presidential veto would be balanced by the committee table.

The changes in the insurgency after the election of 1924 were complex. Although seniority was an increasingly important factor in insurgent power, the movement was not limited to second- and third-term senators. Republicans who had been influenced by populist ideology continued to be elected from the western and Great Plains states. Some of them, like Lynn Frazier (R, North Dakota), behaved like the insurgents of the Taft era. Frustrated by compromise, they relied on public confrontation. Pushed outside the channels of leadership in the Republican party, they relied heavily on denunciations of the conservative agenda.

This dependency on public denunciation was patterned after the political stance of Robert LaFollette, Sr. The Wisconsin politician based his career on his status as a gadfly. Those who followed him in the bolt of 1924 agreed with his belief in the futility of compromise with the conservative elements of the Republican party. When LaFollette died in 1925 others would continue unremitting attacks on party conservatives. However, the heirs of LaFollette would take on a fascinating complexity. The role of gadfly was taken up by those who had been cast out of the party in 1925, not by his son who succeeded to his father's seat in the Senate. Robert LaFollette, Jr., was no less committed to the insurgent ideal than his father. However, LaFollette, Jr., preferred political manipulation to denunciation. The son was more comfortable in the quieter realm of Washington's institutional politics than in the public arena of the press and political rally.

Henrik Shipstead (F-L, Minnesota) best exemplified the political complexity of the new insurgents. His constituency in Minnesota was essentially Republican. The Republican voters of his state had become disillusioned by the conservative dominance of the state party machine, but would not shift allegiance to the Democratic party. After his election to the Senate, Shipstead continued his posture as a Republican reformer who had separated himself from his party's conservative leadership. He supported the legislation of the Republican insurgents, and worked with them both in committee and on the floor of the Senate. However, Shipstead refused to adopt a position of obdurate opposition to the Republican leadership in the Senate. He accepted the status of senior Republican conservatives and became a student of their techniques of political manipulation.

On one remarkable occasion, Shipstead was faced by a classical political

---

(Manufactures), Samuel Shortridge (Privileges and Elections), and Gerald Nye (Public Lands and Surveys as well as the Select Committee to Investigate Contributions and Expenses of Senatorial Candidates).

problem. A group of his loyal constituents demanded a post office, but this service had absolutely no economic justification. In an effort to solve his problem, Shipstead consulted with one of the last remaining members of the Old Guard, Francis Warren (R, Wyoming). Warren suggested waiting until the closing minutes of the congressional session, then suddenly attaching an amendment to a key piece of legislation. The conservative senator told Shipstead to wait for an ideal moment of confusion and suggested the wording that would allow the amendment to pass unquestioned. The confusion erupted; the amendment passed; the village in Minnesota got its post office. The bemused Senator Warren asked Shipstead why he had asked for help from a political rival. Shipstead responded, "After all, thirty-four years in the Senate has taught you a great deal, and I, as I said, want to be educated."[6] The Senate insurgency had changed a great deal since 1911.

---

[6] Ross, *Shipstead of Minnesota*, 60–61.

Selected Bibliography

MANUSCRIPT COLLECTIONS

Anderson, Chandler. Papers. Library of Congress.
Borah, William E. Papers. Library of Congress.
Hughes, Charles Evans. Papers. Library of Congress.
Johnson, Hiram. Papers. Bancroft Library, University of California at Berkeley.
Knox, Philander. Papers. Library of Congress.
LaFollette, Robert, Sr. Papers. Library of Congress.
Lodge, Henry Cabot. Papers. Massachusetts Historical Society.
Pittman, Key. Papers. Library of Congress.
Records of International Conferences, Commissions, and Expositions. National Archives.
Records of the United States Senate. National Archives.
Root, Elihu. Papers. Library of Congress.

PUBLISHED DOCUMENTS

Danielski, David J., and Joseph S. Tulchin, eds. *The Autobiographical Notes of Charles E. Hughes.* Cambridge: Harvard University Press, 1973.
Link, Arthur, et al. *The Papers of Woodrow Wilson.* Vols. 50–65. Princeton: Princeton University Press, 1985–1991.
Lodge, Henry Cabot, and Charles F. Redmond, eds. *Selections from the Correspondence of Theodore Roosevelt and Henry Cabot Lodge, 1884–1918.* Vol. 2. New York: Charles Scribner's Sons, 1925.
Porter, Kirk H., and Donald Bruce Johnson, eds. *National Party Platforms, 1840–1964.* Urbana: University of Illinois Press, 1966.
U.S. Congress, *Congressional Record.* Washington, D.C., December 2, 1918–March 3, 1925.
U.S. Congress, Senate, Committee on Foreign Relations. *Treaty of Peace with Germany: Hearing before the Committee on Foreign Relations.* Washington, D.C., 1919.

U.S. Department of State. *Conference on the Limitation of Armament.* Washington, D.C.
        November 12, 1921–February 6, 1922.
_____. *Foreign Relations of the United States.* Washington, D.C., 1919–1925.
University Publications of America. *Papers of the Republican Party.* Part 1, Series
        A, 1913–1925.

SECONDARY SOURCES

Adler, Selig. "The Congressional Elections of 1918." *South Atlantic Quarterly* 36 (October
        1937): 447–465.
Allen, Howard W. *Poindexter of Washington: A Study in Progressive Politics.*
        Carbondale: Southern Illinois University Press, 1981.
_____. "Republican Reformers and Foreign Policy." *Mid-America* 44 (October 1962):
        222–229.
Ambrosius, Lloyd E. *Woodrow Wilson and the American Diplomatic Tradition.*
        Cambridge: Cambridge University Press, 1987.
Anderson, Chandler. "The Extent and Limitations of the Treaty-Making Power under
        the Constitution." *American Journal of International Law* 1 (July 1907):
        636–670.
Ashby, Darrel. "Progressivism against Itself: The Senate Western Bloc in the 1920s."
        Mid-America 50 (October 1968): 291–304.
Bagby, Wesley. "Progressivism's Debacle: The Election of 1920" (Ph.D. dissertation,
        Columbia University, 1960).
_____. *The Road to Normalcy: The Presidential Campaign and Election of 1920.*
        Baltimore: Johns Hopkins Press, 1962.
Bailey, Thomas A. *Woodrow Wilson and the Great Betrayal.* New York: Macmillan
        Company, 1945.
_____. *Woodrow Wilson and the Lost Peace.* New York: Macmillan Company, 1944.
Billington, Ray. "The Origins of Middle Western Isolationism." *Political Science Quarterly*
        60 (March 1945): 44–64.
Borah, Mary. *Elephants and Donkeys: The Memoirs of Mary Borah.* Moscow: The
        University Press of Idaho, 1976.
Borchard, Edwin. "A Limitation of Armaments." *The Yale Review* 15 (July 1926):
        625–644.
Boyle, Peter. "The Roots of Isolationism: A Case Study." *Journal of American Studies*
        6 (April 1972): 41–50.
Braisted, William. *The United States Navy in the Pacific, 1909–1922.* Austin: University
        of Texas Press, 1971.
Brands, H. W. *TR: The Last Romantic.* New York: Basic Books, 1997.
Broderick, Francis L. *Progressivism at Risk: Electing a President in 1912.* Westport,
        Conn.: Greenwood Press, 1989.
Brown, George. *The Leadership in Congress.* Indianapolis: Bobbs-Merrill Company,
        1922.
Buckley, Thomas. *The United States and the Washington Naval Conference, 1921–1922.*
        Knoxville: University of Tennessee Press, 1970.
Buehrig, Edward H. *Wilson's Foreign Policy in Perspective.* Bloomington: Indiana
        University Press, 1957.
Buell, Raymond Leslie. *The Washington Conference.* New York: D. Appleton and

Company, 1922.

Burke, Robert. "Hiram Johnson's Impressions of William E. Borah." *Idaho Yesterdays* 17 (Spring 1973): 2–11.

Burner, David. *The Politics of Provincialism: The Democratic Party in Transition, 1918–1932.* Cambridge: Harvard University Press, 1986.

Burnstein, Barton, and Franklin Leib. "Progressive Republican Senators and American Imperialism, 1898–1916: A Reappraisal." *Mid-America* 50 (July 1968): 163–205.

Calhoun, Frederick S. *Power and Principle: Armed Intervention in Wilsonian Foreign Policy.* Kent, Ohio: Kent State University Press, 1986.

Caroll, John F. "Henry Cabot Lodge's Contributions to the Shaping of Republican European Diplomacy, 1920–1924." *Capitol Studies* 3 (Fall 1975): 153–165.

Carr, E. H. *International Relations between the Two Wars.* London: Macmillan and Company, Ltd., 1948.

Clark, Joseph S., ed. *Congressional Reform: Problems and Prospects.* New York: Thomas Y. Crowell Company, 1965.

Clements, Kendrick A. *Woodrow Wilson: World Statesman.* Boston: Twayne Publishers, 1987.

Clubb, J. M. and H. W. Allen. "Party Loyalty in the Progressive Years: The Senate, 1909–1915." *Journal of Politics* 29 (August 1967): 567–584.

Cohen, Warren. *The American Revisionists: The Lessons of Intervention in World War I.* Chicago: University of Chicago Press, 1967.

_____. *Empire without Tears: America's Foreign Relations, 1921–1933.* Philadelphia: Temple University Press, 1987.

Coolidge, Archibald C. "Ten Years of War and Peace." *Foreign Affairs* 3 (September 1924): 1–21.

_____. *Ten Years of War and Peace.* Cambridge: Harvard University Press, 1927.

Coolidge, Calvin. *The Autobiography of Calvin Coolidge.* New York: Cosmopolitan Book Corporation, 1929.

Cooper, John Milton. *The Vanity of Power: American Isolationism and the First World War, 1914–1917.* Westport, Conn.: Greenwood Publishing Corporation, 1969.

_____. *The Warrior and the Priest: Woodrow Wilson and Theodore Roosevelt.* Cambridge: Harvard University Press, 1983.

Corwin, Edward. *The President, Office and Powers.* New York: New York University Press, 1940.

Costigliola, Frank. *Awkward Dominion: American Political, Economic, and Cultural Relations with Europe, 1919–1933.* Ithaca: Cornell University Press, 1984.

David, Paul, Ralph Goldman, and Richard Bain. *The Politics of National Party Conventions.* Washington, D.C.: The Brookings Institution, 1960.

DeConde, Alexander, ed. *Isolation and Security.* Durham, N.C.: Duke University Press, 1957.

Dennison, Eleanor. *The Senate Foreign Relations Committee.* Stanford: Stanford University Press, 1942.

Dimock, Marshall. "Woodrow Wilson as a Legislative Leader." *Journal of Politics* 19 (February 1957): 3–19.

Dingman, Roger. *Power in the Pacific: Origins of Naval Arms Limitation, 1914–1922.* Chicago: University of Chicago Press, 1976.

Downes, Randolph C. *The Rise of Warren Gamaliel Harding, 1865–1920.* Columbus: Ohio State University Press, 1970.

Ellis, L. Ethan. *Republican Foreign Policy, 1921–1933.* New Bruswick, N.J.: Rutgers University Press, 1968.

Ervin, Spencer. *Henry Ford vs. Truman H. Newberry, the Famous Senate Election Contest: A Study in American Politics, Legislation, and Justice.* New York: Richard Smith, 1935.

Ferrell, Robert H. *Woodrow Wilson and World War I, 1917–1921.* New York: Harper and Row, 1985.

Fisher, Louis. *Constitutional Conflicts between Congress and the President.* Princeton: Princeton University Press, 1985.

Fitzpatrick, John James. "Senator Hiram Johnson: A Life History, 1866–1945" (Ph.D. dissertation, University of California at Berkeley, 1975).

Fleming, Denna Frank. *The Treaty Veto of the American Senate.* New York: G. P. Putnam's Sons, 1930.

_____. *The United States and World Organization.* New York: Columbia University Press, 1938.

Gardner, Lloyd C. *Safe for Democracy: The Anglo-American Response to Revolution, 1913–1923.* New York: Oxford University Press, 1987.

Garraty, John. *Henry Cabot Lodge: A Biography.* New York: Alfred Knopf, 1968.

_____. *Woodrow Wilson.* New York: Alfred Knopf, 1956.

Gelfand, Lawrence E. *The Inquiry: American Preparations for Peace, 1917–1919.* New Haven: Yale University Press, 1963.

Girard, Jolyon P. "Congress and Presidential Military Policy: The Occupation of Germany, 1919–1923." *Mid-America* 56 (October 1974): 211–220.

Glad, Betty. *Charles Evans Hughes and the Illusions of Innocence: A Study in American Diplomacy.* Urbana: University of Illinois Press, 1966.

_____. *Key Pittman: The Tragedy of a Senate Insider.* New York: Columbia University Press, 1986.

Goodwin, George. "The Seniority System in Congress." In Joseph Clark, ed., *Congressional Reform: Problems and Prospects.* New York: Thomas Y. Crowell Company, 1965.

Gould, Lewis L. *Reform and Regulation: American Politics from Roosevelt to Wilson.* 2d ed. New York: Alfred Knopf, 1986.

Grimmett, Richard F. "Who Were the Senate Isolationists?" *Pacific Historical Review* 42 (November 1973): 479–498.

Guinsberg, Thomas N. "Victory in Defeat: The Senatorial Isolationists and the Four Power Treaty." *Capitol Studies* 2 (Spring 1973): 23–36.

Hansen, John Mark. *Gaining Access: Congress and the Farm Lobby.* Chicago: University of Chicago Press, 1991.

Hawley, Ellis W. *The Great War and the Search for a Modern Order: A History of the American People and Their Institutions, 1917–1933.* 2d ed. New York: St. Martin's Press, 1979.

Haynes, George. *The Senate of the United States.* New York: Russell and Russell, 1938.

Hays, Will. *The Memoirs of Will H. Hays.* New York: Doubleday and Company, Inc., 1955.

Hechler, Kenneth W. *Insurgency: Personalities and Politics of the Taft Era.* New York: Russell and Russell, 1940.

Heckscher, August. *Woodrow Wilson.* New York: Charles Scribner's Sons, 1991.

Hewes, James E. "Henry Cabot Lodge and the League of Nations." *Proceedings of* the *American Philosophical Society* 114 (August 1970): 245–255.

Hicks, John D. *Republican Ascendancy, 1921–1933.* New York: Harper and Row, Publishers, 1960.

Hinckley, Barbara. *Stability and Change in Congress.* New York: Harper and Row, 1977.

Hoag, C. Leonard. *Preface to Preparedness: The Washington Disarmament Conference and Public Opinion.* Washington, D.C.: American Council on Public Affairs, 1941.

Holt, James. *Congressional Insurgents and the Party System, 1909–1916.* Cambridge: Harvard University Press, 1967.

Holt, W. S. *Treaties Defeated by the Senate.* Baltimore: Johns Hopkins University Press, 1933.

Horowitz, David J. *Beyond Left and Right: Insurgency and the Establishment.* Urbana: University of Illinois Press, 1997.

Hughes, Charles Evans. "Some Observations on the Conduct of Our Foreign Relations." *American Journal of International Law* 16 (July 1922): 365–374.

Ichihashi, Yamato. *The Washington Conference and After.* Stanford: Stanford University Press, 1928.

Iriye, Akira. *After Imperialism: The Search for a New Order in the Far East.* Cambridge: Harvard University Press, 1965.

Israel, Fred L. *Nevada's Key Pittman.* Lincoln: University of Nebraska Press, 1963.

Jessup, Philip. *Elihu Root.* 2 Vols. New York: Dodd, Mead and Company, Inc., 1938.

_____. *The United States and the World Court.* Boston: World Peace Foundation Pamphlets, 1929.

Johnson, Claudius. *Borah of Idaho.* Seattle: University of Washington Press, 1936.

Johnson, Evans C. *Oscar W. Underwood: A Political Biography.* Baton Rouge: Louisiana State University Press, 1980.

Johnson, Robert D. *The Peace Progressives and American Foreign Relations.* Cambridge: Harvard University Press, 1995.

Kendrick, Jack E. "The League of Nations and the Republican Senate, 1918–1921" (Ph.D. dissertation, University of North Carolina, 1952).

Knock, Thomas J. *To End All Wars: Woodrow Wilson and the Quest for a New World Order.* New York: Oxford University Press, 1992.

LaFollette, Belle Case, and Fola LaFollette. *Robert M. LaFollette.* 2 Vols. New York: Macmillan Company, 1953.

LaFollette, Robert. *LaFollette's Autobiography.* Madison: The University of Wisconsin Press, 1913.

Latham, Earl, ed. *The Philosophy and Policies of Woodrow Wilson.* Chicago: University of Chicago Press, 1958.

Leopold, Richard. *Elihu Root and the Conservative Tradition.* Boston: Little, Brown and Company, 1954.

Levin, N. Gordon. *Woodrow Wilson and World Politics: America's Response to War and Revolution.* New York: Oxford University Press, 1968.

Link, Arthur. *Campaigns for Progressivism and Peace, 1916–1917.* Princeton: Princeton University Press, 1965.

_____. *Wilson: The New Freedom.* Princeton: Princeton University Press, 1956.

_____. *Woodrow Wilson and the Progressive Era, 1910–1917.* New York: Harper and Row, 1954.

_____. *Woodrow Wilson: Revolution, War, and Peace.* Wheeling, Ill.: Harlan Davidson,

Inc., 1979.

Lippmann, Walter. "Concerning Senator Borah." *Foreign Affairs* 4 (January 1926): 211–222.

Livermore, Seward W. "The Sectional Issue in the 1918 Congressional Elections." *Mississippi Valley Historical Review* 35 (June 1948): 29–60.

_____. *Woodrow Wilson and the War Congress, 1916–1918.* Seattle: University of Washington Press, 1966.

Lodge, Henry Cabot. "Foreign Relations of the United States, 1921–1924." *Foreign Affairs* 2 (June 1924): 525–539.

_____. *The Senate and the League of Nations.* New York: Charles Scribner's Sons, 1925.

_____. "The Treaty-Making Power of the Senate." *Scribners Magazine* (January 1902): 33–43.

Longworth, Alice Roosevelt. *Crowded Hours.* New York: Charles Scribner's Sons, 1933.

Louis, William Roger. *British Strategy in the Far East, 1919–1939.* Oxford: Clarendon Press, 1971.

Lovell, S. D. *The Presidential Election of 1916.* Carbondale: Southern Illinois University Press, 1980.

Lower, Richard. *A Bloc of One: The Political Career of Hiram Johnson.* Palo Alto: Stanford University Press, 1993.

Lowitt, Richard. *George W. Norris: The Persistence of a Progressive, 1913–1933.* Urbana: University of Illinois Press, 1971.

Maddox, Robert. *William E. Borah and American Foreign Policy.* Baton Rouge: Louisiana State University Press, 1969.

Margulies, Herbert F. *The Mild Reservationists and the League of Nations Controversy in the Senate.* Columbia: University of Missouri Press, 1989.

_____. *Senator Lenroot of Wisconsin: A Political Biography, 1900–1929.* Columbia: University of Missouri Press, 1977.

_____. "The Senate and the World Court." *Capitol Studies* 4 (Fall 1976): 37–51.

May, Ernest. *The World War and American Isolation, 1914–1917.* Cambridge: Harvard University Press, 1959.

Mayer, Arno J. *Political Origins of the New Diplomacy.* New Haven: Yale University Press, 1959.

Mayer, George H. *The Republican Party, 1854–1964.* New York: Oxford University Press, 1964.

McCoy, Donald R. *Calvin Coolidge: The Quiet President.* Lawrence: University Press of Kansas, 1967.

McDougal, Myres and Asher Lans. "Treaties and Congressional-Executive or Presidential Agreements: Interchangeable Instruments of National Policy." *Yale Law Journal* 54 (March 1945): 181–351.

McKenna, Marian C. *Borah.* Ann Arbor: University of Michigan Press, 1961.

Mowry, George E. *The California Progressives.* Berkeley: University of California Press, 1951.

_____. *Theodore Roosevelt and the Progressive Movement.* Madison: University of Wisconsin Press, 1947.

Murray, Robert. *The Harding Era.* Minneapolis: University of Minnesota Press, 1969.

_____. *The Politics of Normalcy.* New York: Norton, 1973.

Muskie, Edmund, Kenneth Rush, and Kenneth Thomson, eds. *The President, the Congress, and Foreign Policy.* New York: University Press of America, 1986.

Myers, William Starr. *The Republican Party: A History.* New York: The Century Company, 1928.

Nelson, Keith. *Victors Divided.* Berkeley: University of California Press, 1975.

Neu, Charles E. *The Troubled Encounter: The United States and Japan.* Malabar, Fl.: Robert E. Krieger Publishing Company, 1975.

Nevins, Allan. *Henry White: Thirty Years of American Diplomacy.* New York: Harper & Brothers Publishers, 1930.

Noggle, Burl. *Teapot Dome: Oil and Politics in the 1920s.* Baton Rouge: Louisiana State University Press, 1962.

Norris, George. *The Fighting Liberal: The Autobiography of George W. Norris.* New York: The Macmillan Company, 1945.

Nye, Russel. *Midwestern Progressive Politics: A Historical Study of Its Origins and Development, 1870–1950.* Lansing: Michigan State College Press, 1951.

O'Connor, Raymond G. *Perilous Equilibrium.* Lawrence: University of Kansas Press, 1962.

Osborn, George C. *John Sharp Williams.* Baton Rouge: Louisiana State University Press, 1943.

Overacker, Louise. *The Presidential Primary.* New York: Macmillan Company, 1926.

Parrini, Carl. *Heir to Empire: United States Economic Diplomacy, 1916–1923.* Pittsburgh: University of Pittsburgh Press, 1969.

Paxson, Frederic L. *Postwar Years: Normalcy, 1918–1923.* Berkeley: University of California Press, 1948.

Perkins, Dexter. *Charles Evans Hughes and American Democratic Statesmanship.* Boston: Little, Brown Company, 1956.

Pinchot, Amos. *History of the Progressive Party, 1912–1916.* New York: New York University Press, 1958.

Pollen, Arthur Hungerford. "Three Lessons of the Naval War." *Foreign Affairs* 2 (June 1924): 644–661.

Porter, Kirk H. and Donald Bruce Johnson, eds. *National Party Platforms, 1840–1964.* Urbana, Illinois: University of Illinois Press, 1966.

Pusey, Merlo J. *Charles Evans Hughes.* 2 Vols. New York: Macmillan Company, 1951.

Quigley, Harold S. *From Versailles to Locarno: A Sketch of the Recent Development of International Organization.* Minneapolis: University of Minnesota Press, 1927.

Ripley, Randall. *Majority Party Leadership in Congress.* Boston: Little, Brown and Company, 1969.

Robertson, James Oliver. *No Third Choice: Progressives in Republican Politics, 1916–1921.* New York: Garland Publishing, 1983.

Rochester, Stuart. *American Liberal Disillusionment in the Wake of World War I.* University Park: Pennsylvania State University Press, 1977.

Rogers, Lindsay. "American Government and Politics." *American Political Science Review* 13 (May 1919): 251–263.

_____. *The American Senate.* New York: F. S. Crofts, 1926.

_____. "President Wilson's Theory of His Office." *The Forum* 51 (February 1914): 174–185.

Roots, John McCook. "The Treaty of Versailles in the United States Senate" (Honors thesis, Harvard University, 1925).

Ross, Martin. *Shipstead of Minnesota.* Chicago: Packard and Company, 1940.

Ryley, Thomas W. *A Little Group of Willful Men: A Study of Congressional-Presidential*

    Authority. Port Washington, N.Y.: Kennikat Press, 1975.

Schwabe, Klaus. *Woodrow Wilson, Revolutionary Germany, and Peacemaking,*
    1918–1919. Chapel Hill: University of North Carolina Press, 1985.

Simonds, Frank H. *American Foreign Policy in the Post-War Years*. Baltimore: Johns
    Hopkins University Press, 1935.

Slemp, C. Bascom. *The Mind of the President*. Garden City, N.Y.: Doubleday, Page and
    Company, 1926.

Sprout, Harold and Margaret Sprout. *Toward a New Order of Seapower: American
    Naval Policy and the World Scene, 1918–1922*. Princeton: Princeton University
    Press, 1943.

Stephenson, Nathaniel W. *Nelson Aldrich, a Leader in American Politics*. New York:
    Charles S. Scribner's Sons, 1930.

Stern, Sheldon M. "Henry Cabot Lodge and Louis A. Coolidge in Defense of American
    Sovereignty, 1898–1920." *Proceedings of the Massachusetts Historical Society*
    87 (1975): 118–34.

Stone, Ralph. *The Irreconcilables: The Fight against the League of Nations*. Lexington:
    University of Kentucky Press, 1970.

Sutton, Walter A. "Republican Progressive Senators and Preparedness, 1915–1916."
    Mid-America 52 (July 1970): 155–176.

Tarbell, Ida M. *Peacemakers—Blessed and Otherwise: Observations, Reflections and
    Irritations at an Inter-national Conference*. New York: Macmillan Company,
    1922.

Tillman, Seth. *Anglo-American Relations at the Paris Peace Conference, 1919*. Princeton:
    Princeton University Press, 1961.

Towne, Ruth Warner. *Senator William J. Stone and the Politics of Compromise*. Port
    Washington, N.Y.: Kennikat Press, 1979.

Trani, Eugene P., and David L. Wilson. *The Presidency of Warren G. Harding*. Lawrence:
    The Regents Press of Kansas, 1977.

Trattner, Walter. "Progressivism and World War I: A Reappraisal." *Mid-America* 44 (July
    1962): 131–145.

Uterberger, Betty. "The United States and National Self-Determination: A Wilsonian
    Perspective." *Presidential Studies Quarterly* 26 (Fall 1996): 926–941.

Vinson, John Chalmers. *The Parchment Peace: The United States Senate and the
    Washington Conference, 1921–1922*. Athens: University of Georgia Press,
    1955.

_____. *Referendum for Isolation: Defeat of Article Ten of the League of Nations Covenant*.
    Athens: University of Georgia Press, 1961.

Watson, James. *As I Knew Them: The Memoirs of James Watson*. Indianapolis: The
    Bobbs-Merrill Company, 1936.

Weatherson, Michael A., and Hal Bochin. *Hiram Johnson: A Bio-Bibliography*. Westport,
    Conn.: Greenwood Press, 1988.

White, William Allen. *A Puritan in Babylon*. New York: Macmillan Company, 1938.

Wickersham, George W. "The Senate and Our Foreign Relations." *Foreign Affairs*
    2 (December 1923): 177–191.

Widenor, William. *Henry Cabot Lodge and the Search for American Foreign Policy*.
    Berkeley: University of California Press, 1980.

Williams, Donald. "Dawes and the 1924 Republican Vice Presidential Nomination."
    Mid-America 44 (January 1962): 3–18.

Wilson, Woodrow. *Constitutional Government in the United States*. New York: Columbia

University Press, 1908.

Wimer, Kurt. "Woodrow Wilson's Plans to Enter the League of Nations through Executive Agreement." *The Western Political Quarterly* 11 (December 1958): 800–812.

_____. "Woodrow Wilson Tries Conciliation: An Effort that Failed." *The Historian* 25 (August 1963): 419–438.

Wright, Quincy. *The Control of American Foreign Policy.* New York: Macmillan Company, 1922.

Index

About the Author

KAREN A. J. MILLER is Assistant Professor of History at Oakland University. Her research interests include a history of the Republican Party from 1912 to 1932.

ISBN 0-313-30776-8

90000>

EAN

9 780313 307768